THE
ADMINISTRATION
OF JUSTICE

PRENTICE-HALL INTERNATIONAL, INC., *London*
PRENTICE-HALL OF AUSTRALIA, PTY. LTD., *Sydney*
PRENTICE-HALL OF CANADA, LTD., *Toronto*
PRENTICE-HALL OF INDIA PRIVATE LTD., *New Delhi*
PRENTICE-HALL OF JAPAN, INC., *Tokyo*

THE
ADMINISTRATION
OF JUSTICE

Paul B. Weston
Sacramento State College

Kenneth M. Wells
Sacramento State College

PRENTICE-HALL, INC., *Englewood Cliffs, New Jersey*

A democratic society, in which respect for
the dignity of all men is central,
naturally guards against the misuse
of the law enforcement process.
Zeal in tracking down crime is not itself
an assurance of soberness of judgment.
Disinterestedness in law enforcement
does not alone prevent disregard of
cherished liberties. Experience has therefore
counselled that safeguards must be provided
against the dangers of the overzealous
as well as the despotic. The awful
instruments of the criminal law cannot be
entrusted to a single functionary.
The complicated process of criminal justice is
therefore divided into different parts,
responsibility for which is separately vested
in the various participants upon whom the
criminal law relies for its vindication.

JUSTICE FELIX FRANKFURTER
McNabb v. U.S.

v

Preface

A book about the major stages of the administration of justice from the time a crime is committed until final disposition is primarily concerned with laws and procedures in six functional areas: police protection, prosecution of offenders, criminal court systems, probation services, correctional institutions, and parole supervision of released offenders. Federal laws, court procedures and constitutional law can be discussed with some simplicity because of their uniformity from state to state. This is also true of police techniques, the work of prosecutors and defense counsel, *voir-dire* examination, jury selection, direct and cross-examination, and the correctional process; and to a lesser extent of jeopardy, bail, clemency, extradition and rendition, and writs, motions and appeals. It is not true, however, of the penal codes of each state or procedures in state courts.

To achieve some uniformity in this complex area of differences among state laws and procedures we have used California's recently revised Penal Code and new Evidence Code as major reference sources. We believe this will provide an excellent source for comparison with the laws and procedures in other states and will permit the use of this book in appropriate classes in any state. Selected references at the end of each chapter containing summaries of the cases, books and articles cited also give this book interstate coverage.

We hope our efforts will lead to similar texts by other "teams" of practitioners in law enforcement.

We are very grateful for the help of many friends and associates in the

legal, academic, and law enforcement communities. We wish to acknowl-
edge particularly the help of John J. Horgan, Chairman of the Department
of Police Science, San Bernardino Valley College; Lawrence R. Lawson,
Chairman of the Criminology Department, City College of San Francisco;
A. C. Germann, Professor of Criminology, California State College at
Long Beach; and C. Alex Pantaleoni, Professor of Police Science, Rio
Hondo Junior College. Their prepublication reviews served as both an
incentive to us and as a resource in organizing the material in the text.

PAUL B. WESTON
KENNETH M. WELLS

Contents

I

INTRODUCTION

The prevention, detection, discovery and suppression of crime; the identification, apprehension and prosecution of persons accused as criminals; and the incarceration, supervision and reform and rehabilitation of convicted offenders are accomplished primarily through six major functional areas of government: police, prosecution, criminal courts, probation, prisons and other institutions for the care and treatment of offenders, and parole.

1

Administration of Criminal Justice

The function of the administration of justice in the United States is a sequential crime control process performed by agents and agencies of government with assigned functions and territorial jurisdiction. Statute and case law, defining the essential elements of a criminal act; and the concept of due process of law, preserved for every human being by our Constitution, controls the procedure of determining the guilt or innocence of persons accused of crime. It is a process within a democratic community and a constitutional system dedicated to a program of judicial review which preserves the dignity of individuals and guards against the misuse of law enforcement.

Police officers have the basic obligation of apprehending criminals and share a role with the prosecutor in investigating crime. The prosecutor prepares the formal accusatory pleadings and conducts the court action. Defendants in criminal actions may retain counsel, and indigent de-

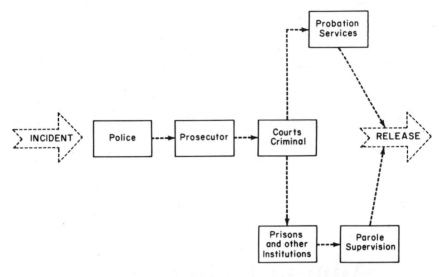

New York State Executive Chamber

FIG. 1.   INCIDENT TO RELEASE; SIX PRIMARY FUNCTIONAL AREAS

fendants will be assigned attorneys as legal assistance essential to a fair trial. Trials proceed with the basic assumption of the innocence of the accused and require proof of guilt beyond a reasonable doubt. There is judicial review of the circumstances of the arrest, the legality of evidence-gathering techniques and the substance and form of the accusatory pleading; courts of appellate jurisdiction may review the record of each case and can, if warranted, reverse the decisions of lower courts. Access to all courts insures petitioners of adequate and speedy legal relief against inquisitorial methods or other infringements of the rights of an accused person, and develops procedures allied with the accusatory rather than inquisitorial nature of American criminal justice. Improved sentencing concepts and rehabilitation as the major objective of the correctional process reject recidivism and project the future good conduct of past offenders.

The prevention, detection and suppression of crime; the arrest and prosecution of persons charged with offenses; and the imprisonment, supervision and rehabilitation of convicted offenders are major problems in the management of federal, state and local government. These public safety responsibilities are assigned to six primary functional areas: police protection, prosecution, criminal court systems, probation services, prisons and other institutions and parole supervision. These public services employ a huge number of people. A recent report surveying the cost of the administration of criminal justice in New York State notes there are more full-time public employees in this state engaged in police work

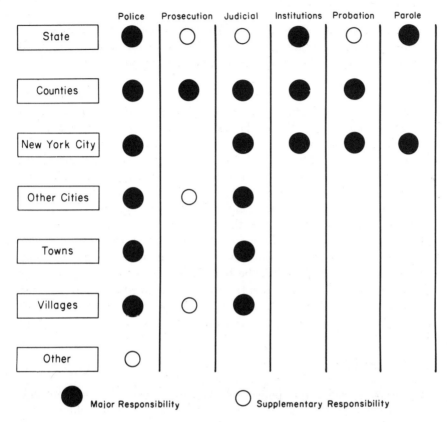

Police   Prosecution   Judicial   Institutions   Probation   Parole

	Police	Prosecution	Judicial	Institutions	Probation	Parole
State	●	○	○	●	○	●
Counties	●	●	●	●	●	
New York City	●		●	●	●	●
Other Cities	●	○	●			
Towns	●		●			
Villages	●	○	●			
Other	○					

● Major Responsibility   ○ Supplementary Responsibility

New York State Executive Chamber

FIG. 2.   LOCAL AND STATE RESPONSIBILITIES; PRIMARY
FUNCTIONAL AREAS

alone than in any major state and local governmental function other than education, health and institutional services.[1]

The cost of the administration of criminal justice varies from state to state, depending upon the incidence of crime and the climate of law and order demanded by the local community. The major portion of the cost to the public is spent for community protection. Police services usually amount to between 60 and 70 percent of the total expenditures; correctional agencies account for the second largest segment of public costs. Probation services, institutions, and parole supervision approximate 20 to 25 percent of overall costs. Most of the costs of the administration of criminal justice are direct, generated and expended by each level of government for its own purposes. Counties, cities, towns and villages accept major responsibility for police, prosecution, judicial and

[1]*Local and State Government Expenditures for the Administration of Criminal Justice in New York State,* New York Executive Chamber (Albany, 1965), pp. 9–16.

probation functions; state governments assume major responsibility for the costs of institutions and parole supervision, as well as providing funds for auxiliary services in supporting or coordinating public safety at local levels.

Police officers, prosecutors, court personnel and other agents of criminal justice, along with statute and case law, provide the raw material for law enforcement in the United States. Basic procedures are established by our separation-of-power doctrine which compartmentalizes the duties of the executive, legislative and judicial branches of government; our dual system of federal and state courts; and an emerging federalism resulting from the incorporation of the basic freedoms and rights guaranteed to individuals by the first eight amendments to the Constitution within the due process clause of the Fourteenth Amendment. However, it is the people who serve the many agencies within the judicial framework and the interrelationships between these individuals and their employing agencies that establish the balance between the police power of the community and the individual's fundamental freedoms—and establish and maintain the administration of criminal justice in America as an accusatory rather than an inquisitorial function.

The Police Role

Collectively, the major police role is a dual one: (1) to "prevent" crime by attempting to create in the mind of the potential offender the fear that the police will apprehend him at the crime scene, therefore, "crime does not pay"; and (2) to detect and investigate crimes that have not been deterred. The San Francisco police force in a recruiting poster, cites the work of policemen as follows:

> *Duties of the position under supervision:* In an assigned district, is responsible for the maintenance of order, the enforcement of laws and ordinances and the protection of life and property; patrols an assigned district or beat on foot; patrols assigned areas in radio cars; directs traffic; prepares reports on work done and unusual incidents observed; when necessary, makes arrests; handles prisoners in police department custody; issues citations; performs duty in bureaus, stations and on other assignments requiring police training and experience; gives advice on laws, ordinances and other matters concerning police administration, and general information to the public; and performs related duties as required.

The nondirective aspect in the attempt to prevent crime by being alert and observant obstructs any real role development; the investigation of crime develops a certain "chase" enthusiasm and a hunter's role. Performance is rated nebulously and accountability for the incidence of

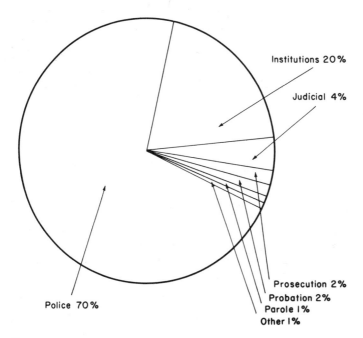

Institutions 20%

Judicial 4%

Prosecution 2%
Probation 2%
Parole 1%
Other 1%

Police 70%

FIG. 3.   TOTAL STATE AND LOCAL EXPENDITURES; FISCAL YEAR
1961 (NEW YORK CITY) AND FISCAL YEAR 1962 (NEW YORK STATE)

crime is difficult to assign. The result is that good but unspectacular
work is often unrewarded.[2]

Police employment is generally a closed career. Hiring is at the entrance level. Job requirements usually set a height standard of no less
than 5 feet 8 inches, with weight in proportion to height; at least 20/30
vision in most cases; over 21 years of age; and a background free of
crime or indications of emotional immaturity. The entrance test is usually one measuring general intelligence only; despite extensive discussion
of psychological and psychiatric testing, little actual testing of this type
exists. There is usually a test of strength and agility, and a medical examination. High school graduation or its equivalent is the ordinary educational requirement. Very few police departments set a two-year college
requirement, and a smaller number ask for a four-year college degree.
These latter requirements are generally found in very small—and select—
police departments, or in federal or state agencies of law enforcement.

Police systems, at the present time, rely on written tests, oral interviews and background investigations as the key to personnel selection.
Even though salaries have increased and are very competitive, the job
classification cites hazardous work, and willingness to work at irregular
hours is a necessity.

[2]Richard H. Blum, "The Problems of Being a Police Officer," *Police* (November-
December, 1960), pp. 10–13 (January-February, 1961), pp. 33–37.

The job announcements of the California Highway Patrol over a period
of several years have remained unchanged. Descriptions of various qualifying tests follow:

> *The Written Test (weighted 6)*[3]: The examination will cover the follow-
> ing subjects: Aptitude for traffic law enforcement work; ability to learn
> rules and regulations; ability to follow directions; ability to think clearly
> and logically; and ability to prepare reports, including ability to spell.
> *The Personal Interview (weighted 4)*:—will be conducted by a qualifica-
> tions appraisal panel and will be supplemented by investigation of the
> educational and employment record and character of competitors.[4]
> The qualifications appraisal will cover education and experience; per-
> sonal traits and fitness, including initiative, integrity, reliability, resource-
> fulness, courtesy, good judgment, ability to analyze situations and people
> accurately, to adopt an effective course of action and to get along well
> with others; neat personal appearance, officer-like bearing and good
> address; willingness to work under strict discipline, willingness to work
> throughout the state, at night and at other unusual hours; ability to
> maintain cooperative relations with city, county and other agencies in
> law enforcement work; satisfactory record as a law-abiding citizen; and
> ability to write legibly.
> *The Physical Performance Test* will be a test of strength, agility and
> endurance.

The Prosecutor (District Attorney)

The prosecutor, or the District Attorney, as he is sometimes termed, is
an elected official chosen by a county-wide vote. In sparsely settled
areas of the country, several counties may unite into a district and elect
a district prosecutor. The role of the prosecutor and his staff is to investigate, to file informations or to secure indictments and to conduct the
prosecutions of accused individuals. Ethically, a prosecutor or a member
of his staff do not have a primary duty to convict. *The primary duty of
these public officials is to see that justice is done.* The canons of the legal
profession point out this duty, and add that the suppression of facts or
the secreting of witnesses capable of establishing the innocence of the
defendant is "highly reprehensible."

The prosecutor has the key role in law enforcement in America. It is
the prosecutor who decides whether to prosecute, to accept a plea of
guilty to a lesser charge or to drop a case for lack of evidence. Crime

[3]On a base of ten.
[4]"Background" investigation.

detection and the arrest of offenders by police can be upgraded or down-graded by the prosecutor and his staff. In 1958, District Attorney Edward Silver of Kings County (Brooklyn), created quite a stir in the New York City Police Commissioner's office. Mr. Silver had been quoted, in reference to his role as prosecutor, as being the "chief law enforcement agent of the county." There is some evidence that the Police Commissioner thought this was *his* role in the city's law enforcement complex. Apparently, though, Silver was not in error. He did not retract his statement, and since that date several New York Police Commissioners apparently accepted the merits of Silver's statement, their silence serving as an acknowledgment of the key role of the prosecutor in law enforcement.

The people who seek the position of prosecutor do not have to meet any physical requirements, but they are usually politically ambitious attorneys. The office of prosecutor has frequently been a stepping stone to higher government positions. Numerous mayors and governors have followed this route. In many areas, the assistant prosecutors who form the legal staff are appointed by the prosecutor and prosper or perish with the political fortunes of the prosecutor. In a growing number of states, a civil service system has been established for the staff of a prosecutor's office, and assistant prosecutors have job tenure despite the political life of their boss. In California, the merit civil service system in the office of the prosecutor has raised the prestige and potential of this office. The basic entrance requirement is a legal education and admission to the state bar. Salaries are excellent[5] and the training potential for trial experience is tremendous.

Expected role behavior is similar to that of the police: there is almost an equal area for developing an enthusiasm for a chase and a hunter's instinct as there is in the police role. Contributing to a normal zest to win trials is the fact that a high percentage of convictions in comparison with cases tried is a performance evaluation technique.

Defense Counsel (Public Defender)

Any practicing attorney may fulfill the role of defense counsel, and it is the right of any attorney to seek and accept clients charged with crime. The attorney's personal opinion as to the guilt or innocence of such clients should not be a factor in whether or not the case is accepted, or in how the case is prepared and presented in court. Once involved in an attorney-client relationship, the attorney should present every defense legally and

[5]Duane R. Nedrud, "The Career Prosecutor," *Journal of Criminal Law, Criminology, and Police Science*, 51, No. 3 (September-October, 1960), 343–55.

factually permissible in order to protect his client from deprivation of life and liberty except through due process of law. This is a necessary role acceptance. Otherwise, innocent persons might become the victims of suspicious circumstances, and be denied the attorney of their choosing and the best trial defense effort.

Attorneys who will accept defendants charged with crime as clients usually have a liking for criminal law. They are individuals who look forward to a day in the trial court, work long hours in preparing a case, have tested skills in pleading difficult causes, and have a fighter's accept-ance of adversary proceedings. This role development extends from the attorney who occasionally takes a criminal case to the defense counsel whose majority of legal work is concerned with defending persons ac-cused of crime. It now includes the government position of public de-fender, where each day's work is concerned with defending the accused in criminal actions. Motivation for the role of defense counsel can be monetary, but the practice of criminal law is not usually lucrative. It may be political ambition. Publicity attending many criminal cases brings attention to the defense counsel. It may be a desire for meaningful work. It may be some combination of these motives, but it necessarily must be a strong urge. The work is hard and the demands for excellence almost overwhelming.

The public defender is a prosecutor-in-reverse. Pay, entrance require-ments and performance evaluation are similar to prosecutors. Interrela-tionships with the police are close, but taut. A public defender is in government, but not within the "we" or "us" group of the police and prosecutor. Public defenders must work with a meager investigatory staff, without the fee-supported organization of regular defense counsel and without the hidden investigative strengths inherent in a cooperating police agency and grand jury. An idea of the difference of this position from that of police and prosecutor, and an overview of the type of per-son accepting this role, is contained in the instructions of one fighting public defender to his clients:

> From this time on do not discuss your case, or any case or any of your affairs with any law officer, or district attorney or fellow prisoner. Until your public defender notifies you, *do not* give any more information of any kind to a law officer or district attorney, and this includes officers from other cities or counties. You do not have to talk to anyone; they cannot make you talk, and you are more likely to hurt yourself than help yourself. *Do not* act on the advice of "jail-house" lawyers; if they were so smart they wouldn't be in jail. Most cases have been lost because the defendant talked too much to the wrong people. *Do not* try to make a "deal" on your own with the district attorney.

Coroner

In many jurisdictions the coroner is also required to serve as public administrator[6] or sheriff. In urban areas, the title of the position is often changed to medical examiner. Delineation of the function of coroner would suggest requirements demanding a practicing physician with some training in pathology. The role of coroner is to find the "cause of death" when a person dies under unexplained or suspicious circumstances.[7] It is a physician who is most capable of probing into the circumstances of death. Within this skill, a skilled autopsy surgeon and pathologist is the person most likely to perform well in this position. Ideally, the position of coroner requires a person with something other than a morbid interest in the mechanics of death; a person honestly dedicated to the mystery of unexplained death. The position pays very well, at the prosecutor or public defender level, and there is no performance evaluation pressure to win trials. The classic coroner's jury report of death at the hands of "person or persons unknown" indicates no particular orientation to either party to a criminal action, although continual contact with police at death scenes creates a favorable rapport with police.

In California, the coroner acts out an investigational and quasi-judicial role. He can summon, or cause to be summoned by any sheriff, constable, or policemen, not less than nine nor more than 15 persons qualified by law to serve as jurors,[8] to appear before him, either at the place where the body of the deceased is or some other convenient place within the county designated by him, and shall convene this jury to inquire into the cause of death.[9]

Grand Jurors

A grand jury is a body of the required number of persons returned from the citizens of a county before a court of competent jurisdiction, and sworn to inquire of public offenses committed or triable within the county.[10] The individual selected to serve as a member of the grand jury is usually a person of some substance in the local community, a citizen

[6]A city or county official responsible for the property of certain deceased persons.
[7]Paul B. Weston and William F. Kessler, *The Detection of Murder* (New York: Greenberg, 1953), pp. 1–9.
[8]Residents of the county who are competent to serve as jurors and not related to decedent, nor charged with or suspected of the killing nor prejudiced for or against the killer.
[9]California Government Code, Section 27492.
[10]California Penal Code, Section 888.

and voter selected by lot from a special "blue ribbon" type of panel. In California, the justices of the superior court in each county submit names of persons known to them and totaling two or three times the number required for the grand jury. The names of the persons who will serve on the jury are then drawn by lot from the grand jury box.[11] This is not an employee role, but it is a role in law enforcement that requires devoting considerable time over a lengthy period to responsible duties. Generally 23 jurors[12] make up a grand jury. Sixteen are necessary to constitute a quorum, and a majority of 12 affirmative votes is necessary for action. The grand jury holds secret meetings to review legal evidence regarding the guilt of persons not usually present. The persuasive arts of the assigned prosecutor and the domination of his technical competence serve to motivate the thinking of many jurors. Now and then, the scope of the role of members of the jury takes on new dimensions, and the jury acts on its own. These "runaway" grand juries often do great civic good.

The role of a grand juror may be as a participant in a lengthy investigation or a brief hearing of witnesses. A basic conflict is involved because ordinary citizens are required to assume a status of subagents in law enforcement.[13] On the one hand, the juror is asked to accept a fractional role as a committing magistrate: along with others on the jury he has to decide if a person, against whom the prosecutor and possibly the police have arrayed a one-sided accumulation of evidence, is to be held in a criminal action. In addition, despite the fact that the term of this "employment" is usually a full year, he is asked to keep his identification as a business or professional man in the community and prevent unwarranted prosecutions from coming to trial. In the history of the grand jury the clue to this role of protector against the arbitrary acts of government, or those of judges subservient to governmental influence, is found time and again in the recurring use of the words "responsible citizens," "approved integrity" and "sound judgment." All grand jurors are thoroughly instructed in the fact that the duty of the grand jury is to screen accusations which are without foundation and only formally accuse those persons against whom the evidence seems to be substantial. It is frequently difficult for most people to distinguish their task from the role of a trial jury in deciding guilt or innocence. Time and again, a grand juror will be cautioned by his foreman or a district attorney that it is only necessary to have *prima facie* evidence to vote for an indictment; the trial of the offender will determine guilt or innocence. Many responsible citizens

11*Ibid.*, Sections 895–902.

12California requires the grand jury to number 23 in heavily populated counties (over four million), and 19 in other counties.

13J. Douglas Cook, "New York Troika: Conflicting Roles of the Grand Jury," *Buffalo Law Review*, 2 (Fall 1961), 42–52.

serving as grand jurors admit that their thinking concerns the guilt or innocence of the person to be indicted rather than the worth of the accusation alone. A common response to a query in this area is: "Who would vote to hold an innocent person?"

Trial Jurors

Trial jurors are the guarantee of the community that the trial defendant will be heard by twelve persons without prejudice or preconceived ideas about the accused. They are unsalaried, compensated only for their expenses and selected at random: once from the list of qualified voters in the county to make up the current jury panel, and then by lot for a particular case. One of the fine things about law enforcement in the United States is the good conscience, devotion to duty and humanitarianism of the trial jurors. They attempt to work within the two basic concepts of a criminal proceeding in the United States: (1) innocence until guilt is proven, and (2) proof of that guilt beyond a reasonable doubt.

It would be fine if trial jurors were *totally* free of discriminatory and prejudicial attitudes or frames of reference, but this is an impossibility because trial jurors are human and have had attitude-shaping experiences throughout their lifetimes.[14] Trial attorneys have learned that physical characteristics, racial and ethnic origins, sex and occupation are factors indicating the different attitudes held by trial jurors. Generally, it is the vocational backgrounds that develop the habits of thought and action brought to this all-important role in dispensing justice. Present or former military personnel, low-salaried "white-collar" workers and management personnel—and their spouses—are generally considered "tough" jurors; salesmen, actors, artists and writers are believed to be more tolerant. Traditionally, representing both the community and an agency in law enforcement, these men and women are people in conflict throughout their jury duty. Some of them do not accept the role of subagent of law enforcement, a necessity if they are to properly relate their tasks to the structure of a criminal action, and at the same time preserve their identity as a member of the community.

Probation Officer

This job classification usually offers employment at the city or county level, and requires a college education in the field of social welfare,

[14]Jack Pope, "The Proper Function of Jurors," *Baylor Law Review*, 14, No. 4 (Fall, 1962), 365–83.

sociology, psychology or a related academic area, together with some casework experience. There are only nominal physical qualifications, and no agility testing. Selection is by competitive written examinations and oral interviews in urban areas, and in many cases appointments without tests in rural areas. The job role consists of two functions, that of staff member in the city or county court system, and supervisor of convicted defendants who have been conditionally released without commitment to custody, or conditionally released with some short-term custodial arrangements. The county of Santa Clara, California, in 1965, issued the following description of this position:

> A probation officer under close supervision investigates cases involving adult offenders. He should be familiar with interviewing techniques, knowledge of the basic principles of applied psychology and have an ability to prepare and present oral and written reports logically and accurately. He should be able to exercise tolerance and good judgment. He supervises individuals placed on probation. This may include counseling and/or the referral of probationers to allied service agencies. He may be responsible for collection of fines, probation costs and restitution to injured parties when ordered by the court as a probation requirement. Responsible also for the supervision of persons paroled from the Santa Clara County Jail by the Santa Clara County Board of Parole Commissioners.

As a member of the court's staff, it is the task of the probation officer to investigate the circumstances *surrounding* the defendant's commission of the crime. His reports extend to the motives for the crime and include a recommendation of whether or not the offender can be rehabilitated without a prison term. Then, as a supervisor of the conditions of probation, this law enforcement employee assumes a semiparental role in his relationships with the convicted person on probation. Because of the conflict between the roles of investigator and supervisor, personnel in some probation departments are assigned primarily to work only in one of these areas.

In the presentence investigation of a criminal offender, the probation officer investigates—but his duties are not intended to aid prosecution. They are concerned with unearthing facts which will indicate all the circumstances pertaining to both the crime and the offender.[15] For this reason, there is a little of the "hunter" in this role or a tendency to the thinking of working police officers. A 1964 court decision[16] in a criminal

[15]Charles L. Newman, *Sourcebook on Probation, Parole, and Pardons* (Springfield, Ill.: Charles C. Thomas, Publisher, 1958), pp. 94–108.
[16]*People v. Quinn,* 393 P 2nd 705 (1964).

action was reversed because the testimony of the probation officer involving promises of leniency in return for a confession was permitted in the trial of an offender. The court commented that there was a history of court rejection of police use of this methodology and expressed considerable amazement to find its utilization by a probation officer.

Prediction about human behavior requires role-playing marked by both stability and adventurousness. A probation officer must excel in his presentence judgments; but the incumbent of this position who refuses to gamble on individuals under investigation is not role-playing in the fullest sense of the functions and duties of his position—an admittedly difficult feat. Performance evaluation may be based on overall work ability, but as in the work of a prosecutor or public defender, there are rewards for "winning," for valid predictions of the future good conduct of offenders recommended for probation.

It is very fortunate for society that the people who are attracted to the role of supervisor appear to be men and women of remarkable maturity and skill. Their task is the supervision of people who have been found guilty of some illegal behavior and in whom the community, through its court and probation agency, has placed a special belief of possible rehabilitation without sentence to prison.[17] People on probation need help, some more than others, but all of them to some extent. This role, alone, has little conflict for the probation officer. An excellent rapport can be established with police officers so long as the probationers don't reengage in criminal activity and thus compromise their probation supervisor.

Parole Agent

Parole units are usually state-wide in operations and heavily professionalized. The role of parole agent is similar to that of probation officer, involving similar conflicts in carrying out investigation of possible criminal conduct or associations likely to lead to criminal behavior. There is, also, a great similarity to the police role. Parole officers often have to return parolees to prison, and this involves procedures akin to summary police arrest. There is not, though, any opportunity to divide the work function to avoid job conflict, as is possible in a probation unit. The investigative and supervisory tasks are forced into a daily blend of suspicion and trust—an unhappy combination. Moreover, while the educational background required for entrance to positions as parole agents is comparable to probation officer requirements, the job specifications also

[17]Newman, *op. cit.*, pp. 109–73.

require an investigative background; many states arm their parole agents in the same manner as policemen.

Unlike their probation counterparts, parole officers work with the poorer risks of law enforcement: individuals whose conduct at the time of the crime or before indicate a need for care and treatment that can be provided only in a custodial institution. These are the offenders who, having served portions of their prison sentence, are eligible for parole. They are all persons who have been exposed to the socialization of prison life, the conflicts of the prison community and the attendant "fringe benefits"—crime schools and group hostility to police and prosecutor.

The same emotional maturity and the same skills common to probation officers are easily identified among parole agents; but there may be considerable erosion of these qualities in time because of the greater incidence of police contacts resulting from the commission of new crimes by parolees. Parole agents, however, must also maintain the same willingness to take calculated risks as probation officers in predicting future human behavior. This usually conflicts with attitudes formed by the high rate of recidivism among convicted offenders.

Correctional Personnel

Treatment and custody personnel differ in both educational requirements and on-the-job duties. Recent innovations joining custodial duties and correctional counseling may be the start of a new role in corrections for all positions except those requiring skilled professional competence in psychology, psychiatry and medicine.

TREATMENT

Entrance requirements call for education and experience in the fields of sociology, psychology, medicine and psychiatry. Behavior expected in these roles depends upon the specific discipline concerned. Professional competence and conduct are expected in contact with the offender. Decision-making is a vital aspect of expected behavior, as is research into the etiology of crime. Each member of the treatment staff is expected to contribute to a prediction consensus about future parole behavior. It is a challenging role and one replete with disappointments. The same conflict that appears among probation officers and parole agents is quite common among these professionals since their work is also concentrated with forecasting future behavior patterns. While job performance is not based on diagnostic success, there is little doubt that continued failure tends to influence attitudes.

CUSTODY

This is probably one of the most demanding jobs in the law enforcement field, and, at the same time, a position offering the least monetary compensation and societal reward. It is hazardous and also tedious duty of a routine nature. It provides the greatest amount of face-to-face contact with the criminal offender of any occupation in the administration of justice. It exposes "free personnel" in prisons to a subculture in which power, cunning, conniving and manipulating are held in greater esteem than abstract concepts of ethics and morality.[18] However, because of extensive contact with offenders, this role in the law enforcement process has a potential completely unrecognized and undeveloped except by persons such as Warden Duffy of San Quentin and Warden Lawes of Sing Sing—and probably an unidentified guard or two or three in every prison. Guard personnel constitute a good percentage of the prison community, and their interrelationships with the inmate population on the one side and their supervisors on the other often require some balancing of role behavior.

The position is usually sought by persons entering the field and preparing for future employment in some area of corrections, either administration, probation or parole; by persons who will later seek work as policemen; by retired men of the armed forces who only seek a sustaining salary in addition to their pension benefits; by local citizens with other jobs or businesses who want to supplement the low income in their major field with other employment; by people who cannot get better jobs in civil service; and—in some states—by people who cannot read or write.

Future professionalization of custody personnel necessarily involves a broadening of job responsibilities to include meaningful work in the treatment of offenders. Pioneer job classification to extend the functions of custody personnel has resulted in a very fine job specification in California's massive system of corrections. The title and other informative data of this position were announced by the California State Personnel Board,[19] and are as follows:

[18]Donald Clemmer, *The Prison Community* (New York: Holt, Rinehart & Winston, Inc., 1958), pp. 181–206.

Elmer H. Johnson, "Sociology of Confinement: Assimilation and the Prison Rat," *Journal of Criminal Law, Criminology, and Police Science*, 51, No. 5 (January-February, 1961), 528–33.

[19]September 15, 1964.

Title: Correctional Counselor I

Salary Range: $619 650 683 717 753

Requirements:

(Note: These are entrance requirements for admission to the examination, which is competitive.)

Either I—Experience: One year of experience in collecting, evaluating and interpreting social, behavioral and vocational data for purposes of counseling and promoting individual adjustment and rehabilitation. This experience must have been gained in one or a combination of the following fields: probation or parole; *or* vocational guidance or rehabilitation; *or* medical, psychiatric or correctional casework; *or* clinical psychology. (Graduate work in sociology, psychology, criminology or in a recognized school of social work may be substituted for the required experience on a year-for-year basis. Applicants substituting education for the entire experience requirements must have had some supervised casework experience during or supplemental to their graduate work. Graduate students in one of these fields will be admitted to the examination, but must produce evidence of completion of one year of graduate work and some supervised casework experience before they will be considered eligible for appointment.) *and* education: equivalent to graduation from college. (Additional qualifying experience may be substituted for two years of the required education on a year-for-year basis.)

Or II—Experience: Two years of full-time paid experience in the supervision of inmates in a California state adult correctional institution; *and* education: equivalent to graduation from college.

Or III—Ten months of full-time paid experience performing the duties of a correctional casework trainee in the California state service. Applicants who meet this experience requirement will be admitted to the examination, but must successfully complete the one year in-service training program for correctional casework trainee before they may be appointed.

The Position: In a correctional institution, a correctional counselor's major responsibility is the study of the individual prisoner for purposes of understanding his needs and outlining a program for his rehabilitation. Following initial classification and assignment of the inmate to a rehabilitation program, the counselor continues individual counseling and participates in the group counseling, study and therapy programs aimed at preparing the inmate for eventual return to the community.

Notably, California personnel technicians and corrections executives have made it possible for existing custody workers to upgrade themselves by combining formal academic programs with their employment and thus eventually qualify for the above position.

Commission on Law Enforcement and Administration of Justice

In July 1965, the Commission on Law Enforcement and Administration of Justice was created by executive order to function within the U.S. Department of Justice. It is composed of distinguished law enforcement officials, judges, attorneys and civic leaders; chaired by the Attorney General; and has been assigned an extensive staff and adequate federal funds. Its task is to study crime in the U.S.; examine the existing operations and methods of police, courts and correctional institutions; and make appropriate recommendations for improved and revised procedures for the control of crime.

In order to examine the entire process of the administration of criminal justice from incident to final disposition, the staff of the Commission has been divided into five major "task forces" with the following objectives:

(1) *The Assessment Task Force*—seeking to assess the volume, nature and causes of crime.

(2) *The Police Task Force*—searching for methods to improve the practices and procedures of the police.

(3) *The Task Force on the Administration of Criminal Justice*—looking for ways to improve the quality of the courts and the work of prosecutors, judges and defense attorneys.

(4) *The Corrections Task Force*—recommend techniques for reducing the recidivism rate.

(5) *The Science and Technology Task Force*—how science and technology can better serve the entire system of criminal justice.[20]

There is a new and growing optimism that important and innovative improvements in the entire system of criminal justice are in the offing. The total knowledge and experience represented by the membership and staff of this new Commission may be the resource necessary to guide nation-wide data collection and study projects; it could possibly build on such executive leadership as exhibited by the administrators of the California Department of Corrections in creating new positions highlighted by minimal conflict of roles and maximal opportunities for meaningful work. This "task force" review of the major functions of the administration of justice is likely to provide the guidelines necessary for new and rewarding concepts of professionalism.

[20]James Vorenberg, "Crime Commission Is Studying the Entire System of Criminal Justice in the U.S.," *California Law Enforcement*, 1, No. 1 (July, 1966), 44–46.

Selected References

CASES

People v. Riser, 47 Cal. 2nd 566 (1956).

> A California case in pretrial discovery, but the majority opinion contains a fine delineation of the role of the prosecutor and, by inference, the associated role of the police. It concludes that the prosecutor should produce evidence or reports upon request where relevant and material; that to deny such production is to lose sight of the true purpose of a criminal trial: the ascertainment of the facts.

Rideau v. Louisiana, 373 U.S. 723 (1963).

> This decision contains a fine discussion of the right of a defendant in a criminal action to a fair trial by unbiased jurors. The petitioner, Rideau, confessed criminal guilt while in jail in response to leading questions of the sheriff and before an array of cameras and recorders. The film and sound track was televised locally prior to trial. The court noted the sheriff had usurped the role of a judicial official.

BOOKS

Biestek, Felix P., *The Casework Relationship*. Chicago: Loyola University Press, 1957. 149 pages.

> The person seeking help and the caseworker form the two-unit team of social casework. It also concerns the working-out of basic convictions about the value and dignity of human relations. Biestek explains, defines and explores the casework relationship, and discusses the controlled emotional involvement, the nonjudgmental attitude and the client self-determination that are vital to successful interrelationship between the caseworker and the person being helped—in either probation or parole, or in prison treatment programs. A text that is very helpful in understanding and developing the role of agents in law enforcement assigned to supervise offenders.

Clark, Donald E., and Samuel G. Chapman, *A Forward Step: Educational Backgrounds for Police*. Springfield Ill.: Charles C. Thomas, Publisher, 1966. 144 pages.

> A text in support of a college education as a prerequisite for the police role. A very fine delineation of the many societal forces acting and reacting upon persons in this law enforcement occupation.

Mitgang, Herbert, *The Man Who Rode the Tiger—the Life and Times of Judge Samuel Seabury*. Philadelphia: J. P. Lippincott Co., 1963. 380 pages.

> Judge Seabury was a crusading reformer who forced an honest mayor upon the people of New York City. A thoroughly researched biography,

the book tells the story of a man and his role in a successful fight against the corrupt and criminal activities of politicians and city employees associated with the Tammany "Tiger"—New York's *Tammany Hall*, the dominant political organization. The role of special prosecutor and district attorney would not have been possible without Seabury's exposures of corruption in government. A fine exposition of the prosecutor's key role in law enforcement.

Newman, Charles L., *Sourcebook on Probation, Parole and Pardons* (2nd ed). Springfield, Ill.: Charles C. Thomas, Publisher, 1964. 335 pages.

Newman has skillfully selected material from many authoritative sources and integrated these extracts into the general continuity of this book. As a result, this combination of readings and basic text is a well organized presentation of probation and parole services. The text presents the role of each of these agents in law enforcement in unusual detail.

Sayre, Wallace S., and Herbert Kaufman, *Governing New York City*. New York: Russell Sage Foundation, 1960. 815 pages.

A definitive text about the people who govern in a large city, their roles in government and their interrelationships. The authors are unusually frank in their reports of corrupt practices, politics as usual and the misuse of official authority.

Sherif, Carolyn W., Muzafer Sherif and Roger E. Nebergall, *Attitude and Attitude Change—The Social Judgment-involvement Approach*. Philadelphia: W. B. Saunders Co., 1965. 264 pages.

A detailing of original research procedures and the results of an exhaustive investigation of attitude and variations by three social psychologists. The social judgment-involvement approach traces the psychological processes of the individual in his acceptance or rejection of persons, groups, ideas and events. This is a new source for a better understanding of attitudes, the frames of reference involved and the vital area of noncommitment as opposed to total rejection or acceptance. An excellent primer about people.

Weston, Paul B., *Supervision in the Administration of Justice*. Springfield, Ill.: Charles C. Thomas, Publisher, 1965. 188 pages.

This text discusses supervision as management centered upon the basic responsibilities of the supervisor to his community, his employing agency, his superiors and his subordinates. It documents supervision as responsibility for performance on the job, and provides a framework for experience in the interdisciplinary exchange of theory and technical skills among the people who work in law enforcement, the courts and correctional agencies.

Prevention and Control of Crime and Delinquency. El Monte, Calif.: Space General Company, 1965. 257 pages.

Report of an extensive study of the administration of criminal justice in California. It is complete with flow charts and typical "aerospace" handling of "input" and "output," but it is also a very fine exposition of the existing structure of occupations and functions of government in the control of crime and delinquency; it contains extensive recommendations for future modernization.

ARTICLES

Cook, Fred J., "Gambling, Treasure Chest of the Underworld," *The Nation* (October 1960), (Special Issue), pp. 1–317.

> Professional gambling is described by Cook as the most lucrative, destructive and tolerated form of crime in the United States, and the greatest single corruptive influence upon a community and its government. This is a careful documentation that day-to-day gambling profits are used to bribe elected officials and to corrupt law-enforcement agents.

Falk, Gerhard J., "The Public's Prejudice Against the Police," *American Bar Association Journal* (August 1964), pp. 754–57.

> A discussion of the police role and image of today. Falk calls for education, improved screening of applicants, better intergovernmental relations and the use of policewomen to overcome negative public opinion concerning urban police in America.

Glueck, Sheldon, "Wanted: A New Legal Profession," *The Police Chief* (August 1965), pp. 24–32.

> A strong plea for a new "West Point" concept in criminal justice. Glueck suggests the professionalization of a new field: specialist criminal lawyer. The plan involves educational institutions located at existing law schools evolving a concept of training law students in a specialized role in law enforcement, either as prosecutor or defense counsel.

Goldstein, Herman, "Police Discretion: Ideal v. Real," *Public Administration Review* (September 1963), pp. 140–48.

> One of the misconceptions about the police administrator's role is the amount of discretion allowed in the execution of the law at the operations level. Goldstein details the vast amount of discretion possible within the role of law enforcement administrator.

Goldstein, Joseph, "Police Discretion Not to Invoke the Criminal Process: Low-Visibility Decisions in the Administration of Justice," *Yale Law Journal*, 69, No. 4 (March 1960), 543–94.

> The theme of this article is that the decision of the police to act or not to act is the starting point of the administration of justice in the criminal process. The decision made by the police officer may be influenced by "departmental policy"—or politics—but varies with each individual, thus Goldstein's terminology: "low-visibility."

Nunnelley, J. P., "When a Trial by Jury?" *Journal of the American Judicature Society* (October 1959), pp. 87–91.

> Nunnelley lists four characteristics of jurors: (1) qualified for the task of evaluating witnesses and determining truth; (2) hold average citizen's view of the crime; (3) not affected by pressure of associates or employment in government; and (4) not concerned with the letter of the law.

This author sums up the role of trial juror as follows: "What is more fundamental to a democracy than the privilege to turn to the people and say, "This is your law; this is your citizen; this is what happened; apply the law to the case as you want it applied."

Rummel, Bartlett, "Police Firearms Training," *The American Rifleman* (August 1963), pp. 9–14.

An inquiry into the governmental duty to provide adequate training for police officers, and a discussion of case law establishing a new concept of governmental liability for failure to adequately train police officers in the proper handling and safe use of weapons. Judge Rummel notes that "government tort immunity is on the way out as part of the American legal system." The implication of the article indicates that new standards of accountability may be emerging for many of the roles in law enforcement. Since judgments against employing agencies are costly, they will serve as motivation to other agencies to expend more funds for training.

II

POLICE

*The protection of lives and property, and
the prevention, detection and suppression
of crime are an old and vital function of
government. The majority of police officers
in the United States are employed by
agencies of local and state governments,
organized within the general "home rule"
concept and relatively autonomous in
operation; these officers account for close to
seventy percent of the total cost of administering criminal justice.*

2

From Incident
to Arraignment

The incident that places a person within the scope of police action may be a positive, affirmative action contributing to a criminal plan or operation, or it may only be an act in preparation for the crime. It may not be legally actionable enough to allow police officers to develop the necessary probable cause for search and seizure or arrest. The person involved in an incident which initiates the chain of police action leading to an arrest must be the "actor," the person who did the acting which created the incident.

Police procedures may be *a priori*,[1] in that officers on police patrol make observations and, as a result of their special training and experience, are capable of predicting that a crime is about to be committed or is in progress. Rules to develop necessary professional police skills by

[1]Predicting an end result from knowledge and experience.

27

establishing the accountability of officers assigned to a specific area for the incidence of observable and avoidable crimes have been instituted; all modern police units offer extensive training programs as to the prompt recognition of suspicious places, people and circumstances.

Police procedures begin with reconstruction when police arrive on the crime scene after the crime has been committed. Police must work *a posteriori*,[2] with the victim as the end result of the basic incident and the criminal as the cause of the action, or at least the individual legally responsible for contributing to the end result.

When the police have completed their procedures following an arrest, every act done from the time of the first incident is open to review by the judicial officer before whom the police are legally required to promptly arraign prisoners.

Crimes and Criminals

A crime is an act committed or omitted in violation of a law forbidding or commanding it and punishable, upon conviction, by death, imprisonment, fine, removal from office or disqualification to hold any office of honor, trust or profit.[3] Law today is wholly statutory. No act is unlawful unless at the time of its commission a valid written law (statute or ordinance) was in force which defines such an act as a crime and sets a penalty for its commission or omission. Substantive law defines the rights, duties and liabilities of the parties involved in a crime, and also defines the essential elements of specific crimes; adjective law enumerates the procedures for proceeding against the accused person. The common law serves merely as a reference in modern law enforcement, and the "unwritten law" is more likely to be a defense of crime utilized by television scriptwriters rather than defense counsel.

Crimes are divided into two major groups: felonies and misdemeanors. Some states, such as New York, add a third noncrime classification of "minor offense" for lesser violations of local (city, town and village) laws and traffic regulations. Classically, a felony is a serious offense and is generally determined by actual service of a "year and a day" in a state prison. However, for the purpose of guiding police officers in the use of proper arrest techniques, the laws of each state name the more serious crimes as felonies. The United States Federal Bureau of Investigation (FBI) classified a group of crimes as serious felonies for the purpose of statistical record and analysis. These crimes are: (1) burglary; (2) larceny ("grand" rather than "petty" theft); (3) aggravated

[2]Reasoning from the end result to the cause.
[3]California Penal Code, Section 15.

assault; (4) rape (forcible); (5) robbery; (6) auto theft; (7) murder and nonnegligent manslaughter.

All persons are capable of committing a criminal act, but the law usually diminishes or relieves an accused of responsibility under the following circumstances: If he is an idiot or insane; if the accused is a child under 14 and in the absence of clear proof of timely knowledge of wrongfulness of the act; when persons act without consciousness or by mistake or ignorance of fact so as to disprove any criminal interest or intent; when otherwise criminal acts are committed through misfortune or accident (where there is no evil design, intention or culpable negligence); if the accused person commits a crime (not punishable by death) because of threats to his life and a belief his life is actually endangered if he refuses to act; and—lastly—if wives commit misdemeanors when acting under the threats, command or coercion of their husbands.[4]

Most states classify the parties to a crime as principals or accessories. In modern law, the "accessory before the fact" is a principal. Police usually term such a person an "accomplice," or more formally, a person described as "acting in concert" with the prime mover of the criminal act. In California, the definition of principals to a crime reads:

> All persons concerned in the commission of a crime, whether it be felony or misdemeanor, and whether they directly commit the act constituting the offense, or aid and abet in its commission, or, not being present, have advised and encouraged its commission, and all persons counseling, advising or encouraging children under the age of 14 years, lunatics or idiots, to commit any crime, or who, by fraud, contrivance or force, occasion the drunkenness of another for the purpose of causing him to commit any crime, or who, by threats, menaces, command or coercion, compel another to commit any crime, are principals in any crime so committed.[5]

California law defines an accessory to a crime by the old definition of "accessories after the fact": "Every person who, after a felony has been committed, harbors, conceals or aids a principal in such felony, with the intent that said principal may avoid or escape from arrest, trial, conviction or punishment, having knowledge that said principal has committed such felony or has been charged with such felony or convicted thereof, is an accessory to such felony."[6]

The penalty for all principals to a crime is in accordance with the provisions of law defining the substantive crime and setting forth the punishment for its violation. Unless the penal code of a state provides a specific penalty for accessories to a crime, they are usually punished in

[4]*Ibid.*, Section 26.
[5]*Ibid.*, Section 31.
[6]*Ibid.*, Section 32.

accordance with a general penal section establishing such penalty. In California the penalty is imprisonment for one to five years, five thousand dollars fine, or both.[7]

The Detection of Crime

The discovery or detection of a criminal act involves an inquiry into the activities of a person or persons or into the nature of things which might be concerned with crime or criminals. It usually begins with a citizen's report or suspicion of a crime, or police observation of a criminal act or suspicious place or person.

Most criminal acts are reported to police by their victims. However, an easily discerned criminal act or circumstance may be discovered and reported by anyone who happens upon the scene of the crime. On the other hand, crimes which are not easily discovered require some professional acumen to uncover the facts constituting the criminal act. This need for trained and professional detection to uncover previously unknown crimes is the major responsibility of police units. It is the reason that modern police forces are divided functionally into two major units: (1) the *patrol division* which acts to discover crime while its roving units, at the same time, tend to deter persons from criminal acts by their presence; this proximity also has the resultant likelihood of apprehending the criminal while a crime is in progress; (2) the *detective division*, which will detect crimes the patrol units have failed to deter, and that are either unreported or undiscovered, and investigate crimes which were previously discovered but are still unsolved. When the perpetrator of the criminal act is not arrested at the scene of the criminal act, or when he is not known to the police at the time of the report of the crime, the standard operating procedure is to question all persons involved and examine the crime scene for evidence.

Local rules for police patrol officers establish their responsibility when criminal acts are discovered on a police "post" or "beat." These rules are generally worded in terms similar to the rules of the New York City Police Department. New York's two rules for discovering crime, while on patrol, have been unchanged since its consolidation of several county-wide departments into one huge (five counties) unit in 1898:

> 47.0   When circumstances warrant, a member of the force on patrol may stop any person or operator of a vehicle for the purpose of identification and to satisfy himself that such person is on legitimate business.
>
> 44.0   A patrolman shall inspect his post as soon as possible and note

[7]*Ibid.*, Section 33.

any condition requiring police attention. Charges shall be preferred against any patrolman who negligently fails to discover, report and take police action in connection with any act or condition which requires police attention.[8]

Court decisions in California are specific in regard to police observation and action.[9] A police officer may make inquiry of anyone upon the public streets late at night to ascertain his identity and the occasion of his presence, if the surroundings are such as to indicate to a reasonable man that the public safety demands such identification. This is known as "field interrogation" by police officers, and the basis for such police action may exist in: (1) crimes recently committed in the locality; (2) the subject acting strangely, loitering or conducting himself in a furtive manner.

California's Penal Code also provides for the search of a person for dangerous weapons.[10] Other states generally permit a police officer to run his hands over a person's clothing when he has reason to fear an attack with a hidden weapon, but most statutes and court decisions tread a bit lightly in granting power to police in this area, despite the fact that the investigation of "suspicious" persons and places are within the scope of the standard police role.

Police in the state of New York petitioned their legislators to enact a special provision of law defining "suspicious circumstances and persons," and delineating the police right to stop such persons for questioning and possible search. Chapter 86, Laws of New York, enacted in 1964, is the result of this police plea for special legislation. It reads in part:

> 1. A police officer may stop any person abroad in a public place whom he reasonably suspects is committing, has committed or is about to commit a felony or any of the crimes specified in section 552 (high misdemeanors: possession of illegal gun, burglar's tools, etc.) of this chapter, and may demand of him his name, address and an explanation of his actions.
>
> 2. When a police officer has stopped a person for questioning pursuant to this section and reasonably suspects that he is in danger of life or limb, he may search such person for a dangerous weapon.

When police fail to deter crime or intercept its progress by alertness to suspicious people and circumstances, the crime scene becomes the place at which police activity is concentrated. The "first officer on the scene" follows a standard police operating procedure which may be summed up as follows: (1) arrest offender, if present; (2) "freeze" the

[8]*Rules and Procedures* (New York: New York City Police Department, 1956), p. 43.
[9]*Gisske v. Sanders*, 9 Cal. App. 13 (1908).
[10]California Penal Code, Section 833.

scene, discover and hold witnesses and others involved until identified and interviewed, and prevent unauthorized persons from entering area; (3) prevent persons present at the scene from destroying evidence; (4) secure all available information; (5) search for and preserve evidence, and (6) record all facts.

The dispatch of police officers to the scene of a crime is usually by radio. If the radio broadcast indicates the crime is still in progress, the first officer to arrive may be any officer in the vicinity; but when the message notes the crime is a "past"[11] burglary or theft, an officer is usually assigned to respond to the scene. When the criminal is not apprehended at the crime scene, discovering and processing evidence and witnesses establish the basic facts upon which detectives of a police unit may base their later investigation of the criminal act. Such detective work is a long-established technique for determining who might have the motive or opportunity, or both, to commit the crime, and developing the probable cause for arrest and prosecution.

The General Investigation

The police investigator will take into consideration all evidence in the case, the character and reputation of the suspect or the premises and information supplied by other law enforcement agencies. An assigned police officer may recall that one of the suspects is a "known criminal" with many previous arrests and a *modus operandi*[12] similar to the crime under investigation. Victims and witnesses will be asked to scan "mug" books of convicted criminals. In these ways, the general investigation seeks to develop meaningful information about the identity of the perpetrator of the criminal act, exclude innocent suspects and direct the investigation toward securing legally significant evidence of the "prime suspect's" guilt.

The general investigation takes cognizance of the policeman's status as a professional, recognizing that through both training and experience the police officer can develop an expert knowledge of the ways in which persons violate laws. It is a conclusion of many courts that police officers have special knowledge, ability and judgment in determining reasonable cause to take action in criminal investigations. Of course, these same courts expect that professionally competent police investigators will be prepared to show the facts upon which they based their action, and that these facts be justifiable.

[11]The time of occurrence of the crime is an hour or more prior to the time of discovery.
[12]Method of operation, habituation to a standard procedure in criminal operations.

The Focus of Investigation

The focal point of an investigation of an unsolved crime occurs when police effort is concentrated on one person as a perpetrator of a crime. It may not occur at the same point in each investigation, but it is an essential point of time in the span of an investigation. This shift in the investigation of a criminal act occurs at the point when the investigation is no longer a general inquiry into an unsolved crime, a "neutral inquiry," but has begun to focus on a particular suspect; when the police or prosecutor initiate a process of interrogation that lends itself to eliciting incriminating statements from that suspect.[13] In *Miranda v. Arizona*,[14] the U.S. Supreme Court states that this focusing of an investigation was meant to describe *custodial interrogation*: "questioning initiated by law enforcement officers after a person has been taken into custody or otherwise deprived of his freedom of action in any significant way." In extensive and unusual comment in *Miranda*, the court's majority opinion cites suggested police procedures in standard texts[15] in support of its belief that any person in custody needs the protection of legal counsel, friends or relatives.

Police Surveillance

Police surveillance techniques have as their basic purpose the securing of information which will successfully advance a criminal investigation to the point where an innocent suspect can be cleared, a suspect not in police custody could be clearly indicated as the guilty person, or additional evidence of guilt can be secured against a person already in custody for the commission of the criminal act being investigated.

A police surveillance may be within the scope of the general investigation, or it may be one of the police investigative techniques utilized after an investigation has focused upon one individual. It is an examination, a viewing, a scanning and an inspection. The police view, optimally without notice, the activities of suspected persons to gather meaningful information. Often they must seek data on words and conduct that a suspect would prefer to keep within the realm of private knowl-

[13]*Escobedo v. Illinois*, 378 U.S. 478 (1964).
[14]384 U.S. 436 (1966).
[15]Inbau and Reid, *Criminal Interrogations and Confessions* (Baltimore: The Williams & Wilkins Co., 1962), pp. 34–55, 87, 111–12.
Charles E. O'Hara, *Fundamentals of Criminal Investigation* (Springfield, Ill.: Charles C. Thomas, Publisher, 1964), pp. 99–112.

edge. Therefore, a police surveillance is usually not performed openly. In fact, it has been termed "snooping." Modern police officers are fully aware that the previously unlimited use of police surveillance is now limited by court decisions in the *Miranda*[16] and the *Massiah*[17] cases when that surveillance is part of in-custody interrogation (Miranda) or a secret police interrogation (Massiah).

Surveillance techniques of police generally fall into two major categories: audio and visual.

AUDIO

Techniques of audio surveillance range from the placing of hidden microphones for eavesdropping to wiretapping for the interception of telephone communications. The recent introduction of long-distance disk or tubular microphones is an extension of the hidden microphone technique. This is a device with which a person may overhear the conversation of others from a distance of several hundred feet. These long-distance microphones negate what was once thought to be a legally sufficient barrier to an overuse of the technique of electronic eavesdropping: the doctrine established in the case of *Silverman v. U.S.*[18] In this landmark case, the U.S. Supreme Court ruled that any physical penetration of the premises constituted a trespass in violation of constitutional guarantee against unreasonable searches and seizures. Police interception of telephone messages as a surveillance technique was outlawed by the court's decision in *Benanti v. U.S.*[19] The court's opinion in *Benanti* called a halt to any surreptitious surveillance by the wiretapping of telephones. The court held that a federal law against the invasion of privacy by wiretapping,[20] which had not been observed by many state agents because of permissive local laws, was binding.

Eavesdropping electronically has some permissive court decisions when there isn't a trespass and police use such devices as a minifon,[21] a miniature microphone and radio transmitter[22] or a detectaphone.[23] However, the use of "spike" microphones which are driven into a wall may be unlawful,[24] and the growing approval of "monitoring" telephone

[16]384 U.S. 436 (1966).
[17]377 U.S. 201 (1964).
[18]365 U.S. 505 (1961).
[19]355 U.S. 96 (1957).
[20] U. S. Communications Act, Section 605.
[21]*Lopez v. U.S.*, 373 U.S. 427 (1963).
[22]*On Lee v. U.S.*, 343 U.S. 747 (1952).
[23]*Goldman v. U.S.*, 316 U.S. 129 (1942).
[24]*Silverman v. U.S.*, 365 U.S. 505 (1961).
   Clinton v. Virginia, 377 U.S. 158 (1964).

conversations requires the special permission of one party to the telephone conversation and the use of an extension telephone.[25]

There is little doubt that many major crimes have been solved with
information gained by police officers assigned to audio surveillances; in
some of the cases there is some belief that the case would not have been
solved by any other known police technique. In 1929, police wiretapping
had the approval of the U.S. Supreme Court. The leading decision of
that day commented that denial of this technique of audio surveillance
to police "would make society suffer and give criminals greater immunity
than has been known heretofore."[26] However, the average citizen has
heard time and again, of many abuses of this surveillance technique.
Stories about blackmail, commercial spying and the use of police "wire-
men" to tap the wires of both politicians and businessmen were not
uncommon.[27] This was not propaganda against police wiretapping, in
the sense that any of the stories were untrue, but it had the effect of
propaganda. Now, the courts appear to have rejected wiretapping as a
valid technique in law enforcement, and despite pleas for a reinstatement
of this practice by police and prosecuting officials, there appears to be
little likelihood of legislative action to amend the federal law.

VISUAL

Ordinary "looking," despite the fact it may be supplemented by optical
or photographic equipment, is the most acceptable form of police surveillance. This is true even when it is observation through windows, over
transoms or through cracks in the walls of buildings. Visual observation
may be mobile, with police officers following a suspect, or fixed, with
police officers manning a "stake-out."

Photographic surveillance has high court and public acceptance. The
many pictures taken of bank robbers in action captured the imagination
of the country, and gave law enforcement agents a new use for an old
technique. Robot or "monitor" cameras are also suitable for every kind
of observation in which a record of visual observation is necessary or
desirable, and lessen the possibility the surveillance will be discovered
and compromised. It is necessary to maintain a chain of evidence in the
taking, processing and presentation of photographic evidence in order to
ensure its admissibility at trial. This is the biggest problem with this
kind of surveillance. However, when admitted in trial, it is a graphic
representation that is likely to be not only demonstrative but decisive.

[25]*Rathbun v. U.S.*, 355 U.S. 107 (1957).
[26]*Olmstead v. U.S.*, 277 U.S. 438 (1928).
[27]Samuel Dash, Richard F. Schwartz, and Robert E. Knowlton, *The Eavesdroppers*
(New Brunswick, N.J.: Rutgers University Press, 1959).

Mail "covers" are a somewhat strange visual examination. The exterior of all mail received by a person is subjected to examination by postal employees and reports made to the law enforcement agency whose request for such surveillance has been approved by a postal official. It is safeguarded by numerous post office restrictions and is a carefully reserved surveillance technique that has not received a great deal of criticism since it is restricted to the listing of the characteristics of the mail and the reporting of any writing or printing, including postmarks, on the outside of such mail. The mail is not opened and examined.

The same type of visual "cover" is often extended to the records of long-distance telephone communications. The toll tickets of a telephone company will identify the subscriber, the telephone called, the duration of the call and the cost of each call. Procurement of telephone records usually requires a court order to the telephone company; it is an excellent source of useful information in certain cases, and it is a police surveillance that appears to have both court and public acceptance.

Arrest

Modern arrest procedures are not techniques of investigation. The casebuilders of today's police units have learned to work within the limits established by the wording of the Mallory decision: "It is not the function of the police to arrest, as it were, at large and use an interrogating process at police headquarters in order to determine whom they should charge before a committing magistrate on probable cause."[28] Each state has its own statutes delegating the power of arrest within its jurisdiction, with some variance in peripheral areas, but with basic harmony in core areas. California's Penal Code[29] clearly and concisely delineates the rights and limitations in this important area of criminal justice. It is cited for this reason and because it is generally illustrative of the law of arrest in other states.

Strangely, the power of arrest without prior notice and approval has never been fully delegated to either private persons or police officers. The warrant of arrest remains a basic court process by which a judicial officer, usually a magistrate,[30] reviews the circumstances of the arrest prior to any summary action and either approves or disapproves of the proposed arrest. In California, a warrant may be issued when a complaint is filed with a magistrate charging a public offense originally triable in the

[28]*Mallory v. U.S.*, 354 U.S. 449 (1957).
[29]Chapters 3–5, Sections 806, 834–851.5.
[30]The judge or justice of a trial court including inferior courts, but sometimes restricted to "courts of record."

superior court of the county in which he sits, if such magistrate is satisfied from the complaint that: (1) the offense complained of has been committed, and (2) there are reasonable grounds to believe the defendant has committed it.

In 1963, the state legislature, "in an urgency measure necessary for the immediate preservation of the public peace, health or safety,"[31] added the following clause to the statutory authorization for warrants of arrest: ". . . provided, that when the magistrate is a judge of the justice court, he may issue such a warrant only upon the concurrence of the district attorney of the county in which he sits or the Attorney General of the state of California." This legislative edict became necessary when judges of this minor court—organized to dispose of minor crimes and arraignments on more serious charges—utilized their designation as magistrates to issue warrants of arrest that, at times, grossly interfered with the processes of justice. Some of the abuses extended to harrassment of public officials and delayed the handling of worthy cases. This action of the lawmakers of a large state is illustrative of the continuing supervision afforded persons to whom the power of arrest is delegated.

An arrest consists of taking a person into custody in the manner authorized by law; it may be made by a peace officer or by a private citizen.

An arrest is made by the arresting officer (or person) giving adequate notice to the individual to be arrested. Such notice should include the intention to arrest, the cause of the arrest and the authority to make it, except when the person making the arrest has reasonable cause to believe that the suspect is engaged in the criminal act or its attempt, or is pursued immediately after its commission or after an escape. Adequate notice also includes the offense for which the arrest is being made whenever the prisoner requests such information.

Peace officers[32] may make an arrest in compliance to a warrant, and they may also arrest without a warrant whenever the arresting officer has reasonable cause to believe that the suspect has committed a public offense in his presence, or a felony—although the felony need not be committed in the presence of the arresting officer and may not have, in fact, been committed.

An arrest by a peace officer acting under a warrant is lawful even though the officer does not have the warrant in his possession at the time of the arrest. The officer may use all necessary means to effect the arrest —after adequate notice of his intention to make the arrest—if the suspect

---

[31]California Penal Code, Section 813, *Note.*

[32]Peace officers are often so defined by law, but the term is generally synonymous with full-time, salaried law enforcement agents such as municipal police, sheriff's deputies and state highway traffic officers.

either flees or forcibly resists. After the arrest, the warrant shall be shown to the arrested person upon his request and as soon as practicable.

A private person may arrest another for a public offense committed or attempted in his presence, may arrest a felon although the felony was not committed in his presence and may arrest when a felony has been committed and he has reasonable cause for believing the person to be arrested has committed it. However, he acts at his peril that a crime has in fact been committed. Also, upon the oral order of a magistrate, an arrest can be made by any person of any individual committing or attempting to commit a public offense in the presence of the magistrate.

If the offense for which the arrest is being made is a felony, the arrest may be made on any day and at any time of the day or night. If it is a misdemeanor, the arrest cannot be made at night, unless upon the direction of a magistrate and endorsed upon the warrant, except when the offense is committed in the presence of the arresting officer.

If an arrested person does not submit to the arrest, he may be subjected to such restraint as is reasonable for his arrest and detention; physical force or any weapon should not be used in resisting arrest when the person being arrested has knowledge—or by the exercise of reasonable care should have knowledge—that he is being arrested by a peace officer. Peace officers with cause to believe that the person to be arrested has committed a public offense may use reasonable force to effect the arrest, to prevent escape or to overcome resistance; they need not retreat or desist because of actual or threatened resistance of the person being arrested—and such officer should not be deemed an aggressor or lose his right to self-defense by the use of reasonable force to effect the arrest or to prevent escape or overcome resistance. However, deadly force is not permitted in making misdemeanor arrests, unless used in self-defense.[33]

Any person making an arrest may take from the arrested person all offensive weapons which he may have about his person, and deliver them to the arraigning magistrate.

Breaking and entering a building to make an arrest may be necessary, and it is lawful if the person making the arrest acts, in general, in emulation of a "reasonable and prudent man."[34] The law also authorizes a breaking out—if detained—from a premises entered for the purpose of making a lawful arrest. In California, this basic law[35] reads:

> To make an arrest, a private person, if the offense be a felony, and in all cases a peace officer, may break open the door or window of the house in which the person to be arrested is, or in which they have reasonable

[33]*Cerri v. U.S.*, 80 Fed. Supp. (1949).
  People v. Hardwick, 204 Cal. 582 (1928).
[34]A just, fair, sensible man with ordinary wisdom, carefulness and sound judgment.
[35]California Penal Code, Section 844–5.

grounds for believing him to be, after having demanded admittance and explained the purpose for which the admittance is desired. Any person who has lawfully entered a house for the purpose of making an arrest, may break open the door or window thereof if detained therein, when necessary for the purpose of liberating himself, and an officer may do the same, when necessary for the purpose of liberating a person who, acting in his aid, lawfully entered for the purpose of making an arrest, and is detained therein.

An officer acting in good faith, as a reasonable and prudent man, may omit the demand for entrance and explanation of purpose whenever: (1) the delay would permit the destruction of evidence or its hiding; (2) the officer is put in hazard of an attack by the person to be arrested; or (3) delay may allow the suspect to escape. California's courts of review have affirmed cases in which officers broke into a building without demand and refusal under the following circumstances: officers heard a swift movement toward the bathroom (possible destruction of evidence); knowledge of prior armed robbery convictions in the criminal history of a person to be arrested for robbery (potential hazard); and the officers heard retreating footsteps (escape).

False Arrest

There is always a liability upon an arresting officer who makes a legally defective arrest. However, there can be no justification of a claim of false arrest when the arresting officer acts in good faith without malice, carelessness or negligence. An officer will incur no liability for false arrest or false imprisonment when: (1) such arrest was lawful or when such peace officer, at the time of the arrest, had reasonable cause to believe the arrest was lawful; (2) when such arrest was made pursuant to a charge made, upon reasonable cause, of the commission of a felony by the person to be arrested; or (3) when an arrest was made of a person charged with crime, on a magisterial order, or upon assisting another in making an arrest when orally summoned to aid in the arrest.

Booking and Detention

In most areas, unless the prisoner requires prompt medical care, rules of police procedure require a peace officer to bring the person he has arrested to a central point for search, recording the details of the arrest (booking) and detention.

The search is under the supervision of the policeman assigned to the booking office, usually a superior officer, and is a thorough examination.

A record is made of all evidence taken from the prisoner and it is appropriately marked and safeguarded. A receipt is prepared in duplicate of all articles of value taken from the prisoner at this time, and a copy of this receipt is delivered to the prisoner by the booking officer at the time of booking.

Booking procedures may vary slightly across the country, but the following rules are in general use by police:

(1) Authority for the arrest and the specific law violated is established and entered on the official arrest records. This includes the name of the victim, the time and place of the occurrence of the crime charged and of the arrest, and enough of the circumstances of the case to establish probable cause for the arrest and a detailing of the essential elements of the crime charged.

(2) The prisoner's fingerprints are taken, and he is photographed. .

(3) When the prisoner's identity is established, a check is made with the records division for outstanding "wants" for other crimes.

(4) The arresting officer admonishes the prisoner regarding his right to remain silent, warns him anything he may say is likely to be used in court against him, and of his right to an attorney, retained or appointed, prior to making any statement, and entry is made to this effect in the arrest records.

(5) The prisoner is informed of the approximate time and date of his arraignment and the name of the court and its location, of the law regarding bail, rules of the detention jail and any other necessary information (but booking and arrest officers cannot recommend bail bondsmen or attorneys).

(6) The prisoner is placed in a cell, permitted release on bail, sent to a hospital (if required) or released as otherwise provided by law.

Prosecutors in California recommend that police use a simple and uniform statement during the arrest process to warn a prisoner of his rights regarding custodial interrogation[36] so they could show some familiarity, when on the witness stand during a trial, with what was said in this advice to the arrested person.

In California, except where physically impossible, from the time immediately following his booking to not later than three hours after his arrest, an arrested person has the right to at least two telephone calls from the booking office. These calls will be at his own expense, in the presence of a public officer or employee, and it is considered adequate when one call is completed to the person called, who may be his attorney, employer or a relative; and the other call is completed to a bail bonds-

[36]A term developed for in-custody police questioning by the U.S. Supreme Court, *Miranda v. Arizona*, 384 U.S. 436 (1966).

man. Any public officer or employee who deprives an arrested person of his rights to such communications is guilty of a misdemeanor.

After arrest, at the request of the prisoner or any relative of such prisoner, any attorney at law entitled to practice in the courts of record in California may visit the prisoner. Any officer having charge of a prisoner who willfully refuses or neglects to allow such attorney to visit a prisoner is guilty of a misdemeanor; any officer having a prisoner in charge, who refuses to allow any attorney to visit the prisoner when proper application is made is liable to a fine of five hundred dollars, to be recovered by action in any court of competent jurisdiction.

A peace officer in California may release a prisoner, arrested without a warrant, from custody whenever: (1) he is satisfied no grounds exist for making a criminal complaint against the accused (and any record of such arrest shall note such release and be deemed a detention rather than an arrest); (2) the person arrested is charged with intoxication only, and no further proceedings are desirable, and (3) the person arrested is charged only with a misdemeanor and has signed an agreement to appear in court or before a magistrate at a place and time designated.

Original Arraignment

When a prisoner is not subject to release in accordance with an established schedule of bail, or is not bailed and is in a condition suitable for court appearance (not drunk, unconscious, ill or mentally incompetent), he must be taken without unnecessary delay to the nearest or most accessible magistrate in the county in which the offense is triable —no longer than two days after his arrest, excluding Sundays and holidays. However, when the two days prescribed expire at a time when the court in which the magistrate is sitting is not in session, the time for this original arraignment of the prisoner is extended to include the duration of the next regular court session on the judicial day immediately following.[37]

Upon the arraignment of the prisoner before an examining magistrate and the filing of a complaint, the case is placed before the court for review of the police action since the time of the criminal act.

The basic "complaint" at this original arraignment before a magistrate, and upon which the examination of the circumstance of the arrest will proceed, must be in writing and subscribed to under oath by the "complainant." In California, when the examining magistrate is only a judge

[37]Usually described as two "court days."

of the justice court, the complaint must be approved by the District Attorney or the state's Attorney General.

In New York State, police of several major cities are permitted by state law[38] to file a "short affidavit" upon the original arraignment. This is in lieu of a complaint, when the illness or injury of vital witnesses prevents the arresting officer from completing his case in time to file a complaint, and the offender can thus be held by the examining magistrate for 48 hours pending the filing of a formal complaint.

Selected References

CASES

Benanti v. U.S., 355 U.S. 96 (1957).
>   The landmark case against wiretapping.

Gisske v. Sanders, 9 Cal. App. 13 (1908).
>   An early California case upholding police procedures regarding suspicious persons and exploring the duty of police to discover, detect and deter crime.

Massiah v. U.S., 377 U.S. 201 (1964).
>   The police practice of equipping a person with a radio transmitter capable of sending conversation to listening officers was held illegal because the defendant questioned was under indictment at the time and did not have the assistance of legal counsel. An informative decision.

McNabb v. U.S., 318 U.S. 332 (1943).
>   This case established the rule that defendants must be promptly arraigned in federal courts. As interesting decision because it foreshadows upcoming decisions likely to make the doctrine of this case enforceable against the states.

BOOKS

Bristow, Allen P., *Field Interrogation*. Springfield, Ill.: Charles C. Thomas, Publisher, 1964. 155 pages.
>   Bristow discusses field interrogation as a procedure in screening suspicious persons encountered by police on patrol, and as a source of useful information.

Gerber, Samuel R., and Oliver Schroeder, Jr., *Criminal Investigation and Interrogation*. Cincinnati, Ohio: The W. H. Anderson Co., 1962. 503 pages.
>   A collection of edited lectures, presented at the Law-Medicine Center, Western Reserve University, that offers a well organized and easily read text detailing investigative and interrogation procedures. An overview of

[38]New York Code of Criminal Procedure, Section 145a.

the pretrial investigation in several excellent chapters permits comparison with police practices in other countries.

LaFave, Wayne R., *Arrest: The Decision to Take a Suspect into Custody.* Boston: Little Brown and Company, 1965. 540 pages. (Published for the American Bar Association.)

A comprehensive review of the current practices in making arrests and attendant problems. The text is divided into five parts: (1) warrants, (2) discretion, (3) alternatives to arrest and delay, (4) prosecution and its purposes and (5) purposes other than prosecution. LaFave has consolidated data gained in an American Bar Association survey of the administration of justice into a definitive treatment of the many important and unresolved issues related to the initial action of police and prosecutor in moving against the accused in criminal proceedings.

O'Hara, Charles E., *Fundamentals of Criminal Investigation.* Springfield, Ill.: Charles C. Thomas, Publisher, 1964. 740 pages.

The significance and application of the basic tools of investigation: information, interrogation and instrumentation. The author develops full appreciation of the crime scene as a core area of police investigation. The text is by an experienced police detective and criminalist familiar with police routines in "the street" and in the laboratory.

Payton, George T., *Patrol Procedure.* Los Angeles: Legal Book Store, 1964. 304 pages.

This is the "how to" book of procedures for policemen on patrol in uniform. It details the acceptable practices for coping with problems encountered by police in the prevention and detection of crime, the apprehension of offenders and the protection of life and property.

ARTICLES

Collins, Robert L., "Improved Crime Scene Investigation," *Journal of Criminal Law, Criminology and Police Science* (November-December 1961), pp. 469–70.

The article examines rising crime rates, court rejection of certain police search-and-seizure and interrogation techniques and increasing professional skills among criminals requiring improved techniques of police investigation. Collins suggests emphasis on the crime scene and physical evidence amenable to scientific analysis.

Meier, Robert, "The Advocate as Investigator," *American Bar Association Journal* (September 1964), pp. 835–37.

An attorney's approach to the role of investigator often results in an investigation pointed toward proving assumed facts. The author analyzes investigation techniques and points out areas of importance in developing legally significant facts.

3

The Exclusionary Rule
and Police Interrogation
and Searches

Fundamental safeguards of liberty, long immune from federal abridgement, are now protected against invasion by state agents through the due process clause of the Fourteenth Amendment. These are the principles of liberty and justice which lie at the base of all our civil and political institutions. The principles recognized initially as fundamental were the First Amendment's freedom of speech, press, religion, assembly, association and petition for redress of grievances. The doctrine of the *Gitlow case*[1] incorporated freedom of speech and press within the operation of the Fourteenth Amendment and thus set a precedent for the later cases which brought the remaining First Amendment freedoms within the scope of the Fourteenth Amendment's protection against state abridgement.

[1]*Gitlow v. New York*, 268 U.S. 652, 666 (1925).

The U.S. Supreme Court and the high courts of individual states, since the *Gitlow* decision, have utilized the Fourteenth Amendment to enforce compliance by state agents with many other guarantees of the Bill of Rights. Police investigatory practices must not be in opposition to the Fourth Amendment's provision for privacy and its prohibition against unreasonable searches and seizures; nor infringe upon the Fifth Amendment's provision that an accused may not be "compelled in any criminal case to be a witness against himself"; nor deny the Sixth Amendment's fundamental premise that the assistance of legal counsel should be available for the defense of any person charged with crime.

There has been a gradual escalation of restrictions placed upon the activities of law enforcement and its agents. Originally, the exclusion of evidence was based on police procedures which were clearly illegal, but in recent years cases have been reversed in which the police investigators were actually following procedures established by their department's book of regulations.

Today, police agencies must develop workable rules which will meet the practical demands of effective criminal investigation and the requirements of the fundamental liberties found in the Constitution. Under this increasing projection of the concept of federalism (or uniformity throughout the U.S.), the same minimal standards must be established in every police agency. If evidence gathered by police during an investigation that precedes, accompanies or follows an arrest is not to be declared inadmissible, it must meet these minimal standards.

There will have to be an increase in professional competence among police officers. This in turn, it is hoped, will improve the image of the policeman with the general public, lead to higher salaries, and not only attract college-educated applicants to the police service but also motivate veteran policemen to undertake off-duty educational programs.

Origin and Growth of the Exclusionary Rule

For many years, the admissibility of evidence upon the trial of a criminal offense was determined by whether or not the evidence might aid the jury in determining the guilt of the accused. If relevant, it was believed that evidence should be admitted and not excluded merely because of the manner in which it was obtained—even if the manner in which the evidence was gathered might be unlawful. Today, however, the fruits of illegal police procedures in gathering evidence are inadmissible in court.

This variation in basic trial procedure stems from the fact that the judicial representatives of modern government believe police officers must not commit illegal acts in gathering evidence against an accused person. This judicial action has resulted in clearly defined areas for rejecting evidence, and is generally termed the "exclusionary rule." Its origin and growth stem from the fact that it appears to be the only means by which meaningful action can be taken to discourage law enforcement officers from practicing illegal means to secure evidence. The exclusionary rule is not a constitutional right, but merely a means of enforcing such legal guarantees. It is a choice offered to police officers: secure evidence by legal means and it is likely to be admissible upon trial; but use illegal evidence-gathering techniques and such tainted evidence is equally likely to be suppressed.[2]

In short, the constitutional provisions guaranteeing certain basic liberties and rights were not being enforced by administrative action. Nor was the right to civil redress, or the law that criminal prosecutions might result from acts related to violations of such rights, a real and practical guarantee of the enforcement of these basic liberties. The lack of concern about either the civil or criminal "safeguards" in our statutory law by police officers in past years is illustrative of the ineffectiveness of "civil redress" or "criminal prosecution" as a deterrent to police illegality in the investigation of crime.

Many public-spirited persons (including numerous police officers who may be justly so termed because the driving motivation in their work against the depredations of crime is based on a sincere desire to serve law and order in the community) believe the judiciary of our appellate courts have erred in freeing guilty persons successfully convicted of crime in a criminal proceeding. However, the fact that the judiciary of our courts of review did not make the majority of their "exclusionary" decisions retroactive is proof that the judges did not contemplate any retrospective effect from their decisions, but only considered the protection of future accused persons from similar invasions of liberties and rights.[3]

Intemperate criticism of the judiciary for its so-called "handcuffing" of the police by the exclusionary rule may have its base—and certainly some support—from the fact that there has been little public hue and cry against the police for conduct infringing upon basic rights. It is not because the general public is aware that such cases are the exception rather than the rule, but a lack of specific aggravation. It is difficult for public outrage and indignation to build up against coerced confessions, unreasonable searches and seizures or arrests without probable cause,

[2]*People v. Cahan*, 44 Cal. 2nd 434 (1955).
 Mapp v. Ohio, 367 U.S. 643 (1961).
 Miranda v. Arizona, 384 U.S. 436 (1966).
[3]*Linkletter v. Walker*, 381 U.S. 618 (1965); *In re. Lopez* 62 Cal. 2nd 368 (1965).

when the person whose rights are violated often has an active association with crime and criminals.

What citizen is going to stand up and protest against the injustice of police pressure of various coercive forms in securing confessions from the "sellers" and "pushers" of the illicit drug traffic? Who is going to demand that police be suspended and even dismissed for searching a person previously convicted several times for armed robbery? And in how many communities is there a man who might feel outraged because police arrested a local bookmaker and found slips and other memoranda after the arrest for its primary justification? Most persons who read of the arrests of these types of individuals probably feel an inner satisfaction that the police finally caught up with them!

Lack of public reaction to past illegalities and infringements of basic rights procedures resulted in police officers becoming habituated to procedures not based upon law, but which are now defended with vigor because they are *de facto*[4] police techniques. However, despite some unwillingness, police officers must now meet the minimal standards established by this judicially declared rule of evidence. Change will be akin to radical surgery for the prevailing police practices in both the interrogation and the search-and-seizure areas of investigation, but the exclusionary rule establishes a set of basic and incontestable guidelines indicating that any illegality by law enforcement officers sworn to support the Constitution of the United States and the Constitution of their "employing" state is likely to seriously impair the prosecution of a criminal case.

The Rule of Derivative Evidence

The essence or force of the exclusionary rule is not that illegally acquired evidence shall not be used before a court during a trial, but that it shall not be used *at all*. The knowledge gained by the wrongdoing involved with involuntary confessions or illegal searches and seizures cannot be used derivatively. The police-prosecutor team is not permitted to make any other use of evidence forbidden at the trial.

Once the defense counsel has established that certain evidence was obtained illegally, he must go on to prove that a substantial portion of the prosecutor's case consists of evidence which can be categorized as the "fruit of the poisoned tree." This claim should be made at the earliest moment, preferably in a pretrial order to suppress the tainted evidence. The prosecutor has the opportunity to dispute this contention, so long

[4]In fact.

as he can convince the court that the evidence in question had an independent origin, removed from the "poisoned tree."

The derivative evidence rule stems from decisions in the case of *Silverthorne Lumber Company v. U.S.*[5] and in the case of *Nardone v. U.S.*[6] In the *Silverthorne* case, the court commented: "The essence of a provision forbidding the acquisition of evidence in a certain way is that not merely evidence so acquired shall not be used before the Court but that it shall not be used at all." In the *Nardone* decision, the fruit of the poisoned tree doctrine was summed up by the court: "To forbid the direct use of methods thus characterized, but to put no curb on their full indirect use, would only invite the very methods deemed inconsistent with ethical standards and destructive of personal liberty."

The Admissibility of Confessions

Police officers have long recognized as appropriate for interrogation the time period starting after the accused person is in custody and ending when the prisoner is arraigned before a magistrate. One nationally known police official stated that this was the only opportunity for the police to develop an understanding in the prisoner of the many facets of his involvement with a criminal charge, and that interrogation was necessary if the police were to proceed on their commitment to protect society against predatory criminals. The police attitude may be summed up as common to any hard-working technician, and indicates nothing more than a desire for a reasonable time to establish a rapport with the prisoner which may lead to a full disclosure of his involvement in the offense charged.

Professor Fred E. Inbau, Northwestern University School of Law, Chicago, Illinois, commented on the attitude of modern police officers when he said he was against any interrogation tactic or technique that would be liable to make an innocent person confess. Dr. Arthur H. Sherry, Professor of Law and Criminology, University of California at Berkeley, advised that the postarrest period deserved a good deal of "thought and consideration" about interrogations, saying any police inquiry after a person was arrested must be conducted in a manner which would not incur the "displeasure or the censure of the courts." "Courts in the United States," Dr. Sherry concluded, "have always had a traditional suspicion and dislike of confessions made to police as evidence. An accusatorial system of justice must provide many enforceable safeguards for the individuals, and the courts of the United States have

[5]251 U.S. 385 (1920).
[6]308 U.S. 338 (1939).

indicated their dislike of the similarity between police-station interrogation of a lone and unadvised suspect and the interrogatory practices of the 17th Century!"

Traditionally, upon trial, prosecuting attorneys question police officers who testify about confessions as to the possible inadmissibility of a confession. The three basic questions utilized to exhibit the basic voluntariness of the confession about to be introduced are usually:

(1) *Did you inform the defendant, at this time, of his right to counsel and his right to remain silent?* In many instances, this question is quickly followed by one concerning the use of responses to questions. This is often put in this form: *Did you inform the defendant that anything he said would be used against him in court?*

(2) *Did you threaten the defendant in any way?* Many prosecutors will probe deeply into this area, using specific questions to develop the basic concept that the confession of the defendant was not the product of fear inspired in some manner by the interrogator or someone under his control.

(3) *Did you make any promises to the defendant?* This question may be less general in some jurisdictions. Usually, the prosecutor confines his query to whether or not the interrogator had made any promises of leniency to secure the confession of the defendant.

While the circumstances of each interrogation will differ, a review of the major factors governing the "voluntary-involuntary" rule for confessions and a gleaning of the controlling cases indicate the conduct by police interrogators which has created the attitude of distrust mentioned by Professor Sherry.

Denial of Rights

The initial factor most likely to invalidate a confession is the denial of basic legal rights to an accused person. Unless a police interrogator can state from the witness stand that the defendant was, in fact, warned of his right to remain silent, warned that if he did respond to questions such answers might be used in court against him upon his trial and told of his right to consult an attorney before he responded to questions, the prosecutor is structuring his case on a weak groundwork. The counsel for the defense may enter a motion to suppress a confession that might otherwise be admissible and contain many legally significant facts. Among the cases illustrating this point are the following:

Escobedo v. Illinois.[7] This is the landmark case in which failure of police interrogators to warn the petitioner of his constitutional rights to

[7]378 U.S. 478 (1964).

counsel and to silence invalidated the results of police diligence and skill. The court's comment indicates that today's test of the voluntariness of a confession must start with an affirmative notice that an accused person has a right to legal advice prior to answering any questions; in fact, he does not have to respond to police questioning at all if the investigation is no longer a neutral inquiry based on the duty of police to inquire about the facts of an unsolved crime. The decision reads, in part: "The simple and peaceful process of questioning breeds a readiness to resort to bullying and to physical force and torture. Thus the legitimate use grows into the unjust abuse. Ultimately, the innocent are jeopardized by the encroachments of a bad system."

People v. Dorado.[8] This California decision clarifies the duty of police officers to warn a person of his constitutional rights to counsel and to silence. The court noted: "Once the investigation has focused on the defendant, any incriminating statements given by him during interrogation by the investigating officers became inadmissible, in the absence of counsel and by the failure of the officer to advise the defendant of his right to an attorney and his right to remain silent. The constitutional right to counsel does not arise from the request for counsel, but from the advent of the accusatory stage itself."

Miranda v. Arizona.[9] On June 13, 1966, the U.S. Supreme Court spelled out in detail the doctrine of *Escobedo* in four related cases in which *Miranda* is the reference case. The decision was similar to the California Supreme Court's holding in *Dorado*, but using a new term: custodial interrogation. In its decision, the court defined this term as follows: "By *custodial interrogation*, we mean questioning initiated by law enforcement officers after a person has been taken into custody or otherwise deprived of his freedom of action in any significant way." In a footnote to this definition, the court added: "This is what we meant in *Escobedo* when we spoke of an investigation which had focused on an accused."

The court's holding in *Miranda* is, briefly: "The prosecution may not use statements, whether exculpatory or inculpatory, stemming from *custodial interrogation* of the defendant unless it demonstrates the use of procedural safeguards effective to secure the privilege against self-incrimination." These safeguards, in accordance with the words of this decision are: "Prior to any questioning, the person must be warned that he has a right to remain silent, that any statement he does make may be used as evidence against him and that he has the right to the presence of an attorney, either retained or appointed. The defendant may waive

[8]62 Cal. 2nd 338 (1965).
[9]384 U.S. 436 (1966).

effectuation of these rights, provided the waiver is made voluntarily, knowingly and intelligently. If, however, he indicates in any manner and at any stage of the process that he wishes to consult with an attorney before speaking, there can be no questioning. If the individual is alone and indicates in any manner that he does not wish to be interrogated, the police may not question him."

However, in regard to this waiver by the accused person, the court's decision established several prerequisites as follows: (1) an individual need not make a preinterrogation request for a lawyer; "While such request affirmatively secures his right to have one, his failure to ask for a lawyer does not constitute a waiver"; (2) a valid waiver will not be presumed simply from the silence of the accused after warnings are given or simply from the fact that a confession was in fact eventually obtained; (3) the fact of lengthy interrogation or incommunicado incarceration before a statement is made is strong evidence that the accused did not validly waive his rights; and (4) any evidence that the accused was threatened, tricked, or cajoled into a waiver will ("of course") show that the defendant did not voluntarily waive his privilege.

The question of an in-custody interrogation being admissible upon trial is spelled out in *Miranda*. The majority opinion notes the court has always set high standards of proof for the waiver of constitutional rights, and states: "We reassert these standards as applied to in-custody interrogation." Specifically, the words of the decision note a heavy burden rests on "the people" to demonstrate that the defendant knowingly and intelligently waived his privilege against self-incrimination and his right to retained or appointed counsel, and adds: "Since the state is responsible for establishing the isolated circumstances under which the interrogation takes place and has the only means of making available corroborated evidence of warnings given during incommunicado interrogation, the burden is rightfully on its shoulders."

The majority opinion in this case contains a strange euphemism for the effects of this decision upon police interrogations: "The presence of counsel at the interrogation may serve several significant subsidiary functions as well." While it's true that the subsidiary functions mentioned in this decision might enhance the value of a confession as evidence, it is equally true that the court is aware that a competent attorney advises his client *not* to talk to the police, and that the effect of this decision is to reject police interrogation.

Massiah v. U.S.[10] This case is concerned with police interrogation of an indicted person without counsel through a codefendant, without informing the accused person his codefendant had been equipped by

[10] 377 U.S. 201 (1964).

police officers with a miniature radio microphone and transmitter, or that police were recording the conversation. It's true that the police secured many incriminating statements in this fashion, but the court ruled they were not usable in court against him: "Any secret interrogation of the defendant from and after the filing of the indictment without the protection afforded by the presence of counsel, contravenes the basic dictates of fairness in the conduct of criminal causes and the fundamental rights of persons charged with crime."

Griffin v. California.[11] While this case relates to the right of the defendant to remain silent at trial and to force the police and prosecutor to prove their case by other evidence, it also serves to show the judicial repugnance to force a person to testify against himself that probably far exceeds any working policeman's concept of the privilege against self-incrimination established by the Fifth Amendment. The court's comment noted that constitutional provisions against self-incrimination not only guarded an accused person's right to remain silent during a trial, but guarded him from any inferences based on his silence. The court ruled that neither the trial judge nor the prosecutor could comment before the trial jury upon a defendant's failure to testify in his own behalf. It's little wonder that prosecutors open the questioning of police who have interrogated defendants with queries concerned with facts which will show the defendant was fully aware of his rights against self-incrimination prior to making the statement about which the police witness hopes to testify.

Force and Threats

A confession that is the product of fear is involuntary and is likely to be declared inadmissible as offending the procedural safeguards of due process of law. No modern police officer ever contemplates the use of physical force, but the willingness of courts of review to recognize the "mental ordeal" of police interrogation is not fully appreciated by police interrogators. The following cases indicate the wide range of actions which may invalidate an otherwise voluntary confession.

Brown v. Mississippi.[12] This was a simple case, with the court ruling the confession was involuntary as actual physical force was used to obtain it. The court put it very plainly: "The rack and torture chamber may not be substituted for the witness stand."

Ashcraft v. Tennessee.[13] A thirty-hour questioning session under lights was ruled as psychological pressure robbing the defendant of

[11]380 U.S. 609 (1965).
[12]297 U.S. 278 (1936).
[13]322 U.S. 143 (1944).

mental freedom. "Such continuous questioning," the decision in this case noted, "is so inherently coercive that its very existence is irreconcilable with the possession of mental freedom by a lone suspect against whom the full coercive force of the police was brought to bear."

Culombe v. Connecticut.[14]   The court's opinion in this 1961 case noted that the task of reconciling the responsibility of the police in ferreting out crime with the right of the criminal defendant, however guilty, to be tried according to constitutional requirements was a recurring problem, touching upon the administration of criminal justice by all states. The decision pointed out that this was a case in which lengthy questioning was presented in an aggravated form as detention and interrogation had spanned four days and five nights. The court's decision concluded with: "Men are not to be exploited for the information necessary to condemn them, and a prisoner is not to be made the deluded instrument of his own conviction, and such an exploitation of interrogation, whatever its usefulness, is not a permissible substitute for judicial trial."

McNabb v. United States.[15]   This was the landmark case in which failure to promptly arraign a prisoner in court following his arrest created a belief that the delay was for the purpose of wrenching from the prisoner by physical force or its threat, or by relentless questioning over a lengthy period, evidence which would not otherwise be available to police. The court's opinion in this case stated a confession must be excluded from federal prosecution if made "during illegal detention due to failure to promptly carry a prisoner before a committing magistrate, whether or not the confession is the result of torture, physical or psychological."

Mallory v. United States.[16]   This 1957 case clarified the decision in the *McNabb* case as far as controlling the admissibility of evidence in trials in federal courts. Together, they are often referred to as the "McNabb-Mallory" rule, which may be stated as: Failure to promptly arraign a prisoner must be accompanied by justification for such delay or such circumstances create a suspicion that the delay was for ulterior reasons related to police interrogation. The state courts are not bound by this rule, but it is likely the doctrine will be carried over to this court system in future years. The court's comment in *Mallory* was as follows: "Circumstances may justify a brief delay between arrest and arraignment, as for instance, where the story volunteered by the accused is susceptible of quick verification through third parties, but the delay must not be of a nature to give opportunity for the extraction of a confession."

[14]367 U.S. 568 (1961).
[15]318 U.S. 332 (1943).
[16]354 U.S. 449 (1957).

Watts v. Indiana.[17]   This is a case delineating the mental ordeal of a police interrogation as a process identifying a confession as involuntary. The court's comment, in part, reads as follows: "When a suspect speaks because he is overborne, it is immaterial whether he has been subjected to a physical or mental ordeal. Eventually yielding to questioning under such circumstances is plainly the product of the suction process of interrogation and therefore the reverse of voluntary."

Promises—Hope of Reward

The last of the trio of factors most likely to invalidate a confession and make it subject to the exclusionary rule relates to the circumstances of any promises made to the defendant. A confession resulting primarily from a promise of some benefit made to the confessor by a person with a real or apparent official capacity, or in the presence of such person, is likely to be declared an involuntary confession since it probably would not have been made without the power of such promise. It is also safely assumed that hope of reward might result in an innocent person confessing to a crime in which he is not involved in any way.

Each state has many cases in which hope of reward has caused a confession to be declared inadmissible. The test is a simple one, whether or not the defendant was influenced by promises when he made the confession. Moreover, two California cases[18] indicate that the "slightest pressure" exerted on the defendant by this hope of reward resulting from a promise aligned in some way with officialdom is sufficient to exclude the confession as not resulting from an expression of free choice by the defendant.

"Hope of reward" does not in itself invalidate a confession. This hope may not originate in a promise negating free choice. Many free and voluntary confessions stem from the fact that at the time of interrogation the accused person talked because of his own belief that this exhibit of cooperation would serve to mitigate the crime or the sentence in some manner.

Totality of Circumstances

It is important that police interrogators also realize that other contributing factors might result in a confession being termed involuntary and therefore inadmissible in the trial of the person making it. It may

[17] 338 U.S. 49 (1949).
[18] *Peolpe v. Berve*, 51 Cal. 2nd 286 (1958).
   People v. Ballard, 167 Cal. App. 2nd 803 (1959).

be the false sympathy of a pretended friend, as in *Spano v. New York*;[19] a basic incapacity resulting from sickness or ill health, as in *Townsend v. Sain*;[20] insanity or mental incompetency, as in *Blackburn v. Alabama*;[21] or the status of the accused as to age, education, intelligence, language problems or lack of experience with police as in *Haley v. Ohio*,[22] *Ward v. Texas*[23] and *Escobedo v. Illinois*.[24] On the other hand, the court may also consider one or more of these factors as indicating the accused person's capacity for resisting police interrogation. This is particularly true of sophistication resulting from a defendant's many experiences with police and with criminal prosecutions.[25]

Many legal minds foresee the extrajudicial confession as a relic of the past. Mr. Justice White said in his dissenting opinion in the *Escobedo* case[26] that the apparent goal of the majority of his associates on the U.S. Supreme Court bench was to bar from evidence all admissions obtained from an individual suspected of crime, whether they were voluntary or involuntary. This does not mean that police interrogation techniques are no longer valuable in the current detection and investigation of crime—and its successful prosecution—but the totality of circumstances of an interrogation must meet the outlined minimal standards when a person being interrogated is the focus of an investigation or is detained in some form of police or governmental custody.

Reasonableness in Search and Seizure

It has taken almost half a century for the exclusionary rule to be extended to protect the privacy of all persons in the United States. In 1914, the U.S. Supreme Court reversed a lower court in *Weeks v. U.S.*,[27] and the majority opinion stated that evidence which had been the fruits of an unreasonable search and seizure by federal agents should not have been admitted into evidence upon the trial. Forty-one years later, in 1955, a state court acted and restricted state officers. This was the decision of the California Supreme Court in *People v. Cahan*.[28] In 1961, six years after the *Cahan* decision, the U.S. Supreme Court ruled in *Mapp*

[19]360 U.S. 315 (1959).
[20]372 U.S. 293 (1963).
[21]361 U.S. 199 (1960).
[22]332 U.S. 596 (1948).
[23]316 U.S. 547 (1942).
[24]378 U.S. 478 (1964).
[25]*Stein v. New York*, 346 U.S. 156 (1953).
[26]378 U.S. 478 (1964).
[27]232 U.S. 383 (1914).
[28]44 Cal. 2nd 434 (1955).

v. *Ohio*[29] that unlawfully obtained evidence is inadmissible in any court. The majority opinion in *Mapp* reflected the court's belief that no approval could be made of "convictions obtained by unlawful seizures." Support of such an invasion of privacy, the court commented, was "lending its aid to a dirty business" and noted that the guarantee against unlawful search and seizure contained in the Fourth Amendment might as well be stricken from the Constitution if the court continued to permit unlawfully obtained evidence to be used against a defendant.

Justification for this judicial action in excluding the evidence gathered in these three cases can be established by a brief review of the facts of each case. In the *Weeks* case, the federal officers entered the defendant's room without a search warrant, seized and carried away papers connecting the defendant to an interstate gambling operation—a lottery. The court held that the tendency of law enforcement agents to enforce the criminal law by unlawful seizures could not be sanctioned by courts which were also charged with the maintenance of fundamental rights such as privacy. In the California *Cahan* case, the police recorded evidence of unlawful bookmaking by illegally placed microphones. The court held that it was "morally incongruous" for the state to flout constitutional rights—and admit such evidence—at the same time that it demanded that its citizens observe the law, and that it was a "dirty business" which the court did not want to aid or abet in any manner. Lastly, in the *Mapp* case, police officers forcibly entered the defendant's residence, physically overcame her resistance and confiscated allegedly lewd and lascivious material. The Supreme Court's action in this case established the minimal standard that evidence must be obtained by reasonable means, and if the search and seizure was determined by a court to be unreasonable, the fruits of such search and seizure would be inadmissible in *any* court, federal or state, against the defendant who suffered the trespass.

Application for a search warrant by a police officer is the finest safeguard against later claims about unreasonable search and seizure of evidence. Court review, prior to overt police action, protects the policeman concerned against unjust charges of oppressive police action. It takes the police action out of the do-it-yourself category and interposes the services of a legal technician—a judge.

However, time is often a factor in police investigations and they may have to act without the delay incidental to applying to a court for such process. In such cases, searches and seizures without a warrant are not unreasonable when incidental to a lawful arrest. Police may seize things connected with the crime, as well as weapons and other things which

[29]367 U.S. 643 (1961).

might be used to effect an escape from custody, but the search cannot be an "exploratory" search[30] *prior* to an arrest, nor can the premises searched be distant from the site of the arrest, or the "fruits" of such search be unrelated to the arrest.

Whether the police officers involved apply to court for a search warrant or make a summary arrest, they must still satisfy the constitutional requirement for showing probable cause for their request for court process or for their summary action in making an arrest without court process. The probable cause which will ensure the reasonableness of seizure, or a summary arrest, is more than a mere suspicion. A set of circumstances might only emerge as a suspicion of criminal activity to an untrained and inexperienced person, but to the experienced law enforcement officer the same circumstances might not only spell out a budding criminal activity, but very likely the nature of the specific crime involved. Courts recognize this fact and when the doctrine of the "reasonable and prudent" man is applied to any set of circumstances it is applied along the lines of: "Is the evidence available sufficient to warrant a trained and experienced policeman of reasonable caution in believing that a crime has been committed?" The policeman of reasonable caution may be better described as a man of ordinary caution and prudence; and "believe" in the above test is probably better expressed by the phrase, "conscientiously entertain a strong suspicion."

Probable cause is most often based on known facts which corroborate the policeman's initial belief. However, when probable cause is based partly on information received from others, the training and experience of police officers must also be extended to their capability in judging the reliability of informers. Often, information may be supported only by the knowledge of the police that the informant had been reliable and trustworthy in the past, and such informant's previous information had resulted in legal arrests.

Probable cause is a test for reasonableness and is based upon a totality of circumstances. Each case must be decided on its own facts and circumstances. There is no formula for reasonableness. Whether or not a search (or an arrest) is based on probable cause turns on the circumstances presented in a particular situation, as a matter of substantive decision.[31]

Consent to a search is a substitute for probable cause, and a waiver of the constitutional provisions of the Fourth Amendment, but the burden of proving consent rests with the prosecution. It must be shown that no duress or coercion, actual or implied, accounted for the consent; that it

[30]*Go-Bart v. U.S.*, 282 U.S. 344 (1931).
[31]*Chapman v. U.S.*, 365 U.S. 610 (1961).

was specific consent, freely and intelligently given; and emanated from the defendant or someone in control of the premises to be searched or the property to be seized.[32] The question of the voluntariness of consent to search is generally evaluated on the language and attitude of the policeman and response—or lack of it—by the defendant, but failure to object is not consent.

However, no showing of probable cause or affirmative consent will warrant court approval of electronic "snooping" when there is a trespass amounting to an unauthorized physical penetration of premises for this purpose. In the case of *Silverman v. U.S.*,[33] the court held that the attaching of an electronic device, a "spike mike," to the heating duct of a house constituted a violation of the Fourth Amendment, and conversations overheard by police officers were inadmissible: "The Fourth Amendment, and the personal rights which it secures, have a long history. At the very core stands the right of a man to retreat into his own home and there be free from unreasonable governmental intrusion."

Minimal Standards for Police

Under the increasing projection of the concept of federalism, the same minimal standards for police interrogation and searches and seizures must now be established in each of the states to ensure that evidence gathered by police during questioning sessions or searches will not be declared inadmissible against an accused person with standing to complain.

The police officers of the nation dominate this area of gathering evidence by these two methods, but the fruits of their labors are reviewed in our sequential arrangement of criminal justice by the assessment and adjudication process; responsibility in this area has been placed in the judiciary by court supervision of police operating procedures. It is part of our system for administering justice not to entrust the enforcement of law to a single functionary. And it is within the judicial power to object to evidence-gathering methodology believed to be lawless, and well within the assigned role of the judiciary to exclude evidence from their courts which they believe was secured by lawless means.

Many investigations of crime will be impeded, the efficacy of police in making apprehensions will be impaired and past successes in interrogating suspects made impossible or unlikely; existing levels of professional competence should be improved to meet this challenge; police and prosecutor should no longer bring accused persons into court under

[32]*Amos v. U.S.*, 255 U.S. 313 (1921).
[33]365 U.S. 505 (1961).

circumstances which will permit claims of improper police interrogating or searching procedures to result in the release of guilty persons.

Selected References

CASES

Ashcraft v. Tennessee, 322 U.S. 143 (1944).
> Extended interrogation (36 hours) negates confession as being voluntary.

Brown v. Mississippi, 297 U.S. 278 (1936).
> A confession secured by physical violence is in violation of the Fourteenth Amendment to the U.S. Constitution (due process) and is inadmissible as evidence against the accused.

Escobedo v. Illinois, 378 U.S. 478 (1964).
> The right to an attorney develops when the police investigation focuses on a defendant, and statements obtained after denying the defendant his right to counsel will not be admitted against him at his trial. Police must effectively warn the accused of his absolute right to remain silent.

Mapp v. Ohio, 367 U.S. 643 (1961).
> A violation of the Fourth Amendment is a denial of the due process required by the Fourteenth Amendment and is thus enforceable against the states; evidence obtained by searchers in violation of the Constitution is inadmissible against the defendant in a state court.

Miranda v. Arizona, 384 U.S. 436 (1966).
> The prosecution may not use statements stemming from custodial interrogation of the defendant unless it demonstrates the use of procedural safeguards effective to secure the privilege against self-incrimination. Prior to any questions, the person in custody must be warned that he has a right to remain silent, that any statement he does make may be used in evidence against him and that he has the right to the presence of an attorney. Any indication by the person in custody that he wishes to consult with an attorney before speaking, or when alone that he does not wish to be interrogated, prevents the police from questioning him.

BOOKS

Dash, Samuel, with Robert Knowlton, and Richard Schwartz, *The Eavesdroppers.* Newark, N.J.: Rutgers University Press, 1959. 484 pages.
> Wiretap devices are used not only by the police, but also by agents of business, labor and politics. This is a definitive study of wiretapping based on interviews with law enforcement officers, private detectives, newspaper men, convicted racketeers, lawyers, jurists, judges, cab drivers and manufacturers of technical electronic equipment. The authors include a former

prosecuting attorney, a law professor and a technical expert. The first section concerns the practitioners and victims of wiretapping devices; the second, a technical review of listening devices; and the third, an analysis of state and federal statutes regarding wiretapping and controlling court decisions.

Douglas, William O., *The Anatomy of Liberty*. New York: Trident Press, 1963. 194 pages.

A very clear delineation of the rights of the individual which are usually summed up as "liberty," their importance, erosive action seeking diminishment and protective actions.

Kamisar, Yale, Fred E. Inbau, and Thurman Arnold, *Criminal Justice in Our Time*. ed. A. E. Dick Howard. Charlottesville: University Press of Virginia, 1965. 161 pages.

This book contains essays (pp. 1–135) by two diametrically opposed exponents of modern criminal justice, with each essay serving as a digest of thousands and thousands of words published previously in many articles in police and legal periodicals. Yale Kamisar is an advocate of individual rights and constitutional guarantees; Fred E. Inbau has written forcefully for years about the social responsibility of police and the overriding need of the community to successfully prosecute persons accused of crime. This juxtaposition of opposing spokesmen for divergent views of criminal justice, in paperback form, conserves and digests much research time.

ARTICLES

Ashley, Maurice, "Constitutionalism and the Sovereign State in the Seventeenth Century," *Chapters in Western Civilization*, Vol. I, 3rd ed., ed., Contemporary Civilization Staff, Columbia College, Columbia University Press, New York, 1954, pp. 438–83.

An article about the origin of constitutional systems and the mechanics of their development.

Fabian, F. M., and Harry W. Moore, Jr., "Admissibility of Evidence Obtained by Wiretapping," *Police* (January-February 1965), pp. 30–35.

A study of the admissibility of evidence secured through "wiretapping" of telephones. Fabian and Moore do an excellent review of controlling cases from *Olmstead* in 1928 to *Benanti* in 1957.

Herman, Lawrence, "The Supreme Court and Restrictions on Police Interrogation," *Ohio State Law Journal* (Fall 1964), pp. 449–500.

Probably the finest article to-date on a major problem in the procedural area in criminal justice. Herman assesses the impact of all controlling court decisions by subject matter: (1) the coerced confession rule; (2) Fourth Amendment restrictions on police interrogations; (3) the privilege of self-incrimination and (4) right to counsel.

Jones, S. Bruce, "Heartbreaks for the Constitution," *American Bar Association Journal*, 50 (August 1964), 758–61.

Jones writes that, historically, the first eight amendments were a bill of rights placing limitations on the powers of the federal government, but judicial interpretations making these limitations applicable to the states by applying the doctrine of their incorporation into the Fourteenth Amendment extend the power of the federal government and have made the federal courts the supervisors of the states' affairs, contrary to the intent of the adoptees of the Constitution.

Klotter, John C., "The Expanding Right to Counsel," *Police* (November-December 1964), pp. 67–70.

A historical study of the right to counsel by accused persons. Klotter traces every aspect of this basic right from pre-Constitution days to the *Escobedo v. Illinois* decision.

Lynch, John T., "Electronic Eavesdropping: Trespass by Device," *American Bar Association Journal* (June 1964), pp. 540–44.

Sophisticated electronic devices now offer gross trespasses on the individual's right to privacy. Often without a physical trespass, listeners may hear and even record the conversations of a man with his wife, attorney or religious advisor. Any evidence resulting from such eavesdropping, the author notes, is not admissible because of its privileged nature, but that the harm often occurs in the listening—and not in any attempt to drag such evidence into court. He makes a strong plea not to lower the rights of the individual but to raise the standards, competence and integrity of law enforcement and its agents.

Monahan, Ellsworth A., *Search and Seizure*. New York: New York City Police Department, 1962, 18 pages.

A brief study reviewing the leading cases on search and seizure as they concern police procedures. Monahan writes: "In *Mapp v. Ohio*, the U.S. Supreme Court applied the exclusionary rule against a state. The court said that the Fourteenth Amendment to the U.S. Constitution, through its due process clause against the states, binds the courts of the states to exclude all evidence obtained as a result of an "unreasonable" search in violation of the Fourth Amendment. Since this decision, it is vital for police officers to have complete familiarity with the laws of evidence, of arrest and of search and seizure."

Waite, John Barker, "Whose Rules? The Problem of Improper Police Methods," *American Bar Association Journal* (November 1962), pp. 1057–59.

An excellent article about the manner in which the U.S. Supreme Court's monitorship of criminal justice is making rules of conduct for all police. The author does not believe the Court is adequately equipped for this purpose and recommends that the entire area covered by recent cases in exclusion and reversal be handled by appropriate legislative action.

"Admissibility of a Confession," *Defender Newsletter*, 2, No. 5 (September 1965), pp. 1–11.

A review of major case law excluding the use of confessions in criminal actions in state courts.

PROSECUTOR

Prosecution is the development of criminal actions or other proceedings for violations of law punishable by penal sanctions. The prosecutor is the supervising county law enforcement official. He is often termed the "key" official in law enforcement because his function is to initiate criminal charges, no matter how minor the penalty may be, and to serve as trial attorney for "the people" at the trial of offenders.

4

Arraignment to Trial

A criminal action is best defined as the proceedings by which a person is charged with a criminal act ("crime" or "public offense") and brought to trial and convicted or acquitted. The accused person who is prosecuted in a criminal action is termed the "defendant," and the prosecution is in the name of the "people" of the state in which the proceedings are held.

Court procedures in the sequential stages of the administration of justice, from the time of the original arraignment to immediately prior to trial, preserve the rights of a defendant in a criminal action and establish the concept of an accusatory proceeding rather than an inquisitorial action. They provide multiple means for dismissal of the charges prior to trial, if warranted.

Initially, a member of the prosecutor's staff makes the fundamental decision to charge, and either a magistrate or a grand jury reviews the basic complaint against the accused person. If the prosecutor succeeds in establishing a *prima facie* case, the formal accusatory pleading is placed before the court having jurisdiction to try the offense charged by the filing of an indictment or information. In this formal charging, the defendant is informed of the nature of the charges, and can initiate any response suitable to the circumstances of the case. In many states, particularly California, state's evidence is available to him upon request before the trial, in order to better inform him of the state's case against him.

Rights of a Defendant

The rights of a defendant in a criminal action are guaranteed by the Constitution of the United States. While most states have similar provisions for protecting the rights of an accused person, our dual system of federal and state courts created some problems regarding equal rights in all courts. However, the recent trend in the decisions of the U.S. Supreme Court indicates that the Fourteenth Amendment's guarantee of the due process of law will ensure defendants, in criminal actions prosecuted in state courts, rights equal to those common to federal courts.

The major substantive and procedural rights of a defendant in a criminal action may be reviewed by scanning California's Penal Code. It contains a fine working summary of these rights. The defendant in a criminal action is entitled to the following:

1. To a speedy and public trial;

2. To be allowed counsel or to appear and defend in person and without counsel; and

3. To produce witnesses on his behalf and to be confronted with witnesses against him in the presence of the court, except:

   a. Hearsay evidence may be admitted to the extent it is otherwise admissible, and

   b. The deposition of a witness taken in an action may be read to the extent that it is otherwise admissible.[1]

4. No prosecution for a crime of which the accused person has been once prosecuted and convicted or acquitted.[2]

5. No more restraint prior to conviction than necessary for detention to answer the charge.[3]

6. No person shall be convicted of a crime (public offense) unless:

   a. By verdict of a jury accepted and recorded by a court;

   b. By a finding of a court in a case where a jury has been waived; or

   c. By a plea of guilty.[4]

[1]California Penal Code, Section 686.
[2]*Ibid.*, Section 687.
[3]*Ibid.*, Section 688.
[4]*Ibid.*, Section 689.

7. Prosecution must be by indictment or information, except:
    a. For removal of state civil officers,
    b. For offenses arising in the organized militia,
    c. For offenses triable in municipal and justice courts,
    d. For misdemeanors triable in juvenile courts, and
    e. For felonies in which it is lawful for the defendant to plead guilty to the complaint before a magistrate.[5]

8. To preliminary examination of the case by an examining magistrate and an order holding the defendant to answer signed by such judicial officer, when prosecution is to be by filing of an information.[6]

9. When prosecution is by indictment, the grand jury shall receive sufficient competent evidence to support the indictment and no other evidence than such as is:
    a. Given by witnesses produced and sworn before the grand jury;
    b. Furnished by writings, material objects or other things presented to the senses; or
    c. Contained in a deposition admissible under the laws of the state.[7]

10. To release on bail if the offense charged is bailable.[8]

11. A proceeding to conditionally examine material witnesses.[9]

12. Not compelled to be a witness against himself.[10]

13. That the burden of proving guilt beyond a reasonable doubt be borne by the "people."[11]

Actually, today's greatest guarantor of a fair criminal action is not found in the explicit wordings of law, but rather in the many court decisions, particularly in California, relating to a defendant's right to pretrial "discovery" permitting access, upon request, to much of the "people's" evidence in the case.

Original Arraignment

Historically, a great deal of importance has been placed upon prompt arraignment of a prisoner following an arrest. In past years this court proceeding was the first official opportunity for warning, informing and advising the prisoner. At this arraignment, the court explains the charge; it advises the defendant of his right to communicate with counsel, relatives and friends; to testify or remain silent; and to subpoena witnesses. In proper cases, the court will assign counsel to indigent defendants.

[5]*Ibid.*, Section 682.
[6]*Ibid.*, Section 738.
[7]*Ibid.*, Section 939.6.
[8]*Ibid.*, Section 1270 and 1271.
[9]*Ibid.*, Section 1335–45.
[10]*Ibid.*, Section 688.
[11]*Ibid.*, Section 1096.

It was the first notice many accused persons had concerning these rights. It was also the first opportunity of persons charged with serious offenses to secure their release on bail. Today, because of recent court decisions requiring police officers to inform an accused person of his rights to remain silent and to legal counsel at the time of arrest, the original arraignment is concerned mostly with informing the defendant of the charge against him and setting bail. Even the duty of setting bail has been relegated to police officers having custody of the prisoner by the establishing of a schedule of bail upon which prisoners can be released by their police custodians in less serious criminal cases.

There is often some debate as to what court has jurisdiction over an accused person. It may be that the crime is of a continuing nature such as larceny and kidnapping; or one committed on an airplane, boat or railroad train; or close to a dividing line between cities, counties or states. Jurisdiction is first a matter of law, then it is largely a matter of convenience. Budgets are limited in all agencies concerned with the lawbreaker, and crimes originating in other counties are considered a statistical and moral responsibility of the agencies of justice in the "home" county. The examining magistrate will usually examine the complaint closely for the "place of occurrence" or the criminal act, and will note in the court minutes which court has jurisdiction of the case, if it can be determined at this initial stage of the criminal action.

In addition to ascertaining the territorial jurisdiction of a criminal action upon original arraignment, the examining magistrate also must decide whether or not the defendant is a minor and direct the case to juvenile court when the crime charged and the age of the accused permit this processing.

When the court of original arraignment is in the county in which the crime charged is triable, the examining magistrate shall deliver a copy of the written complaint to the defendant, advise him of his right to legal aid, ask him if he desires the aid of counsel and allow him a reasonable time to send for counsel. If the defendant is unable to employ counsel and requests court help, the court will assign legal aid. This is usually the public defender, if such office exists. The old rule that such counsel would only be assigned in serious felony cases was extended to all felonies after the Gideon case;[12] it has been extended to all misdemeanor cases in California, when requested by an indigent defendant, and where the circumstances of the case indicate legal aid is necessary for an adequate and effective defense.

At his original arraignment, a defendant may be asked to answer to the accusation set forth in the complaint if the case is a minor one and the

[12]*Gideon v. Wainwright*, 372 U.S. 335 (1963).

defendant has counsel or intelligently waives his right to counsel. In vagrancy, and drunk and disorderly cases, the magistrate may, in most jurisdictions, dispose of the case on a plea of guilty and may act as trial judge on a not guilty plea if the defendant waives the transfer of the case to another time or different court.

However, in felony cases, modern legal procedure requires a defendant to be represented by counsel at the time he responds to the complaint. For this reason, most of the felony cases require another arraignment at which the defendant answers the formal accusatory pleading (complaint, indictment or information).

The Decision to "Charge"

A decision to charge a suspect or prisoner in a criminal proceeding is based upon a professional belief that there is sufficient evidence of guilt to warrant the filing of a formal accusatory pleading and a trial of the

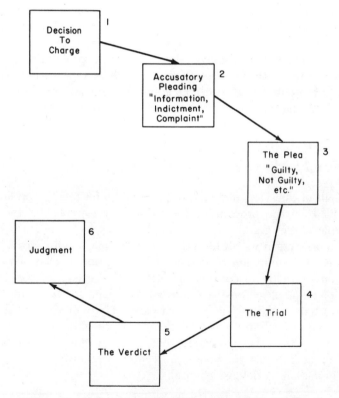

FIG. 4.   SIX BASIC STEPS IN A CRIMINAL ACTION

defendant for the offense charged.[13] The charging decision is made by the prosecutor or an assigned member of his staff.

It may appear that police officers who make a summary arrest are making this decision to charge the offender, but the continuation of the case after the original arraignment depends upon the circumstances of the arrest and the evidence upon which the arresting officer based his summary arrest; the assigned member of the prosecutor's staff must decide whether the facts at hand, or available before trial, warrant prosecution. The arresting officer confers with the assigned member of the prosecutor's staff, and the police unit forwards all police reports and other data on the case to the prosecutor's office. It is, in a sense, a "team" review. The prosecutor brings a legally trained mind to this review, and he may advise continued prosecution or he may advise against it because the evidence gathered by police, and the evidence likely to be developed in support, do not amount to enough legally significant facts to ensure a reasonable expectation of a successful prosecution.

The review, in cases involving a serious crime, often occurs prior to the arrest. Police and the assigned member of the legal staff of the prosecutor's office, often assisted by investigators assigned to the prosecutor's office, may accomplish the case preparation prior to arrest and continue their cooperation through the subsequent proceedings. This is particularly true when the arrest is made pursuant to a warrant or when the case is presented to the current grand jury for an indictment of the offender and the arrest made pursuant to, and after, the grand jury finding.

Accusatory Pleading

Over half of the states now permit prosecution for felonies on an information filed by the prosecutor; the prosecutor can reserve the secret review role of the grand jury for complex cases, or cases such as rape or child molesting in which he wishes to spare major witnesses from the probing cross-examination of defense counsel prior to trial. The grand jury is too unwieldy to convene as often as necessary in our growing number of criminal actions. It often will complain to the court that its time is wasted on the review of minor cases. The procedure of filing an information is a fairly recent innovation; it is probably closer to the due process of law than the indictment route since it requires a preliminary hearing in open court in which prosecution witnesses are subject to cross-examination by defense counsel.

[13]Wayne R. LaFave, *Arrest: The Decision to Take a Suspect Into Custody* (Boston, Mass: Little, Brown & Co., 1965), pp. 320–23.

The accusatory pleading, whether it is an indictment or information, should be filed in a court of competent jurisdiction;[14] it must contain the title of the action, specifying the name and location of the court in which the pleading will be presented, the name of the accused person or description by a fictitious name if the true name is unknown, and a statement of the crime or crimes charged.

In charging an offense, the accusatory pleading is sufficient when it contains, in each of its "counts" or specifications regarding an offense charged, a statement that the accused has committed some specified crime. This statement must be phrased with sufficient clarity to give the accused notice of the offense of which he is accused. The language may be ordinary, should be simple and concise, without technical embellishments or allegations of matters not essential to the proof.

In jurisdictions where a prior conviction of a crime is a factor in determining the degree of the crime charged—or the maximum or minimum sentence on conviction—a statement of the conviction of such prior crime or crimes should be contained in the accusatory pleading. There are also approved statutory procedures for the consolidation or joinder of offenses or defendants in accusatory pleadings, such as New York's "omnibus" indictment law.

There are benefits which exist in the basic requirements of an accusatory pleading in felony cases. The prosecutor of a criminal action must establish a *prima facie* case to the satisfaction of a required number of grand jurors, or to a magistrate conducting a preliminary examination (which is the prerequisite for filing an information in the trial court). This procedure requires the prosecutor to test his case by the production of legally admissible evidence. The defense counsel is informed of the facts of the case through the indictment and the minutes of the grand jury, or by his participation in the preliminary examination. The courts are able to screen out a number of cases before trial by acting favorably on defense counsel's motion to dismiss for the failure of the prosecutor to establish sufficient cause; or a grand jury, likewise, can favor an accused person and refuse to vote an indictment. On the other hand, pleas of guilty often result from the erosive action of this formal inquiry before court or grand jury upon a guilty person's claim of innocence.

Grand Jury: The Indictment

The prosecutor, or one of his staff, serves as an advisor to the grand jury, and to some extent the moderator of its proceedings. Witnesses are subpoenaed, put under oath and questioned by the prosecutor or any

[14]The court which has authority to try and sentence defendant.

juror. Physical evidence is marked as an exhibit, authenticated in a manner similar to a trial court and examined by grand jurors. This is an *ex parte* proceeding that excludes the public, the defendant and defense counsel. The grand jury may, however, listen to a defendant as a witness and may deny a witness' attorney attendance at the proceedings. Witnesses may have counsel in the hallway and consult such attorney each time the questioning probes a different area of inquiry.

An indictment results from a vote of members of a current grand jury who have heard and examined legal evidence and requires the vote of a specified number of jurors. In California, it is at least 14 jurors in heavily populated counties, and at least 12 in other counties.[15]

A grand jury is authorized to find an indictment when all the evidence before it in its judgment, if unexplained and uncontradicted, would warrant a conviction by a trial jury. This is the standard *prima facie*[16] case which is required to move ahead with any criminal action. The evidence should be legally admissible under the local rules of evidence. As long as the admissible evidence resulting from the sworn testimony of witnesses (or depositions admissible under law), or physical evidence heard or examined by the grand jury, is sufficient to show a reasonable belief in guilt, the grand jury may indict any accused person. In many jurisdictions the names of the witnesses testifying before the grand jury, or whose depositions have been read to it, must be inserted as an endorsement upon the jury's affidavit.

The indictment is signed by the foreman of the grand jury and presented in its presence to the trial court. The court will verify the attendance of a quorum of grand jurors, accept the sworn statement of the foreman that an indictment has been voted by the required number of grand jurors, and order it filed with the clerk of the court.

The Preliminary Examination: The Information

The examination of a criminal action before a magistrate's court of jurisdiction, following the original arraignment of the defendant, is for the purpose of determining whether or not there is sufficient evidence to justify holding the accused for trial on the charge or charges specified in the felony complaint filed by the policeman or the victim. This examination requires the prosecutor to present such witnesses and evidence as necessary to raise a reasonable belief (probable cause) that the crime specified in the felony complaint has been committed and that the accused person committed that crime.

Unlike a grand jury, normally not required to hear evidence for the

15California Penal Code, Section 940.
16On the face of it.

defendant, the magistrate conducting a preliminary examination must examine under oath any witness produced by the defense immediately following the examination of the witnesses for the prosecution. Defense counsel also has the opportunity at a preliminary hearing to cross-examine prosecution witnesses and to make appropriate motions: (1) a motion to dismiss because of vagueness and indefiniteness in the felony complaint; (2) a motion to dismiss for failure to establish a *prima facie* case; (3) a motion to reduce the original charge; and (4) a motion to secure low bail for his client.

If the committing magistrate is satisfied that the evidence constitutes a *prima facie* case, he will hold the prisoner "to answer" to the trial court and commit him to the custody of the sheriff, or permit his release on bail when the offense is bailable.

The defendant, after being advised of his right to legal counsel, may waive this right if he is acting knowledgeably and not in ignorance. If he does not have counsel to represent him, he may not, however, waive the formal preliminary examination. If he is represented by counsel before the magistrate, he may waive a formal preliminary examination and be held to answer to the trial court without the production of evidence by the prosecutor. The prosecutor, from the time of the magistrate's holding order, has a limited amount of time to file the information with the trial court. In California, it must be filed within 15 days.

Arraignment for Pleading

A defendant in a criminal action must be arraigned before the court in which the felony or misdemeanor complaint or felony indictment or information is filed, unless the action is transferred to some other court for trial. A defendant in a misdemeanor case may appear through his attorney, but the personal appearance of a defendant is required in felony cases. If in custody, the officer having custody of the defendant will be directed to deliver him to court; if the defendant is released on bail, he will be informed of the time and place of arraignment for pleading. Bench warrants are issued for the arrest of indicted defendants and may specify release on bail, in appropriate cases, until appearance is necessary at this arraignment. Persons released on bail, but who fail to appear as directed, are usually rearrested on a bench warrant and held until arraignment.

A defendant who appears without counsel must be informed by the court, before being arraigned, of his right to have counsel and must be asked if he desires the assistance of counsel. If he desires legal assistance and is indigent, the court must assign counsel for his defense.

A defendant who requires additional time to consider his response to the accusatory pleading, particularly one who has appeared without counsel and requested court assignment of legal aid, will be allowed a continuance to afford him a reasonable time to answer the charge.

The arraignment consists of the in-court reading and delivery of the accusatory pleading to the defendant; he is asked to plead either guilty or not guilty to the charge.

In misdemeanors triable in lesser courts, the accusatory pleading upon which a defendant is arraigned is usually the simple complaint used at the original arraignment of the prisoner and a copy is not delivered to the defendant unless requested by him.

The Plea

The first pleading of the accused person is the defendant's answer (plea) to the charges made against him. It must be oral, made in open court and recorded in the court's minutes. The basic pleas are either guilty or not guilty. In the case of crimes punishable upon conviction by death or life imprisonment, many jurisdictions will not permit a plea of guilty, but will automatically enter a plea of not guilty and set a trial date. A like plea is entered when the prisoner stands "mute" instead of pleading. In some states, and in the federal courts, the accused person can plead *nolo contendere* (a no-contest plea that limits the admission of guilt to the facts of the case at trial). Most states extend their list of pleas from the basic guilty or not guilty to include: (1) not guilty by reason of insanity; (2) a plea of former judgment or acquittal; and (3) having once been in jeopardy. California permits these six pleas, providing that a defendant who does not plead guilty may enter *one or more* of the other pleas. The defendant may also file a demurrer in lieu of a plea. This provision for multiple pleas, or the filing of a demurrer, is proper in that they are all general or particular denials of the right of the state to bring the accused to trial.

Accusatory pleadings can be amended, and the plea of the defendant can be amended or withdrawn; these actions generally must have the permission of the court, and often the permission of the opposing counsel.

Guilty

The plea of guilty in California moves the criminal action to the pre-sentence probation hearing. Judges will often refuse to accept a plea of guilty, until satisfied the defendant is intelligently aware of the nature of the plea, the decision is voluntary and that no promises of leniency have been made to the defendant.

This plea is also a process by which the accused person may secure some slight advantage. Leniency may not be promised, but it may be implied. The prosecutor may agree that a lesser charge is more appropriate. The offender's strategy may be pointed toward the presentence investigation report and a plea of guilty may convince the probation officer handling the investigation that the offender has taken the first step toward rehabilitation. Lastly, there is the age-old feeling that a plea of guilty won't "bother" the police, prosecutor and courts, and this willingness to save the community the expense of a trial will gain the defendant some advantage.

Not Guilty

The plea of not guilty moves the criminal action toward the trial and puts into issue every material element of the offense charged. It requires the prosecutor, at trial, to prove by admissible evidence, and beyond a reasonable doubt, every essential element in the crime charged and the identity of the perpetrator.

Nolo Contendere

This plea requires the consent of the district attorney and the approval of the court. The legal effect of such plea shall be the same as that of a plea of guilty, but the plea may not be used against the defendant as an admission in any civil suit based upon or growing out of the act upon which the criminal prosecution is based.

Insanity

The plea of not guilty by reason of insanity should usually be joined with the plea of not guilty. Standing alone, the plea of not guilty by reason of insanity admits the commission of the acts alleged in the accusatory pleading but denies legal responsibility for the acts.

Double Jeopardy or Previous Judgment of Conviction or Acquittal

Lastly, a defendant can plead "double jeopardy" or claim a previous judgment of conviction or acquittal. To conform with the constitutional protection of the Fifth Amendment (". . . nor shall any person be sub-

ject for the same offense to be twice put in jeopardy of life and limb"),
the defendant must show he has been put in jeopardy by being regularly
charged with the crime before a similar court of like jurisdiction, and
acquitted or convicted, or otherwise put "once in jeopardy." A successful
plea of prior jeopardy is a bar to another prosecution for the same
offense, its attempt, or for an offense necessarily included in the previously charged offense. However, the defendant is deemed to have waived
the privilege regarding "double jeopardy" by taking an appeal from the
crime for which he was convicted, and, on reversal, must face his original
criminal responsibility in the new trial as if no previous trial had been
held.

Whenever a defendant is acquitted on the merits,[17] he is acquitted of
the offense, notwithstanding any defect in form or substance in the
accusatory pleading on which the trial was had. It is not deemed a former
acquittal of the offense charged if: (1) the defendant was previously
acquitted on the grounds of a variance between the accusatory pleadings and the proof, or (2) the accusatory pleadings were dismissed upon
an objection to its form or substance, or in order to hold the defendant
for a higher offense, without a judgment of acquittal.[18]

The court majority in *U.S. v. Tateo*[19] held that no double jeopardy
was involved when a defect in the proceedings leading to conviction
constituted reversible error, and upheld the 1896 doctrine established in
U.S. v. Ball.[20] That doctrine holds that defendants can be reindicted
after the original indictment has been found defective. "It would be a
high price indeed for society to pay were every accused granted immunity from punishment because of any defect sufficient to constitute
reversible error in the proceedings leading to conviction."

Courts also support a plea of "double jeopardy" when there is a
"carving," the taking of one trial out of another. California has a specific
statute[21] which bars successive prosecutions, convictions or punishments
where a single criminal act or a continuous criminal transaction violates
more than one penal section. This section of law requires a choice to be
made by the prosecutor, and an acquittal or conviction under the selected section of law named in the accusatory pleading upon which the
trial is based bars a successive prosecution or additional sentence for a
different offense arising out of the same act, omission or continuous
transaction.

New York, California and about half of the other states have statutes

[17]The actual substance or fundamentals of a case.
[18]California Penal Code, Sections 1021 and 1022.
[19]377 U.S. 463 (1964).
[20]163 U.S. 662 (1896).
[21]California Penal Code, Section 654.

forbidding a second prosecution for an act or omission that has been the subject of a prosecution in another jurisdiction by deeming such "foreign" conviction or acquittal as a "sufficient defense."[22]

The Demurrer

An accused person may file a demurrer to the information or indictment. The demurrer is an attack on the technical integrity of the formal accusatory pleading. California law[23] lists either response for the use of defendants before courts in that state: "The only pleading on the part of the defendant is a plea or a demurrer."

Classically, demurrers must be filed in writing and must specify the grounds upon which the objections to the accusatory pleading are based. The grounds usually fall within the following areas: (1) illegal source; that is, the grand jury acted without legal authority to inquire into the alleged offense, or the court (in which the prosecutor filed the information) does not have jurisdiction; (2) facts as stated do not list all the essential elements of a crime; (3) statute of limitations bars charge of crime; (4) accusatory pleading contains legal justification of the alleged offense; and (5) crimes or other defendants have been joined or consolidated without authority.

Pretrial Discovery

One of the most underrated but most helpful changes in the law from the standpoint of the defendant and defense counsel is the breakthrough of pretrial discovery in California. Most of the states and the federal government have extremely limited discovery of the prosecution's evidence, or none at all. Prior to 1956, California discovery available to the defendant or his attorney was limited to receipt of the transcript of the grand jury proceedings and the autopsy report, and the inspection of notes used by a witness to refresh his memory during his testimony on the witness stand, and then only if the defense counsel could show that such notes would be contradictory to the testimony of the witness.[24] In order for the prosecutor or witness to prevent discovery of notes the witness needed only to refresh his recollection prior to his testimony and not refer to his notes while testifying. In addition, as a practical matter it proved difficult to show that the notes would contradict the testimony without first seeing or reading the notes.

[22]*Ibid.*, Section 656.
[23]*Ibid.*, Section 1002.
[24]*People v. Gallardo*, 41 Cal. 2nd 57 (1953).

In December, 1956, the breakthrough came in an appeal from a first degree murder, death-penalty conviction.[25] Prior to trial, the defendant's attorney moved to inspect the fingerprint evidence as well as reports made to police by witnesses to the homicide. These motions were denied by the trial court. During the course of the trial, after a showing by use of newspaper articles that the reports made to police by witnesses conflicted with their testimony, the defendant's attorney issued a subpoena *duces tecum*[26] for the production of the police reports of the witnesses' statements, but this subpoena was vacated by the trial court on motion by the prosecutor.

The Appellate Court affirmed the conviction, noting the common law objection: "That to compel the prosecution to reveal its evidence beforehand would enable the defendant to secure perjured testimony and fabricate evidence to meet the state's case . . . that to require the prosecution to reveal, but to deny the prosecution to learn of defendant's evidence would unduly shift to the defendant a balance of advantage already heavily weighted in his favor." However, after stating the common law objection, the Appellate Court went on to say: "To deny flatly any right to production on the ground that an imbalance would occur between the prosecution and defense would be to lose sight of the true purposes of a criminal trial, the ascertainment of the facts. The possibility that defendant will obtain perjured testimony or fabricate evidence as a result of disclosure during trial is too remote and slight to justify denying production on that basis."

A few months later, the language of the *Riser* decision was used in a petition for a writ of mandate, at trial court level, to order pretrial discovery of statements made by the defendant to the police and prosecutor. The motion for pretrial discovery was accompanied by an affidavit by the defendant declaring that he could not recall for his attorney the questions asked or the answers he gave police and that he needed these recorded statements to refresh his recollection. The trial court denied the motion, thus laying the foundation for a petition for a writ of mandate to the appellate court.[27] This court of review applied the reasoning of the *Riser* case and added:

> For the prosecutor to keep evidence undisclosed partakes of the nature of a game rather than judicial procedure. The state in its might and power ought to be, and is, too zealous of according the defendant a fair and impartial trial to hinder him in intelligently preparing his defense and in availing himself of all competent, material evidence that tends to throw light on the subject matter of the trial.

[25]*People v. Riser*, 47 Cal. 2nd 566 (1957).
[26]Appear with specified records, documents, or other evidence in the possession of the person subpoenaed.
[27]*Powell v. Superior Court*, 48 Cal. 2nd 704 (1957).

The floodgates were completely opened by this decision and pretrial opinion came flooding out of the appellate courts. Subject matter and reference cases in this area are as follows:

SUBJECT MATTER	REFERENCE CASE
1. Statements of witnesses given to police before the trial.	*People v. Carter,* 48 Cal. 2d 737 (1957).
2. Reports of expert witnesses concerning their examinations.	*People v. Walker,* 155 Cal. App. 2d 134 (1957).
3. Specimens taken from the body of deceased for examination by defense expert.	*Schindler v. Superior Court,* 161 Cal. App. 2d 513 (1958).
4. "Raw notes" of interrogator of defendant.	*McCarthy v. Superior Court,* 162 Cal. App. 2d 755 (1958).
5. Disclosures (pretrial) of name and whereabouts of an informer.	*Castiel v. Superior Court,* 162 Cal. App. 2d 710 (1958).
6. Names and addresses of witnesses to elements of the crime, and photographs of the investigation.	*Norton v. Superior Court,* 173 Cal. App. 2d 133 (1959).
7. Statements of witnesses (made during precourt interviews to police or prosecutor) who testified at a preliminary hearing or grand jury proceeding.	*Funk v. Superior Court,* 52 Cal. 2d 423 (1959).
8. No requirement that defense show a conflict between testimony and reported statements before discovery granted.	*People v. Cooper,* 53 Cal. 2d 755 (1960).
9. Statements to police or prosecutor of witnesses or possible witnesses at any court proceeding who would not be called by prosecutor at trial. ("We believe that it was not only the right, but it became the duty of petitioner's counsel to demand inspection of said statements in order to properly prepare for trial.")	*Vetter v. Superior Court,* 189 Cal. App. 2d 132 (1961).

The prosecutor has not been forgotten in this discovery explosion and has opportunities for discovery of defense evidence if he will only put forth the effort. In the case of *Jones v. Superior Court*,[28] the majority opinion comments on discovery as follows: "Absent the privilege against self-incrimination or other privileges provided by law, defendant in a

[28]58 Cal. 2nd 56 (1962).

criminal case has no valid interest in denying the prosecution access to evidence that can throw light on the issues in the case."

New York and some other states have, by statute, required the defendant to give the prosecutor notice and the names of witnesses when alibi is to be the defense in the case.[29]

Discovery in California is now a routine matter between defense counsel and prosecutor. A request by defense counsel, oral or written, will usually suffice. This development has brought the defense and prosecution much closer in their mutual goal of justice, American style. The fight theory is still present, but the hidden or unproduced evidence is not now a deciding factor, nor is the element of surprise as great in the eventual outcome of the criminal action. The defense has been given a new interest in on-the-spot police investigation of crime. It has been given the opportunity to review, before trial, the police investigation and evaluate that investigation in the light of its weaknesses and strengths, and to move to efficiently direct its own investigation into areas in which the police investigation was delinquent.

Pretrial discovery, within certain legal and constitutional limits, can procedurally implement a fair and impartial presentation of the facts at the trial of a criminal action and dramatically improve court procedures in the administration of justice.

Selected References

CASES

U.S. v. Tateo, 377 U.S. 463 (1964).

A review of the concept of "double jeopardy" in the administration of criminal justice. In this case the "people" sought legal relief against the dismissal of an indictment for placing the accused twice in jeopardy.

Powell v. Superior Court, 48 Cal. 2nd 705 (1957).

California's leading case upholding the right of a defendant to pretrial discovery of evidence in the possession of police or prosecutor. The opinion notes that when a prosecutor keeps evidence undisclosed, it is akin to gamemanship rather than the act of a court official preparing a case for court presentation.

BOOKS

Berman, Harold J., *Justice in the U.S.S.R.* Cambridge, Mass.: Harvard University Press, 1963. 450 pages.

This is a text about the Soviet system of justice and its coexistence with

[29]New York Code of Criminal Procedure, Section 295.

a system of force in government. Berman notes the most obvious difference between Soviet and Anglo-American criminal procedure is the conduct of the pretrial investigation by the examining magistrate and the active participation by the court in the trial itself. Berman highlights the accusatory nature of our American system of justice by his comparison analysis of Soviet inquisitorial procedures.

Ginsberg, Morris, *On Justice in Society*. Ithaca, New York: Cornell University Press, 1965. 248 pages.

A fine text on the concept of justice and the relationship of rights, claims and duties. Ginsberg explains complex relationships with unusual simplicity and remarkable coherence.

ARTICLES

Bodin, Harry Sabbath, "Marshalling the Evidence, and Pleading and Practice Before Trial," *Trial Practice*, 2 (1962), 1–64.

The proper pretrial preparation of criminal actions. Bodin writes of the need for a thorough evaluation and gathering of facts as preparation for the best defense and the best moves at the proper time.

Louisell, David W., "Criminal Discovery: Dilemma Real or Apparent," *California Law Review* (1961), pp. 56–103.

Louisell notes that reciprocity and mutuality between adversaries are not possible in criminal cases in the United States because of the constitutional guarantee against self-incrimination; discovery may erode the adversary system because defense attorneys may lose their zeal for investigation when a mere court order will, in effect, do their investigation for them—and the dual investigatory process of the adversary system will turn into a unilateral process.

Sears, Roy W., "Illinois Double-Jeopardy Act: An Empty Gesture," *Journal of Criminal Law, Criminology and Police Science*, 51, No. 2 (July-August 1960), 236–40.

The Illinois statute barring the state from further prosecution after a federal prosecution for the same crime is discussed. Sears makes a comparison analysis of similar laws across the nation.

Styn, Ronald L., "California Extends Double-Jeopardy Policies to Punishment," *Stanford Law Review*, 16, No. 4 (July 1964), 1108–13.

Discussion on doctrine of limiting punishment for a crime to the level of the previous sentence when a case has been remanded back to the lower court for retrial. Styn notes the "gamble" inherent in some motions and appeals seeking a new trial was a handicap to petitioners in seeking redress in the courts for an injustice.

"The Prosecutor's Constitutional Duty to Reveal Evidence to the Defendant," *Yale Law Journal* (November 1964), pp. 136–50.

An article on criminal discovery, the suppression of evidence by the prosecutor, and the prosecutor's duty to reveal evidence to the defense.

The author points out that "honest" pretrial discovery ensures against later reversal of cases on the grounds that the defendant did not have the opportunity for a fair trial, having been denied "due process" because of the pretrial imbalance of investigatory facilities.

5

Extradition and Rendition

Interstate rendition is the correct description of the procedure by which one sovereign state would give up, yield, return or surrender persons who have committed a criminal act in another state; interstate extradition is the procedure which initiates such action. The word extradition, however, embraces not only the requisition or demand for the return of a fugitive from justice but the rendition itself, and often refers to a return of persons from other nations.

Extradition in the public interest is to prevent the successful escape of any person who has been accused of crime. It is defined as the surrender by one state or nation to another of an individual accused or convicted of an offense outside its own territory and within the territorial jurisdiction of the other, which, being competent to try and punish him, demands the surrender. It should not be confused, on the international scene, with transportation, deportation or banishment procedures which result in the removal of a person from a country, but differs from the specific return of a person as contemplated in extradition.

Article IV of the U.S. Constitution cites the need for each of the states to recognize with "full faith and credit" the public acts, records and judicial proceedings of every other state, and specifically provides for a procedure of extradition and rendition among the states: "A person charged in any state with treason, felony, or other crime, who shall flee from justice, and be found in another State, shall on demand of the executive authority of the State from which he fled, be delivered up, to be removed to the State having jurisdiction of the crime."[1] This early recognition of the need for procedure for transferring criminals from one state to another guards against one state becoming a sanctuary for persons who are engaged in criminal acts in other states; it is in furtherance of the basic concept that all of the states must be equal in power and dignity and authority as a necessary essential to the American scheme of government.[2]

Under the terms of international treaties for the extradition of fugitives from justice, it is not necessary that the fugitive flee to the asylum nation. All that is required is that the accused person has committed an extraditable offense under the provisions of the treaty and is found within the jurisdiction of the asylum nation. Under federal statutes[3] a "fugitive from justice" is a person who, having within the state committed an act which by its laws constitutes a crime, has left its jurisdiction and is found in the territory of another state. The Uniform Criminal Extradition Act under which most states now operate,[4] includes, as a "fugitive," a person who was not in the demanding state at the time of the commission of the criminal act charged.

Uniform laws based on agreements between the states[5] have facilitated the return of persons charged with crime from other states, the compulsory attendance of out-of-state witnesses, and given extraterritorial authority to peace officers of the state in which the crime took place when they are in "fresh pursuit" of the perpetrator of a crime. The interstate control of crime prevents criminals from utilizing state lines to handicap local police officers, and is supplemented by federal legislation for removal warrants, and against unlawful flight to avoid prosecution, confinement or giving testimony in felony cases.[6]

[1]U.S. Constitution, Article IV, Section 2, Clause 2.
[2]*Coyle v. Smith*, 221 U.S. 559 (1911).
[3]Title 18, United States Code, Section 3182.
[4]Forty states.
[5]The Uniform Criminal Extradition Act.
  The Uniform Act to Secure the Attendance of Witnesses.
  The Uniform Act on Interstate Fresh Pursuit of Criminals.
[6]Title 18, United States Code, Sections 1073 and 3041.

International Extradition

The obligation of one sovereign nation to surrender a fugitive from justice to agents of a demanding nation is not mandatory unless previously negotiated and the subject of a treaty between the nations concerned. Because of the Constitutional limitation upon presidential power in dealing with foreign nations,[7] the United States cannot surrender fugitives upon the demand of other nations unless a valid treaty is in effect. For this reason, mutual agreements have been sought which will remove the uncertainties of national discretion and comity[8] when this country requests the extradition of a fugitive from justice. These treaties have many minor stipulations which sometimes handicap efforts at international extradition, but they are generally more than adequate in their detailing of extraditable criminal offenses. Many of the recent treaties have a retroactive clause covering crimes committed before the effective date of the treaty, and have resulted in the return of fugitives who had previously found haven from criminal prosecution in foreign countries.

Local prosecutors initiate the return of accused or convicted persons from outside the continental limits of the United States by a request to their governor. This state executive forwards the necessary papers to the U.S. Secretary of State, who, in turn, assigns the prosecution of the proceedings to the U.S. consul in the nation in which the fugitive is located; this foreign service official is the proper party to defend any judicial review of the request for extradition or to appeal from any adverse ruling. If a demand is made on the United States by another nation, the proceedings for surrender are subject to review in federal courts, or state courts of record with general jurisdiction. If sufficient evidence is produced to sustain the charge under the provisions of the treaty, the presiding judge must certify this fact to the Secretary of State, and forward this determination, along with a true copy of all the testimony in such hearing, so that a warrant may be issued upon the requisition of the proper authorities of the demanding nation; the magistrate should commit the prisoner to a proper jail pending such action.

Interstate Extradition

Interstate extradition begins with a written application to the governor, by the prosecutor or the confinement official having jurisdiction in the case, for a requisition or demand upon another state for the rendi-

[7]Article II, Section 2, Clause 2.
[8]Mutual recognition; official courtesy.

tion of the fugitive. The application should contain the name of the person charged, the crime charged against him and the approximate time, place and circumstances of its commission; or the circumstances of the accused person's escape from custody or of the violation of the terms of his bail, probation, or parole; and the name of the state in which the fugitive is believed to be, along with the location of the accused at the time of the application. In addition, the prosecutor's application must contain the certification that the ends of justice require the arrest and return of the accused to the demanding state for trial and that the proceeding is not instituted to enforce a private claim. The application is executed in duplicate, and is to be accompanied by two certified copies of court papers involved. Upon the governor's verification and approval, indicated by endorsement directly on the application, one copy of the application and supporting documents is to be filed in the office of the Secretary of State, and the other copy and supporting papers shall be forwarded, with the governor's formal demand, to the asylum state.[9]

Two procedures are established in California for returning fugitives to demanding states, one for the classic fugitive from justice, and the other for the person placed in this classification by the uniform extradition statute. In the first instance, the papers constituting the demand must allege that the accused person was present in the demanding state at the time of the commission of the alleged crime, and thereafter fled from that state, and a duty is placed upon the governor (subject to the provisions of law) to have such person arrested and delivered up to the executive authority of the demanding state. The governor should not inquire into the guilt or innocence of the accused, except for necessary inquiries in identifying the person in custody as the individual charged with crime. In the second instance, the papers merely charge the accused person with an act in the demanding state or in a third state intentionally resulting in a crime in the demanding state, even though the accused was not in the demanding state at the time of the commission of the crime and has not fled therefrom; but in this type of demand the action of the governor is permissive rather than mandatory.[10]

In any event, the demand must be accompanied by proof that a crime is charged, or that there has been a conviction of a crime, in the demanding state. This evidence must be in writing and shall consist of either: (1) a copy of an indictment found, an information filed or an affidavit executed before a magistrate in the demanding state charging the accused person with having committed a crime under the laws of the demanding state, together with a copy of any warrant issued; or (2) a

[9]California Penal Code, Section 1554.2.
[10]*Ibid.*, Section 1548.1.

copy of a judgment of conviction or of a sentence imposed in execution, together with a statement by the executive authority of the demanding state that the person claimed has escaped from confinement or has violated the terms of his bail, probation or parole. Accompanying papers in support of this demand must be certified as authentic by the executive authority making the demand.[11]

When the executive authority of a state is satisfied that the demand is within the provisions of the extradition law, he will issue a governor's warrant for the arrest of the person named in the papers of the demanding state. Often, an arrest is made before this formal demand is verified and a governor's warrant issued. When an arrest is made upon a warrant issued by a magistrate upon the filing of a verified complaint, or without a warrant upon reasonable information that the accused stands charged in the courts of any other state with a felony, there is a preliminary hearing before a magistrate. If it appears that the accused is the person charged with having committed the crime alleged, the magistrate must, by a warrant reciting the accusation, commit him to the county jail for a period not exceeding 30 days, which will enable the arrest of the accused to be made under a warrant of the governor on a requisition or demand of the executive authority of the state having jurisdiction of the offense charged. The prisoner may be admitted to bail at this arraignment, pending issuance of the governor's warrant of arrest, if the offense charged is not punishable by death or life imprisonment. The examining magistrate must promptly notify the local prosecutor of the arrest, and he, in turn, is responsible for the notifications which will initiate formal extradition proceedings.[12]

When the accused person is formally held on the governor's warrant of arrest, he cannot be turned over to the agent of the demanding state unless he is first taken forthwith before a magistrate informing him of the demand made for his surrender, the crime with which he is charged and his right to demand and procure legal counsel. If the accused or his counsel desires to test the legality of the arrest, the magistrate may fix a reasonable time to apply for a writ of *habeas corpus,* and a copy of the accused's application for this writ is served upon the local prosecutor and the agent of the demanding state. In addition, if this first test of the legality of the proceedings is adverse to the accused person, a reasonable time is fixed by the presiding magistrate in which to apply to the next higher court.[13]

Any officer or other person entrusted with a governor's warrant in extradition proceedings who delivers to the agent of the demanding state

[11] *Ibid.,* Section 1548.2.
[12] *Ibid.,* Sections 1551–1552.1.
[13] *Ibid.,* Section 1550.1.

a person in his custody under such warrant, in willful disobedience to the legal requirements for the protection of the person being extradited (such as his arraignment before a magistrate, informing him of the circumstances of the arrest and his right to legal counsel, and allowing him to test the legality of the demand for his extradition), is guilty of a misdemeanor, punishable upon conviction by imprisonment for not more than 6 months, a one thousand dollar fine, or both.[14]

All of the above proceedings are for the purpose of maintaining the public interest without infringing upon the rights of any accused person. However, nothing in these formal procedures limits the right of an accused person to return voluntarily and without formality to the demanding state; or upon arrest and after an arraignment before a magistrate in which he is advised of his rights to formal extradition procedure, to intelligently waive the issuance and service of the governor's warrant and all other procedures incidental to the extradition proceedings by signing a written waiver in the presence of the magistrate.[15]

Generally, extraditees are immune from civil actions arising out of the crime charged in the requisition and demand, until convicted or upon the expiration of a reasonable time for return to the asylum state after acquittal; they may be charged with other crimes in addition to, or in lieu of, the crime or crimes for which extradition was instituted. No fee or reward can be paid or accepted for services rendered in extradition proceedings, except as provided by law for necessary official expenses.[16]

The review of an extradition arrest and subsequent custody for the purpose of turning over an accused person to an agent of the demanding state has, as its objective, the determination of whether the accused person may lawfully be removed to the demanding state, rather than any inquiry into the guilt of innocence of the prisoner.[17] Direct attacks in applying for discharge from detention in the asylum state under a writ of *habeas corpus* usually allege the validity of detention is defective because: (1) extradition papers are not in order or are without the necessary authentication by the governor of the demanding state; (2) the charge is inadequate to support extradition, whether by indictment or affidavit, or is insubstantial; (3) petitioner is not the person named in the extradition papers; or (4) petitioner is not a fugitive from the demanding state's justice because he was not within its jurisdiction at the time of the alleged offense.

A collateral attack upon the validity of the detention for the purpose of extradition is that the constitutional rights of the fugitive will be vio-

[14]*Ibid.*, Section 1550.2.
[15]*Ibid.*,Section 1555.1.
[16]*Ibid.*, Sections 1555–58.
[17]*Shoemaker*, Ex parte 25 Cal. App. 551 (1914).

lated by the demanding state if he is extradited, that the demand for rendition carries no more validity than the proceedings upon which the demand was based, or that the asylum state would be an active participant in violating the accused person's constitutional rights by subjecting the fugitive to cruel and unusual punishment if he were returned.[18]

Wrongful Refusal to Grant Extradition

The governor of California has a duty to grant extradition upon the request of a demanding state when the fugitive is a person who was present in the demanding state at the time of the commission of the crime charged and then left. This is not true of the executive authority of many other states. In fact, several executives of Middle Atlantic and New England states have refused to approve extradition requests from governors of the southern states because of an unwillingness to return a person who might become the subject of cruel and unusual punishment in the demanding state. Knowing that reciprocity requires cooperation, most of the executives in charge of state governments grant extradition upon legal requests in accordance with the basic concept that no state should be a sanctuary for criminals. There is a belief that our dual federal and state court system assures any petitioner of an opportunity for adequate and speedy legal relief when necessary, and that the fugitive would have access to these courts through traditional writs, motions and appeals after his return from the asylum state. However, when a lawful demand for the extradition of an accused person is refused by the governor of the asylum state, the courts have no apparent power to compel the extradition of fugitives in criminal cases.[19]

Attendance of Out-of-State Witnesses

A uniform compact between states requiring reciprocal arrangements for the demand and attendance of material witnesses in criminal cases is known as the "Uniform Act to Secure the Attendance of Witnesses from Without the State in Criminal Cases."[20] It is very similar to extradition in that a certificate showing the need of the witness is prepared by the "demanding" judicial officer and forwarded to a judicial officer in the state in which the witness is located; a hearing is provided to determine if the certificate (acting as a requisition) is justified. The

[18]"Extradition Habeas Corpus," *Yale Law Journal*, 74, No. 1 (November 1964), 91.

[19]*Manchester*, Ex parte 5 Cal. 237.

[20]California Penal Code, Chapter 3a, Sections 1334–1334.6.

attendance of the witness is secured either through court process directing the witness to appear or an order of arrest. In the latter case, the
witness is arrested and delivered to an agent of the demanding state for
transportation to the requesting judicial officer.

In any state which is a signatory to this uniform compact,[21] a judge
with authority to command persons within such state to attend and
testify before courts, may issue a certificate under the seal of his court
that: (1) a criminal prosecution is pending in the court or there is a
grand jury investigation; (2) a specific person is a material witness in
such prosecution or investigation; and (3) his presence will be required
for a specified number of days. This certificate naming the witness whose
attendance is required should be considered by the receiving judge as
prima facie evidence; he should convene a hearing within a reasonable
time to determine if the witness' attendance is material and necessary
and will not cause undue hardship to such person. The laws of the
requesting state protect the witness from arrest and the service of civil
and criminal process during such attendance and necessary travel. If
the judicial determination is affirmative, the magistrate or judge issues
a subpoena, with a copy of the certificate from the requesting judicial
officer attached, directing the witness to attend and testify in the court
or grand jury investigation. Failure to appear, after tender of payment
of witness fees and mileage (five dollars a day and ten cents a mile), is
punishable in the same manner as the failure to attend in any court of
record when under subpoena.

However, an endorsement on the certificate may recommend the witness be taken into immediate custody and delivered to an officer of the
requesting jurisdiction to assure his attendance; in this instance, the
receiving judicial officer may order the witness to be brought before
him for a hearing, and if satisfied as to the desirability of the custody
and delivery, he may order the witness taken into custody and delivered
to an officer of the requesting state.

"Fresh Pursuit" of Criminals

Time is essential in law enforcement. Continued pursuit by police
officers often results in the arrests of persons who might otherwise never
be identified as criminals or never apprehended. "Fresh pursuit" was
recognized in twelfth-century England as the common law practice of
apprehending persons by a "hue and cry" raised upon a felony committed. This was a pursuit with horn and voice from town to town and
county to county until the felon or felons were taken and delivered to
the sheriff.

[21]Forty-two states and Puerto Rico.

The Uniform Act on Fresh Pursuit grants peace officers of one state, who enter another state in fresh pursuit of a felon or suspected felon, the same authority to arrest and hold such person in custody as possessed by peace officers in the other state. Fresh pursuit does not necessarily mean instant or "in sight" pursuit, but rather pursuit without unreasonable delay.[22]

The rapidity of modern transportation has armed the criminal with the means to promptly move across state lines after the commission of a crime. The usual reason for flight is that distance, and particularly state boundaries, circumvents the efficiency of police agencies. Police officers not only lack authority outside of their own locality, but they are also without the ready and knowing cooperation of fellow workers. Outside their own jurisdiction, police officers must seek the cooperation of other police forces and this is never quite as efficient as unit operations.

In California, the major sections of the Penal Code related to this extension of the arrest power of peace officers follow the provisions suggested by the Uniform Act on Fresh Pursuit, granting the out-of-state peace officer the same power possessed by peace officers of California when making an arrest. It also provides for the prompt arraignment of the prisoner before a magistrate in the California county in which the arrest was made; for the conduct of a hearing by the magistrate for the purpose of determining the lawfulness of the arrest; and for the commitment of the prisoner to await the issuance within a reasonable time of an extradition warrant by the governor of the demanding state if the magistrate finds the arrest lawful. The magistrate may admit the prisoner to bail if the offense is bailable under California law, and may discharge the prisoner from custody if he finds the arrest was unlawful.[23]

Federal Removal Proceedings

The purpose of federal removal proceedings is to accord to defendants arrested for a violation of the laws of the United States the necessary safeguards against an undesirable and inconvenient removal to a distant point for trial; and at the same time it removes any opportunity for delaying prosecution by preventing or postponing transportation from the district of arrest to the district in which the criminal action is pending, thus turning the district of arrest into a sanctuary for the commission of crimes elsewhere.

United States territory has been divided into districts in which the federal courts exercise original criminal jurisdiction. For the purpose of

[22]*The Handbook on Interstate Crime Control* (Chicago, Ill.: The Council of State Governments, 1949), pp. 1–7.
[23]California Penal Code, Sections 852.2 and 852.3.

removal proceedings, these districts are classified into two groups and a procedure established to remove prisoners from a district of arrest to the district in which the prosecution is pending.[24] It should be noted that this division of federal districts turns removal proceedings into a system very similar to interstate extradition.

A federal arrest is situated in a "nearby district" when the place of arrest is in another district in the same state, or less than one hundred miles distant from the place where the prosecution is pending when the place of arrest is in another state. A federal arrest is situated in a "distant district" when the place of arrest occurs in other than the state in which the prosecution is pending, and the site of the arrest is one hundred or more miles from the place in which the criminal action is pending.

A person arrested in a "nearby district" on federal charges must be arraigned before the nearest available commissioner,[25] who informs the prisoner of the complaint against him, of his right to retain counsel and to have a preliminary examination, and of his right to silence. He must warn the prisoner that any statement made by him may be used against him, and allow the defendant reasonable time and opportunity to consult with counsel. The defendant is not required to plead, and if he waives the preliminary examination, the commissioner holds him to answer in the district court in which the prosecution is pending—or in which the offense was committed, if no prosecution is pending. If the prisoner does not waive, the commissioner should conduct a preliminary hearing within a reasonable time. This hearing is similar to the type conducted in state courts. If from the evidence at the hearing, the commissioner finds probable cause to believe that an offense has been committed and that the defendant has committed it, he holds the defendant to answer in the district in which the prosecution is pending.[26]

If a person is arrested for an offense against the laws of the United States in a "distant district," he is to be taken without unnecessary delay before the nearest available commissioner or a nearby judge of the United States in the district in which the arrest was made. Original arraignment and the opportunity to waive a hearing are conducted in the same manner as in the case of an arrest in a nearby district; the commissioner or judge issues a warrant of removal to the district where the prosecution is pending if the defendant waives a hearing.

When a defendant does not waive a hearing in a "distant district," the commissioner or judge hears the evidence, with the defendant given

[24]Title 18, U.S. Code, Section 3041 and Appendix, Rule 40.
[25]Or any other nearby officer empowered to commit persons charged with federal offenses.
[26]Title 18, U.S. Code, Appendix, Rule 40 (a) and 5 (a-c).

the opportunity to cross-examine witnesses and introduce evidence in his own behalf. Only a judge can make the final decision in these cases. Therefore, if a commissioner conducts this hearing he has to report his findings and recommendations to the judge concerned. A defendant is discharged when it appears that insufficient grounds have been shown for such warrant of removal. A warrant of removal is issued upon: (1) sufficient grounds based on evidence presented at the hearing; (2) production of a certified copy of an indictment and proof that the defendant is the person named therein; and (3) production of a certified copy of an information or complaint and proof that there is probable cause to believe that the defendant is guilty of the offense charged.[27]

A defendant arrested without a warrant cannot be removed until a warrant issued in the district in which the offense was committed is presented; a defendant may be admitted to bail if the offense is bailable under federal laws; and all papers and other documents, and any bail taken, are transmitted to the clerk of the district court to which the defendant has been transferred by the warrant of removal.[28]

It should be noted that in the federal hearings for a warrant of removal, a defendant prosecuted by indictment of a federal grand jury does not enjoy the review of the grand jury action by the judicial officer of the district in which the arrest was made. The federal grand jury, as an arm of the U.S. district court, has already found probable cause to believe the person named is guilty as charged, and this action is not reviewable by judges of the "home" district. Therefore it would be illogical to permit such review just because the arrest was made in a "distant district."

When the arrest is made in a "nearby district," the federal defendant has the same rights and the proceedings are handled in the same manner as when a person charged with a crime under the laws of a state is arrested within such state. Any necessary transfer from the jurisdiction of the place of arrest to the place where prosecution is pending, or in which the crime was committed, is accomplished with just the normal original arraignment in the county of arrest. However, federal arrests in "distant districts" are safeguarded in the same manner as extradition and rendition between states: the judicial officer is assigned the role of the governor of a state in uniform extradition proceedings between states; the judicial hearing in a U.S. court in the district of arrest is substituted for the *habeas corpus* hearing in the asylum state under interstate extradition procedures.

[27]Title 18, U.S. Code, Appendix, Rule 40 (b).
[28]Title 18, U.S. Code, Appendix, Rule 40 (c).

Federal Action: Unlawful Flight

In an unusual action in support of local law enforcement and its need to extradite persons from other states or secure the attendance of out-of-state witnesses, Congress enacted a federal statute against unlawful flight to avoid prosecution or giving testimony. This law provides primarily for the return of persons who take flight to avoid prosecution, or custody or confinement after conviction, for a crime or attempt to commit a crime which is a felony, or to avoid being a felony case witness. The place of return is the federal district in which the original crime was committed or the person confined. As a matter of practice, these apprehended fugitives are usually released to local authorities.[29] The federal attorney cannot prosecute except with the written approval of the Attorney General or one of his assistants. Local authorities seek extradition of the prisoner and compulsory attendance of the witness. It is cooperative action and contributes to the interstate control of crime. The federal statute reads:

> Whoever moves or travels in interstate or foreign commerce with intent either (1) to avoid prosecution, or custody or confinement after conviction, under the laws of the place from which he flees, for a crime or an attempt to commit a crime, punishable by death or which is a felony (or a "high misdemeanor" in New Jersey) under the laws of the place from which the fugitive flees, or (2) to avoid giving testimony in any criminal proceedings in such place in which the commission of an offense punishable by death or which is a felony (or "high misdemeanor" in N.J.) is charged, shall under the laws of such place be fined not more than $5000, or imprisoned not more than five years, or both. Violations of this section may be prosecuted only in the Federal judicial district in which the original crime was alleged to have been committed or in which the person was held in custody or confinement and only upon formal approval in writing by the Attorney General or an Assistant Attorney General of the United States.[30]

Unlawful flight to avoid prosecution or giving testimony is synonymous with "fugitive from justice," and this new law and the excellent work of the Federal Bureau of Investigation in making apprehensions is providing local law enforcement with a new methodology for the return of fugitives from other states.

[29]*Know Your FBI* (Washington, D.C.: Federal Bureau of Investigation, U.S. Dept. of Justice, 1966), p. 23.
[30]Title 18, U.S. Code, Section 1073.

Selected References

CASES

Ex parte Morgan, 78 Fed. Supp. 758 (1948).
  An extensive decision on extradition and fugitives.
Roberts v. Reilly, 116 U.S. 80 (1885).
  A classic decision exploring the designation of "fugitive."

BOOKS

Fitzgerald, Maurice J., Col., U.S. Army, *Handbook of Criminal Investigation.*
  New York: Arco Publishing Co., 1957, 212 pages.
  Contains an excellent chapter on tracing of fugitives.
The Handbook on Interstate Crime Control (rev. ed.). Chicago: The Council
  of State Governments, 1949, 144 pages.
  Ways and means of overcoming loopholes in the criminal law in relation
  to the "no-man's" land of crime control.

ARTICLES

Cardozo, Michael H., "When Extradition Fails, Is Abduction the Solution?"
  American Journal of International Law, Vol. 55, 127–35.
  A review of available means for returning fugitives.
Evans, Alona E., "New Extradition Treaties of the United States," *American
  Journal of International Law,* Vol. 59, 351–62.
  Extradition treaties recently negotiated with Brazil and Sweden, and
  a general discussion of international treaties and their requirements.
"Extradition Habeas Corpus," *Yale Law Journal,* 75, No. 1 (November 1964),
  78–135.
  This article discusses the use of the writ of *habeas corpus* as a legal
  method of avoiding extradition to another state, basing the argument for
  the denial of the demanding state's requisition on constitutional questions
  of past or prospective deprivations of the fugitive's rights by the demanding state.

IV

JUDICIAL SYSTEMS

*The judicial function is supervision with
responsibility. It has a high duty and a solemn
responsibility to overview the work of police
and prosecutor, opposing counsel and jurors;
to preserve the due process of law throughout the arrest-to-release procedures in the
administration of criminal justice; and to
translate into living law the sanctions which
may be imposed upon offenders after a
fair trial.*

6

Bail

Bail is a procedure in the administration of justice for securing temporary liberty after arrest or conviction through a written promise to appear in court as required. It may be necessary to deposit cash bail, a surety bond or evidence of an equity in real property—as well as the written assurance of another person or persons—in support of the basic promise to appear. In recent years, a rejection of ancient bail procedures has been evident, and there is a trend toward releasing detained individuals upon their own recognizance[1] or through the issuance of a citation (summons) to appear in court at a specified time in lieu of continued custody after arrest in misdemeanor cases.

The basic concept of bail is to provide reasonable means for releasing detained persons while their cases are pending, whenever the accused person is willing to give reasonable and sufficient assurance of his willingness to appear in court when required.

[1]Recognition of detained person as an individual who will appear in court as required in accordance to a signed agreement.

The custom of bail originated in the ancient English practice of requiring the oath of responsible persons for the release of accused individuals detained while awaiting trial. In 1275, the Statute of Westminster formalized bail procedures in England and protected the person held in custody from excessive bail.

In the United States, the system for release on bail was established by the Judiciary Act of 1789 and became a Constitutional guarantee when the first ten amendments were adopted in 1791. This legislation provides, in substance, as follows: upon all arrests in criminal cases, bail shall be admitted, except when the punishment may be death, in which cases bail is discretionary, depending upon the nature of the circumstances of the offense, the evidence, and usages of law. The Eighth Amendment of the Constitution only provides guidelines: "Excessive bail shall not be required."

The fixing of pretrial bail depends upon the facts of each individual case; but whenever bail is set in an amount greater than usually fixed for serious crimes it is reasonable to expect the presentation of some evidence justifying the need for high bail to guard against allegations of arbitrary judicial action. Bail set at a higher amount than fulfilling the purpose of assuring that the accused will stand trial and submit to sentence if found guilty is "excessive" under the Eighth Amendment.[2]

In providing for release on bail, the basic presumption of innocence goes beyond its role upon trial in demanding the burden of proof of guilt, and places emphasis upon the accusatory nature of American criminal procedures and the fact that "guilt" is the verdict of a court and not inherent in the accusatory pleadings.

Admission to bail always involves a calculated risk that the defendant will not appear. From its very inception as a procedure in administering justice, bail has proved to be a thorny concept. Courts and legislative bodies have recognized this by providing for the revocation of bail, the surrender of the defendant, and the forfeiture of posted security. California law notes the potential of flight to avoid prosecution in citing the matters to be considered by a judge in fixing the amount of bail, or in allowing it at all in discretionary cases: a court should take into consideration the previous criminal record of the defendant and the seriousness of the offense charged, and should weigh them in connection with the defendant and "the probability of his appearing at the trial or hearing of the case."[3]

Admission to bail also involves the calculated risk that a criminal career might continue during liberty. Bail is not a device to prevent

[2]*Stack v. Boyle*, 342 U.S. 1 (1951).
[3]California Penal Code, Section 1275.

anticipated, but unconsummated crimes; to protect witnesses or evidence; or to punish or treat persons accused of crimes.[4] On the other hand, the fruits of crime are not to be used for the purpose of bail, and any offer of bail will be denied unless the magistrate is convinced no portion of the security or bail costs has been feloniously obtained by the defendant.[5]

"Preventive Detention" After Arrest

Police officers who must face the hazards of arresting armed opponents are not in favor of the prompt release of prisoners when there is a calculated risk that the defendant will continue his criminal operations upon release. In every jurisdiction, police officials can cite several instances of serious crimes by bailed offenders awaiting trial. Aaron Mitchell's case, in Sacramento, California, is illustrative: Mitchell, on bail pending the trial of a robbery charge, committed an assault and robbery. In the process of fleeing the crime scene, he shot and killed a Sacramento police officer, Arnold Gamble. Mitchell has been tried and convicted, but the officer's wife is a widow and their children fatherless.

Experienced police officers know many career criminals do not have access to necessary funds to defray the costs of release on bail and legal assistance; but, because release on bail is considered a vital expense and career criminals don't relish the idea of being defended by an assigned counsel or a representative of the public defender's office, it is not uncommon for the original arresting officer to make a second apprehension while the defendant is at liberty on bail.

Release of an offender on probation or parole provides the assignment of a probation or parole agent to supervise the convicted offender's readjustment to the community and a life without crime; but release upon bail provides for release without supervision at a time when the offender is emotionally disturbed. Bail may, in fact, subvert the arrest and accusatory proceedings by permitting an offender the opportunity to destroy evidence which could mean conviction at trial.

In the future it may be possible for all courts to accept the police view of the great need for "preventive detention" in many cases in which bail is now a matter of right. At the present time in most localities, jurists at the lower court levels who daily face the realities of crime and criminals often refuse bail when it is within their discretion to do so,

[4]Senate Committee on the Judiciary, *Constitutional Rights and Federal Bail Procedures*, 88th Congress, 2d sess., December, 1964 (Washington, D.C.: Government Printing Office, 1965), p. vi.
[5]California Penal Code, Section 1275.

within the concept of what the police term "preventive detention." A possible answer to the police dilemma might be a special tribunal for a *really* speedy trial of offenders. In this way, the community would receive protection, while the offender would not be held in custody without trial for any lengthy period.

Of course, such action may place onerous handicaps upon a defendant. He cannot assist in locating witnesses, he cannot consult with his attorney in the privacy of his law office, he enters the courtroom from a cell block rather than through the corridor door and his attorney might not have sufficient time to prepare the defense. With the elimination of the bail procedure, the career criminal cannot destroy evidence or suborn perjury and he cannot murder witnesses for the prosecution.

Persons at the operational level believe the admission to bail must be based upon other factors in addition to the mere guarantee of an appearance in court when required. However, the late Mr. Justice Jackson, prior to his elevation to the Supreme Court bench, favored a climate of law and order and worked for greater authority by police, but in relation to the purpose of bail, he was opposed to its use for any reason other than that of ensuring the appearance of the defendant in court. In the *Williamson* case he wrote: "Imprisonment to protect society from predicted but unconsummated offenses is so unprecedented in this country and so fraught with danger of excesses and injustice that I am loath to resort to it."[6]

Bail as a Right

At the federal level, release on bail in noncapital cases is viewed as a right; at the state level, the Constitution does not specifically delineate bail as a right. In *Stack v. Boyle*,[7] the U.S. Supreme Court upheld the right to bail in noncapital cases. The late Mr. Justice Jackson, in preparing a concurring opinion in this case commented:

> From the passage of the Judiciary Act of 1789 to the present federal rules of criminal procedure, federal law has unequivocally provided that a person arrested for a noncapital offense shall be admitted to bail. This traditional right to freedom before conviction permits the unhampered preparation of a defense and serves to prevent the infliction of punishment prior to conviction. Unless this right to bail before trial is preserved, the presumption of innocence, secured only after centuries of struggle, would lose its meaning.

California supports the position of the U.S. Supreme Court in viewing bail as a matter of right in noncapital cases, and extends bail as a matter

[6]*Williamson v. U.S.*, 184 F. 2nd 280 (1950).
[7]342 U.S. 1 (1951).

of right to the defendant convicted of a misdemeanor when an appeal has been filed from a judgment imposing a fine only or imprisonment. It also allows its judiciary a humanitarian approach to releasing offenders upon bail; it establishes release at the court's discretion when a person is accused of an offense punishable with death, or awaiting action upon an appeal from a judgment and sentence in a felony case. These sections of the California Penal Code are numbered and entitled as follows:

1270. *Offense Not Bailable.* A defendant charged with an offense punishable with death cannot be admitted to bail, when the proof of his guilt is evident or the presumption thereof is great. The finding of an indictment does not add to the strength of the proof or the presumptions to be drawn therefrom.

1271. *In What Cases Defendant May Be Admitted to Bail Before Conviction.* If the charge is for any other offense, he may be admitted to bail before conviction, as a matter of right.

1272. *Admission to Bail Upon Appeal.* After conviction of an offense not punishable with death, a defendant who has appealed may be admitted to bail:

1. As a matter of right, when the appeal is from a judgment imposing a fine only.

2. As a matter of right, when the appeal is from a judgment imposing imprisonment in cases of misdemeanor.

3. As a matter of discretion in all other cases.

California also provides procedures for review when a person is imprisoned or detained in custody on any criminal charge for want of bail. Such person is entitled to a writ of *habeas corpus* for the purpose of giving bail; the applicant need not allege he is being illegally confined, but only that he is held for want of bail.[8] The judge before whom the application for the writ is heard may take an undertaking of bail from the applicant, if the charge upon which he has been imprisoned or detained is bailable, and file the agreement in the proper court. When the applicant is at the preconviction level, and the charges do not involve: (1) a crime of violence, (2) a crime committed with a deadly weapon, or (3) a crime involving the forcible taking or destruction of the property of another, the judge must immediately set the amount of bail, if no bail has previously been fixed.[9] Because a person who applies for a writ of *habeas corpus* may be unnecessarily restrained of his liberty while the processing of his application is being conducted, the court in which such a petition is presented may admit the detained person to bail pending a hearing, if the offense for which he is being held is bailable.[10]

[8]California Penal Code, Section 1490.
[9]*Ibid.*, Section 1491.
[10]*Ibid.*, Section 1476.

Forms of Bail

Release upon bail may require the posting of a formal bail bond[11] for the amount of the bail, along with sureties as "guarantors"; the deposit of cash bail without sureties; or release upon the personal recognizance of the defendant ("O.R."). These forms of bail were handed down from the original colonial states during the westward movement of the frontier across the United States. Legal provisions regarding the more formal aspects of admission to bail in California are practically the same as in New York and several New England states. The following requirements are specified in California for the various types of bail, but they are also illustrative of the same provisions of law in other states.

BAIL BOND

The bail bond is a written undertaking, executed by two sufficient sureties (with or without the defendant, in the discretion of the magistrate) and acknowledged before the court or magistrate admitting the defendant to bail. In its opening section, the bail bond cites the name of the defendant, the time, date and circumstances under which the defendant is held in custody and a brief description of the crime charged. The major portion of the bail bond is a statement of the contract. It names the sureties, their places of residence and occupation and states that such sureties undertake that the defendant will appear as required (specifying the level of the proceeding, from answering the charge to awaiting action on appeal), in whatever court the proceeding may be assigned; it adds that the defendant "will at all times hold himself amenable to the orders and process of the court." Failure to perform on the bond contract will result in the sureties having to forfeit to the people of the state of California the sum specified as defendant's bail.[12]

In the terminology that has been handed down in this legal area, the two sureties on a bail bond are known collectively as the "bail." The qualifications of the "bail" is:

> 1. Each of them must be a resident, householder or freeholder within the state; but nonresidents of the county may be rejected.
> 2. They must each be worth the amount specified in the undertaking, exclusive of property exempt from execution, except that if any of the sureties is not worth the amount specified in the undertaking, a hearing must be held before the magistrate to determine the value of such equity,

[11]An "undertaking."
[12]California Penal Code, Section 1278.

and witnesses may be examined until the magistrate is satisfied that the value of the equity is equal to twice the amount of the bond such surety must justify. (Magistrates may permit additional sureties if necessary to justify severally the equivalent of sufficient bail.)

3. In all cases, the magistrate may further examine the "bail" under oath concerning their sufficiency, and must require justification that they each possess the qualifications necessary—and if such justification is based upon real property, the affidavit must contain full details of ownership and equity, the number of times such property has been posted as collateral and whether or not such previous undertakings are still in effect.[13]

Undertakings of bail by admitted surety insurers should meet all the other requirements of law and the obligation of the insurer is clearly stated in the same manner as any "bail," and is signed by the bondsman representative as attorney in fact for the admitted surety insurer.[14]

CASH BAIL

A misdemeanant may be released after arrest and booking, and any person may be released at any time after an order admitting them to bail has been made, upon depositing with the clerk of the court—in which further proceedings are scheduled against the person in custody—cash bail in the amount specified in the order, or—if no order—then in the schedule of bail as established by law. Delivery to the officer in whose custody such individual is held of a certificate of the deposit of cash bail requires release from custody.[15] If a person has entered into a formal undertaking for bail, he may, at any time before the forfeiture of the undertaking, in like manner deposit the sum mentioned in the undertaking, and upon the deposit being made, the formal bail bond is exonerated.[16]

A receipt is given upon the deposit of cash bail. After the person for whom the money was deposited has appeared in court and the proceedings concluded with a judgment, the bail is exonerated and the money returned to the depositor upon submission of the receipt. However, if the defendant is also the depositor and the final judgment calls for the payment of a fine, the court will direct that the cash bail be applied in satisfaction of the fine, but will refund any surplus to the defendant-depositor. United States or California Bonds, or a surety bond executed by a certified, admitted surety insurer as required in the in-

13*Ibid.*, Sections 1279–1280a.
14*Ibid.*, Section 1459.
15*Ibid.*, Section 1295.
16*Ibid.*, Section 1296.

surance code, of the same value as cash bail may be deposited in lieu
of cash; this deposit must also be returned or relinquished to satisfy a
fine after judgment. A bill of sale and title deed for real property in
which the defendant owns an equity may also be deposited in the same
manner as cash bail, but the court must hold a hearing in this event to
determine if the equity is equal to twice the amount of cash bail necessary; such equity will also be returned or relinquished as would cash
or bonds.[17]

While the rates of professional bail bondsmen are either established
or supervised by state insurance departments, they do charge high fees.
In California, the cost of bail when the deposit is less than $500.00 is a
flat fee of $10.00 plus 10 percent of the amount fixed as bail. When the
amount of bail is $500.00 or more, only the 10 percent fee is charged
the person seeking a surety bond for deposit in lieu of cash bail. However, no accused person has any right to a surety bond; it is always
within the discretion of the bondsman to decide whether or not to write
the bond.

RECOGNIZANCE

In 1959, California made provision for releasing any defendant upon
his written promise to appear, without the deposit of any valuable consideration in the form of a bail bond or cash bail. Upon good cause
being shown for this informal type of bail, the judge of any court (or a
magistrate) with authority to set bail for a defendant can now release
him on his own recognizance. This procedure does not grant a right to
the defendant, but rather a permissive and discretionary procedure to
the judiciary.[18] The judicial officer releasing the defendant requires him
to file a signed agreement with the court, in which he agrees that: (1)
he will appear at all times and places as ordered by the court or magistrate releasing him, and as ordered by any court in which, or any magistrate before whom, the charge is subsequently pending; (2) if he fails
to so appear and is apprehended outside of the state of California, he
waives extradition; and (3) any court or magistrate of competent jurisdiction may revoke the order of release and either return him to custody
or require that he give bail or other assurance of his appearance.[19]

The court in which the criminal proceeding against the defendant is
pending may require a defendant, who has been released as above, to
give bail in an amount specified by it, or to deposit cash bail in lieu
thereof. Such court, and any court to which the case against a defendant

[17]*Ibid.*, Sections 1269b, 1296–1298.
[18]*Ibid.*, Sections 1318 and 1318.2.
[19]*Ibid.*, Section 1318.4.

at liberty on his own recognizance may be transferred, may direct his arrest:

(1) when he has failed to appear as he agreed

(2) when he was required to give bail or other security upon the revocation of his own recognizance and has failed to do so

(3) upon an indictment being found or an information filed in felony cases.[20]

Willful failure to appear as agreed in a personal recognizance results in the defendant being charged with an additional crime of the same seriousness as the charge of crime upon which he had been released. Punishment when a misdemeanor defendant fails to appear as agreed is not specified, but a felony defendant who fails to appear is guilty of another felony with a maximum punishment of a $5,000 fine, five years in state prison or one year in county jail, or both.[21]

Schedule of Bail

The schedule of bail contains a list of misdemeanors and the amount of bail necessary for release, and may list one amount as standard bail for all misdemeanors not listed in the schedule. This schedule and its preparation are the function and duty of the municipal and justice court judges in each county. A bail schedule must be adopted by a majority vote; it is subject to revision, and its application is countywide—copies are sent to all jails in the county. The senior judge in each county shall call not more than two, nor less than one, meetings each year for necessary action in establishing or revising this schedule of bail.[22]

Amount of Bail

During the postarrest period of detention, the amount of bail depends upon the grade of the offense, whether the arrest is with or without a warrant and whether or not the defendant has been arraigned upon the charge. When the arrest is on a warrant alleging a public offense, bail should be in the amount specified in the indorsement upon the warrant by the issuing magistrate.[23] When the arrest is for a misdemeanor, the amount of bail should be fixed by the magistrate at the time of arraignment; and if prior to arraignment, bail should be as fixed in the warrant of arrest; and if arrested without a warrant, then the amount of bail should

[20]*Ibid.*, Sections 1318.6 and 1318.8.
[21]*Ibid.*, Sections 1319.4 and 1319.6.
[22]*Ibid.*, Section 1269b.
[23]*Ibid.*, Section 1269a.

be in accordance with the countywide schedule of bail for misdemeanants. When the arrest is for a felony, the bail should be as fixed by the judge before whom the prisoner is arraigned upon the formal complaint, and if prior to such arraignment, the amount of bail is to be as indorsed upon the arrest warrant.[24] Generally, when the arrest is without a warrant directing an arrest for the commission of a bailable offense, and the defendant is neither arraigned nor the subject of a warrant fixing the amount of bail, a magistrate or a commissioner of a court having jurisdiction of the offense should fix the amount of bail.[25]

When a defendant has been held to answer upon an examination for a public offense, bail may be established by the examining magistrate, the judge of any municipal court within the county where a felony charge is pending, or a judge who has power to issue the writ of *habeas corpus*.[26]

In the period following the finding of an indictment or the filing of an information, but preceding conviction, in offenses not punishable by death, the bail is fixed by the magistrate before whom the defendant is arraigned on the bench warrant, or before whom the defendant is arraigned upon voluntary surrender prior to service of a bench warrant. The court in which the charge is pending may, upon good cause shown, change the amount of bail. If an application for reduced bail is made by the defendant, a notice must be served upon the district attorney. If bail is increased, the defendant may be ordered into custody unless bail is given in the new amount.[27]

When a defendant is awaiting action on an appeal, the amount of bail may be fixed by the trial judge or by any judge having the power to issue a writ of *habeas corpus*.[28]

Persons Authorized to Accept Bail

Persons authorized to accept bail in accordance with a schedule of bail or the order of a competent court or magistrate, to issue and sign an order for the release of the arrested person and to set a time and place for appearance before the appropriate court are the officer in charge of a jail wherein an arrested person is held in custody, or the clerk of the court in which a person is admitted to bail.[29] When a person arrested for a misdemeanor is bailed in accordance with a schedule of bail, it is often termed "police" bail, as it is administered by police or sheriff's personnel in charge of local detention facilities.

[24]*Ibid.*, Section 1269b.
[25]*Ibid.*, Section 1276.
[26]*Ibid.*, Sections 1277 and 1281a.
[27]*Ibid.*, Sections 1284 and 1289.
[28]*Ibid.*, Section 1291.
[29]*Ibid.*, Section 1269b.

Surrender of Defendant

A defendant at liberty on bail may surrender himself to the officer having custody prior to release, or he may be surrendered by his "bail" or the depositor of cash bail (for the exoneration of the posted security). Standard procedures are: (1) upon the presentation of a certified copy of the bail bond (undertaking) or the deposit receipt, the defendant is surrendered to the original place of custody where the officer in charge of the jail must accept the defendant (as upon a commitment) and acknowledge the surrender by a certificate in writing; (2) the "bail" or depositor files the certified copy of original bail papers along with the receipt for surrendering the defendant with the court in which the action or appeal is pending; and (3) upon a five-day notice to the district attorney, the court may order the security or deposit exonerated. Bail is also exonerated when a defendant is committed by court order to a state hospital for the care of the insane. Exoneration permits the person posting any security or other deposit of value to recover it in its entirety.[30]

Arrest for Surrender of Defendant

In another reflection of the patterns of early America in bail procedures, the defendant is considered "bonded" into the custody of his bondsman or depositor, and may be arrested and returned to his original custody from anywhere in the United States by the bondsman, depositor or authorized agents.

In California, for the purpose of surrendering a person released upon bail, the bondsman or any person who has deposited money or bonds to secure the release of the defendant (at any time before such bail or deposit is finally exonerated) may arrest the defendant; by written authority indorsed on a certified copy of the undertaking or of the certificate of deposit, he may also empower any person of suitable age to do so, and the arrest may be made outside of the state. The defendant must be delivered without unecessary delay and within 48 hours of the time of arrest, or the time the defendant is brought into the state, to the court or magistrate before whom the defendant is required to appear, or to the police or sheriff of the county in which such court is located. The defendant and his bondsman (or depositor) may enter into a written agreement waiving the 48-hour requirement, but such an agreement is revocable. This time limit may also be extended when the 48 hours ends on a Saturday, Sunday or holiday, but only until noon of the following business day.[31]

[30]*Ibid.*, Sections 1300 and 1371.
[31]*Ibid.*, Section 1301.

Traditionally, when the bondsman or authorized agents have arrested a fugitive defendant outside the state they may remove the fugitive into this state, in restraint, without extradition proceedings of any kind, so long as they have a certified copy of the bail bond or certificate of deposit. Some states, however, do not believe in this ancient authority of a bondsman and restrict it by law to guard against injustice. California makes it a misdemeanor for a bondsman to seize a fugitive person in this state who has been admitted to bail in another state without securing a warrant of arrest and an order to return the fugitive from a competent court in California. The bondsman or other person is required to file with a magistrate a request for an arrest warrant and an order authorizing the affiant to return the fugitive to the jurisdiction in which bail was given. An affidavit stating the name and whereabouts of the fugitive, the offense with which the alleged fugitive was charged or convicted, the time and place of court action and the particulars of the manner in which the fugitive has violated the terms of his bail agreement must be filed in support of the requests. The magistrate may issue the arrest warrant, but only after probable cause is established that the fugitive is the person for whom the warrant is sought, and he may require evidence under oath as he deems necessary to make this decision. The magistrate must notify the district attorney of the issuance of the warrant, and direct him to investigate the case and determine the facts. After the arrest of the fugitive, the magistrate holds an arraignment where the prisoner is advised of his right to counsel and to produce evidence at the hearing. The magistrate may admit the fugitive to bail pending the hearing. The magistrate conducts the hearing and the district attorney is present. If the magistrate is satisfied from the evidence presented that the person arraigned before him is the fugitive, he may issue an order authorizing affiant to return the fugitive to the jurisdiction from which he escaped bail.[32]

Professional bail bondsmen may suffer a severe financial loss when a person at liberty on a surety bond becomes a fugitive. In past years, organized crime rings would assist their friends in this business, but today's bondsmen appear to prefer regular "collection agencies" that trace these fugitives, despite charges likely to equal 50 percent of the surety bond's face value.

Arrest on Recommitment Order

The order for the recommitment of the defendant is signed by the judge of the court before which the action or appeal is pending, is entered upon

[32]*Ibid.*, Section 847.5.

the court's minutes, recites generally the facts upon which it is founded, and directs that the defendant named be arrested by any peace officer or policeman in the state and be committed to the officer in whose custody he was at the time he was admitted to bail, to be detained until legally charged. The defendant may be arrested in any county as upon a warrant of arrest without need for specific authorization for arrest.[33]

Forfeiture

If, without sufficient excuse, a defendant neglects to appear as required in his bail agreement, or upon any other occasion when his presence in court is lawfully required, the court will direct the fact to be entered upon its minutes and the undertaking of bail, or the cash bail deposited, will be declared forfeited. If the amount of the security or deposit exceeds $50.00, the bondsman or depositor must be adequately notified. After the date of forfeiture and notice, the bondsman or depositor is permitted 180 days in which to adjust the forfeiture. The three possible procedures are: (1) defendant and bondsman or depositor appear in court and satisfactorily excuse defendant's neglect or satisfactorily indicate to the court his absence was not with the connivance of the bondsman or depositor; (2) bondsman or bail appear in court and satisfactorily indicate to the court that the defendant is dead or physically unable (ill, insane, detained by other authorities, etc.) to appear in court during this 180-day period; and (3) surrender the defendant.

In the first two instances, the court will direct that the forfeiture be discharged upon such terms as may be just. When the defendant has surrendered, a motion can be made to the court to set aside the forfeiture and revoke the admission to bail. If action is not taken within this 180-day period, a summary judgment against each bondsman shall be entered in the court records, and the district attorney or civil legal adviser in the county is required to assist in satisfying this judgment.[34]

Citation in Lieu of Bail

The Manhattan Summons Project by the New York City Police indicated the efficacy of the greater use of summonses (citations) in lieu of arrests in misdemeanor and minor offense (ordinance violation) cases. Recent reports on this project revealed that a great deal of money could be saved in the reduction of the time policemen must spend on post-

[33]Ibid., Sections 1310–1312.
[34]Ibid., Section 1306.

arrest procedures when summons were used in place of physical restraint.

Citations in lieu of arrest do solve many of the problems associated with bail because the defendant is not in physical custody and can be released without the formality of posting a bail bond or cash bail. However, it is in California that a whole new concept of using citations in lieu of bail in misdemeanor cases is being pioneered. In this new procedure, the citation is used in lieu of bail in misdemeanor cases in accordance with uniform countywide regulations. The importance of this new procedure is not only humanitarianism—and lowered costs which can be projected from the New York City project—but also the fact that the arrested person does not have to post cash bail, or seek the help of friends or professional sureties to post a bail bond, as a prerequisite to admission to bail.

California's Penal Code provides for this new procedure in two instances: (1) misdemeanor offenses in violation of a county or city ordinance, and (2) misdemeanor offenses in violation of state law.[35] Unless the offender is immediately arraigned or demands such arraignment, the officer making the arrest may prepare a written notice to appear in court (the time must be within 5 days of the arrest and the place the court of arraignment). The arrested person must sign the notice as his written promise to appear as specified. After the prisoner's signature is secured, he is given a copy of the notice to appear and is released from custody, and the officer forwards the signed notice to the court of arraignment.

The second step in this procedure, taken without cost or red tape while the arrested person is at liberty, is made by the magistrate of the court of arraignment within the five-day limit of the notice; this consists of indorsing upon the duplicate copy of the notice the amount of bail he believes will be reasonable and sufficient for the appearance of the defendant in court at a later date. Next, the arrested person may appear in court at any time from the date the magistrate set bail until the expiration of the five days specified in the notice of appearance and arrange for admission to bail in the amount specified by the magistrate.

In concluding this procedure, the alternative steps are: (1) if the arrested person fails to arrange bail and does not appear as agreed, he is guilty of a misdemeanor regardless of the disposition of the charge upon which he was originally arrested, and the magistrate shall issue and have delivered for execution a warrant for the arrested person within twenty days after his failure to appear as promised; or (2) if the arrested person has been admitted to bail in the amount specified by the magistrate, but does not appear in court when the case is called for arraignment,

[35]*Ibid.*, Sections 853.1 and 853.6.

the magistrate may declare the bail forfeited, and may order that no further proceedings shall be had in such case.[36]

This procedure is in extensive use in Contra Costa County in northern California. Police officials, supported by an interagency County Bail Bond Committee encourage the use of this citation-in-lieu-of-bail procedure in all authorized circumstances with the following exceptions:

1. Imminent danger the violation will continue after release.

2. Hazard to police or public because of arrested person's mental or physical condition.

3. Identity or residence cannot be adequately ascertained.

4. Unusual circumstances of violation offer reasonable grounds for concluding the release should be reviewed by a magistrate or be processed in accordance with countywide bail schedule.

This new procedure not only has solved many of the problems formerly associated with an arrested person arranging for bail at night —when many of these minor offenses occur—but it has also solved many of the problems associated with indigent defendants who are without sufficient funds to arrange even nominal bail, or to pay the fees of a professional bondsman. (An interesting and possibly very important side action is that the police and sheriff's officers are cast in a new and helping role likely to earn them the good opinion of these offenders.)

Bail and the Indigent Accused

The vaunted guarantees of "equal treatment" and "due process" are certainly absent when the financial status of the accused, in whole or in part, determines his fate before the bar of justice. Originally, efforts to ensure a fundamental fairness to the indigent accused were directed at the trial and posttrial periods in the administration of justice. *Gideon v. Wainwright*[37] and *Douglas v. California*[38] both place emphasis on these two periods. More recently, numerous cases have advanced the importance of the pretrial period. Court decisions in right-to-counsel, right-to-silence and pretrial discovery cases all indicate a learned belief that a defendant can be so prejudiced during the pretrial period that his subsequent trial lacks the necessary fundamental fairness essential to the basic concepts of justice. Continued detention of any defendant after arrest precludes any meaningful contribution to his own defense. It is faulty dispensation of justice when an accused person can be held in detention because he is too poor to afford to post cash bail, or to pay a fee to a

[36]*Ibid.*, Sections 853.1–853.8.
[37]372 U.S. 335 (1963).
[38]372 U.S. 353 (1963).

professional bondsman for a surety bond for deposit as bail; unable to marshall among his friends in the lower socio-economic group in the community any sureties who can fulfill the requirements of a "bail"; or because of nomadism or chronic unemployment, typical of indigent persons, he is unable to qualify for a release on bail on his own recognizance.

Since he is unable to secure a release upon any form of bail, the indigent accused is the victim of a chain reaction which further weakens his basic ability to prove his innocence upon trial. He cannot work to earn the money to hire an attorney; he cannot expend the necessary expenses in seeking out witnesses and other relevant evidence; and his indigency indicates a lack of financial resources to support his family while he is not working; therefore, he must borrow money for their support or seek welfare help.

In 1961, in New York's Manhattan Borough, the Vera Foundation initiated the Manhattan Bail Project. Law students were utilized to interview felony defendants and develop a background investigation which would support a recommendation, by these investigators, to the court of arraignment, that a release on the defendants' own recognizance would not be likely to defeat the ends of justice.[39]

These investigators began their screening of likely prospects by interviewing defendants who were financially unable to hire an attorney to assist in their defense. The initial interview was held in or about the detention area of New York's felony courts in which these prisoners were arraigned after arrest, and sought information in five basic areas: (1) residence in New York City for ten years or more; (2) whether occupancy at a present residence or next most recent residence exceeded six months; (3) whether present or immediately previous employment spanned six months or more; (4) whether relatives resided in New York City and extent of recent contacts; and (5) no previous conviction of a crime.

If the questioning of the indigent accused indicates further investigation is likely to develop some indications of stability in one or more of the above areas, the verification is sought by telephone, courtroom interviews with relatives and friends and by old-fashioned leg work. If the accused person is considered a good risk, the investigator reports this fact to the court, in an *amicus curiae*[40] role, for the information of the magistrate in releasing the defendant on his own recognizance.

Similar "O.R." projects now span the United States. Preliminary reports show that careful investigation will indicate many indigent accused persons who may be released on their own recognizance without the

[39]Herbert Sturz, "An Alternative to the Bail System," *Federal Probation*, 26 (December 1962), 50.
[40]Friend of the court.

posting of one penny of bail—and with considerable confidence in such persons appearing in court as required. In the December 1965 issue of *State Bar of California Reports*, it is noted that San Francisco's "O.R." project (by VISTA—Domestic Peace Corps Volunteers) released 300 persons, over a period of five months, representing 98 percent of the project's recommendations, and only five persons (1.7 percent) failed to appear at trial.

Cost accounting, however, has not been a part of these "O.R." projects. Therefore, there is presently little or no information as to the cost of screening these defendants. There is every indication an accounting survey will show that government could conduct these "O.R." investigations and show an overall profit because of the reduction of existing overcrowding in local detention facilities, the lowered costs of transporting prisoners and the multiple savings possible when a defendant does not have to be imprisoned, possibly contributing to the support of himself and his family and the expenses of his defense. The Vera Foundation's success with the problem of the indigent accused has highlighted the basic stability of people—even when faced with accusations of crime—and there's hope that officials in the administration of justice throughout the United States will develop modern bail procedures along the lines of the issuance of citations in lieu of bail, and expanded use of "O.R." as an overall cost-saving device and a measure of equality in the ability of the rich and poor alike to aid in their own defense.

Selected References

CASES

Hudson v. Parker, 156 U.S. 277 (1895).

> An early case reviewing the traditional right to freedom before conviction and the need for release on bail to prepare an adequate defense and to guard against the unnecessary infliction of punishment pending final disposition of the charge of crime.

Stack et al. v. Boyle, 342 U.S. 1 (1951).

> This decision contains an excellent discussion of the proper methods for fixing pretrial bail.

BOOKS

Rules and Procedures—Police Department, City of New York. New York: Police Department, City of New York, 1956 (particularly Chapter XI, "Bail," pp. 137–44).

> An excellent text in developing the relationship between arrest and

bail, and the need for specific procedures to guard against corrupt practices in accepting bail.

Senate Committee on the Judiciary, *Constitutional Rights and Federal Bail Procedures*, 88th Cong., 2d sess. Washington, D.C.: Government Printing Office, December, 1964, 19 pages.

A summary report of hearings on proposed legislation to modify federal bail procedures.

ARTICLES

Ares, Charles, and Herbert Sturz, "Bail and the Indigent Accused," *Crime and Delinquency*, 8 (January 1962), 12–20.

Does the bail system work for the poor man as well as the rich man? Should a man's liberty depend primarily upon his purse? Cannot a democratic society find a more equitable solution to the problem of securing the attendance in court when required of persons charged with crime? The author discusses these questions in theory and practice, and describes the New York City project as a search for an alternative to bail.

Breslin, James, "Best Bet for Bail: A Good Crook," *Life* (March 29, 1963), pp. 15–17.

A brief article on the relationships between "good crooks" and professional bail bondsmen. Its delineation of the bondsman and his equally "professional" client highlights everything that is wrong with the existing system of bail.

Kunstler, William M., "Fair Bail for All," *The Nation* (July 27, 1963), pp. 52–53.

A brief report of the Vera Foundation's Manhattan Bail Project for the pretrial "parole" of accused persons who cannot afford bail.

Smith, Talbot, "A New Approach to Bail Practice," *Federal Probation*, 29 (March 1965), 3–6.

A discussion of the need for strict bail practices and the possible justification for the elimination of bail, wholly or in part. The writer discusses the abuses of today's bail procedures and the differences between practice and theory.

"Bailbondsman and the Fugitive Accused—The Need for Formal Removal Procedures," *Yale Law Journal*, 73 (May 1964), 1098–1111.

A review of prevailing practices in the return of fugitives by bail bondsmen, and a delineation of desirable procedures to ensure procedures similar to extradition and rendition.

"Pretrial Release Programs," *Defender Newsletter*, 2, No. 6 (November 1965), 1–9.

A review of programs for pretrial release of indigent defendants in criminal cases in lieu of bail.

7

Court and
Judicial Systems

The judicial power emanating from the court systems of the United States has its origin in the constitutional separation of powers, its growth in the fact that America's judiciary has maintained an independence beyond its heritage of rejecting domination by king and church and its present role of high social acceptance in the community from a continuing acceptance of professional responsibility for the integrity of the judicial process.

In a country which declared its independence on the proposition that all men are created equal, and in which all judicial personnel are sworn to support and defend a Constitution guaranteeing equal protection of the laws, it is no more than reasonable to expect a court system of both law and justice: A system which will establish procedures to protect the innocent, discover and initiate appropriate action against the guilty and afford "due process" to all litigants.

Separation of Powers

The trilogy of government embraced within Constitutional provisions for the separation of legislative, executive and judicial powers neither fragments nor compartmentalizes the governing power, but rather divides the totality of responsibility into three segments capable of functioning together effectively. In the Constitution of the United States, Article I delineates the legislative powers and vests them in a Congress consisting of a Senate and a House of Representatives; Article II enumerates and limits the executive power vested in the President; and Article III sets forth the judicial power of the United States. This traditional system of checks and balances may not coincide with maxims for the effective practice of modern management, but it is in furtherance of the doctrine of government by law—and government under law is an important measure of liberty. However, the unchecked ability to make law can and does lead to infringement and destruction of the basic freedoms and liberties of the people. The Constitution not only creates a government of law rather than tyranny, but also provides limits whereby the law itself cannot become a tyranny.

U. S. Supreme Court Justice Van Devanter, in *Evans v. Gore*,[1] notes that these separate departments of government were provided for in the Constitution to ensure an operating independence which would serve as a check or balance upon the operations of each department. It was his opinion that the judicial power was both the weakest and the most important of the three powers of government: "Of the three, the judiciary is the weakest, possessing only the power of judgment. However, it is the balance wheel of the entire system, preserving an adjustment between individual rights and governmental powers."

Judicial Power

Prior to April 30, 1789—the effective date of Constitutional government in the United States—each of the sovereign states exercised an autonomous judicial power through its state courts. The Articles of Confederation (ratified in 1781) did assign a limited federal judicial power, but it was little used.[2] Article VI of the Constitution establishes the base for a government by law in which the judicial power of each

---

[1]253 U.S. 245 (1920).
[2]Lewis Mayers, *The American Legal System* (New York: Harper & Row, Publishers, 1964), pp. 4–5.

state is bound to the Constitution and laws of the federal government. Article VI reads:

> This Constitution, and the laws of the United States which shall be made in pursuance thereof; and all treaties made, or which shall be made, under the authority of the United States, shall be the supreme law of the land; and the judges in every state shall be bound thereby, anything in the constitution or laws of any state to the contrary notwithstanding.

Article III of the Constitution, in Sections 1 and 2, vests the judicial power of the United States in a federal court system headed by one supreme court and inferior courts instituted and established, as necessary, by Congress; it establishes an independent judiciary through adequate tenure and undiminished compensation and provides for an extensive original and appellate jurisdiction over all cases in both law and equity:

> Section 1. The judicial power of the United States, shall be vested in one supreme court, and in such inferior courts as the Congress may from time to time ordain and establish. The judges, both of the supreme and inferior courts, shall hold their offices during good behavior, and shall, at stated times, receive for their services, a compensation, which shall not be diminished during their continuance in office.
>
> Section 2. The judicial power shall extend to all cases, in law and equity, arising under this Constitution, the laws of the United States, and treaties made, or which shall be made, under their authority;—to all cases affecting Ambassadors, other public Ministers and Consuls;—to all cases of admiralty and maritime jurisdiction;—to controversies to which the United States shall be a party;—to controversies between two or more states;—between a state and citizens of another state—between citizens of different states—between citizens of the same state claiming lands under grants of different states, and between a state, or the citizens thereof, and foreign states, citizens or subjects.
>
> In all cases affecting Ambassadors, other public Ministers and Consuls, and those in which a state shall be party, the Supreme Court shall have original jurisdiction. In all the other cases before mentioned, the Supreme Court shall have appellate jurisdiction, both as to law and fact, with such exceptions, and under such regulations as the Congress shall make. . . .

Immediately following this grant of judicial power, the Constitution makes provision in Article IV (Section 1) to ensure the power of state courts, despite the new subordination of these courts to the supremacy of the federal power. This section of the Constitution calls for each of the states to fully recognize the judicial power of their sister states. This "Full Faith and Credit" provision reads as follows:

> Section 1. Full faith and credit shall be given in each state to the public acts, records, and judicial proceedings of every other state. And

the Congress may by general laws prescribe the manner in which such acts, records and proceedings shall be proved, and the effect thereof.

On September 24, 1789, less than six months from the inauguration of government by Constitution, Congress enacted a Judiciary Act creating the "one supreme court" and a system of "inferior courts" as ordained in Section 1, Article III, of the Constitution. This act not only provided for a top court at the apex of a new pyramid of federal courts, but also extended the federal judicial power into every geographic area of the new nation in its establishment of inferior courts. However, Congress was unusually selective in its grant of jurisdiction to this new system of federal courts. It did not choose to grant all the judicial power possible under the provisions of Section 2, Article III of the Constitution, but it did indicate an intent to preserve the continuity and integrity of the court systems of the various states making up the new nation by allocating concurrent jurisdiction in many instances to the two systems of courts. This dual jurisdiction ranges from actions involving a "diversity" of citizenship, to cases against federal officials, instances of state failures in civil rights and cases involving a "federal question": a dispute "arising under this Constitution, the laws of the United States, and treaties."[3]

Judicial expansion of the Constitutional concept of "due process" was provided for in the Fourteenth Amendment and has imposed new limitations upon state court systems by requiring observance of basic liberties and various individual rights in state court criminal proceedings. By a process of incorporation, the U. S. Supreme Court has utilized the Fourteenth Amendment to protect persons from the actions of state courts which are in violation of certain liberties guaranteed by the First Amendment.[4] Since the *Gitlow* doctrine reversed the court's previous decision in *Barron v. Baltimore*,[5] which limited the force and effect of the first eight amendments to federal court procedures, there has been case after case delineating the rights which cannot be infringed upon by a state or its agents because of the Fourteenth Amendment. The court has not as yet held that the Fourteenth Amendment's due process clause makes all the provisions of the first eight amendments applicable to the states, but the case law in this area indicates a definite trend in this direction. In *Malloy v. Hogan*,[6] the self-incrimination protection of the Fifth Amendment was applied to the states; in *Mapp v. Ohio*,[7] the Fourth Amendment's protection of privacy was found ap-

[3]*Ibid.*, pp. 7–9.
[4]*Gitlow v. New York*, 268 U.S. 652 (1925).
[5]7 *Peters* 243 (1833).
[6]378 U.S. 1 (1964).
[7]367 U.S. 643 (1961).

plicable to the states; and in *Gideon v. Wainwright*,[8] it was made obligatory upon the states to make certain a defendant in a criminal trial was not denied the Sixth Amendment's "assistance of counsel."

Judicial Process

A court can only proceed through judicial process. In reality, any court is a passive thing, to be moved only by the initiative of a legal proceeding. Any person can be the force which overcomes the basic inertia of America's judicial system of justice: applicant, petitioner; plaintiff, defendant; or the community as represented by "the people." The action of a court also has a remarkable directness in that a judicial decision, in most instances, only applies to the litigant or litigants involved. Of course, when new and unusual areas of law are affected by the decision, it is a warning for the future that legal proceedings having similar circumstances are likely to be affected by it. Judicial process, therefore, in our American system of courts is the end result of an examination under judicial control of a particular legal matter appropriately placed before the court involved by one or more litigants.

There are six basic advantages of the judicial process:

1. It is a process of applying a logical and systematic approach to a body of knowledge developed by both reason and experience;
2. Guidance is provided by a judge whose legal training relates actions in specific cases to known principles and standards;
3. Judicial decisions are subject to review by other legally trained persons, often sitting *en banc*[9] to mitigate individual prejudices and misconceptions;
4. Case records of judicial action are public;
5. Decisions, as well as the grounds and reasons for them, are published by appellate courts for the information and guidance of every interested person or agency; and
6. Judges can resist public excitement and hysteria.[10]

Contempt of Court

The power to punish interference with the conduct of judicial proceedings or willful disobedience of court process not only ensures the orderly conduct of the court hearing, but also contributes to the effective-

[8]372 U.S. 342 (1963).
[9]As a group.
[10]Roscoe Pound, *Justice According to Law* (New Haven, Conn.: Yale University Press, 1952), pp. 88–91.

ness of the judicial process and supports the power of the judiciary. While some acts constituting traditional criminal contempt of court are likely to be processed as regular criminal proceedings, it is the prompt invoking of the power of holding any person in contempt of court when the conduct is committed in the presence of the court that affects both the order of the proceedings and judicial process and power. Disobedience to any direction of the court by any person concerned in the conduct of the proceedings may be punished.

In most jurisdictions, when a judge holds a person in contempt for an act or omission committed in his presence in court, there is usually a preliminary warning that such conduct—if continued—will be held in contempt of court. When the warning is rejected and the action repeated the judge can act as prosecutor, witness and judge. In a summary proceeding, the judge may impose punishment without affording the offender any opportunity for defense or argument. Some judicial officials follow the practice in these cases of ordering the offender to show cause why such summary action should not be taken, and this affords the offender an opportunity to present evidence and to cross-examine witnesses, if any.[11]

In California, criminal contempt is classified as a misdemeanor. The Penal Code[12] of this state also provides for a sheriff or other officer to command as many male inhabitants as may be necessary to assist in seizing, arresting and confining persons resisting the execution of the court process, their aiders and abettors, and such officer shall certify the names of these persons to the court for contempt proceedings. In general, the behavior described as within the meaning of "criminal contempts" in California is as follows:

1. Disorderly, contemptuous or insolent behavior committed during the sitting of any court of justice, in immediate view and presence of the court, and directly tending to interrupt its proceedings or to impair the respect due to its authority.

2. Behavior of like character in the presence of any referee or jury while holding hearings authorized by law.

3. Any breach of the peace, noise or other disturbance directly tending to interrupt the proceedings of any court.

4. Willful disobedience of any process or order lawfully issued by any court.

5. Resistance willfully offered by any person to the lawful order or process of any court.

6. The contumacious and unlawful refusal of any person to be sworn as

[11]Mayers, *The American Legal System*, pp. 37–40.
[12]California Penal Code, Sections 723–724.

a witness; or, when so sworn, the like refusal to answer any material question.

7. Publication of a false or grossly inaccurate report of the proceedings of any court.

8. Presenting to any court—or any member of it—with the power to order judgment after conviction any representation of any kind in aggravation or mitigation of the punishment to be imposed, except as provided by law.[13]

The Federal Court System

This court system is divided between constitutional and legislative courts. A constitutional court is one created under the provisions of Article III (the judiciary article) of the Constitution, while a legislative court is one created through the authority of the legislative power as established in Article I of the Constitution. In addition to minor technical differences between the two types of courts, a legislative court is endowed with administrative and quasi-legislative power in addition to its judicial authority. However, three of the legislative courts—the Court of Claims, Customs Court, and the Court of Customs and Patent Appeals—all have had their status changed to that of constitutional courts in unusual action by Congress during 1953 to 1958. In addition, there are several territorial courts established by Congress under the power granted by Article IV of the Constitution, under its provisions regarding a territory or other property of the U.S.

The three constitutional courts which make up what is generally termed the federal court system are: (1) the U.S. Supreme Court, (2) the U.S. Courts of Appeals, and (3) the U.S. District Courts. Acting as a magistrate for district courts is the U.S. Commissioner—one in each of the U.S. federal districts.

The U.S. Supreme Court has nine justices, one of whom is the Chief Justice. Six judges constitute a quorum, and a majority of no less than four judges must concur for a valid decision. It has both original and appellate jurisdiction. Its original jurisdiction is in actions (1) between the U.S. and a state, or between two states; (2) involving certain foreign ambassadors, ministers, consuls and their servants; and (3) commenced by a state against persons not citizens of such state or against a foreign country. It has appellate jurisdiction over (1) cases tried or reviewed in all other Constitutional and territorial courts, and the majority of the legislative courts, and (2) cases from the highest state courts

[13]*Ibid.*, Section 166.

when a "substantial federal question" is involved. When access to the court is not clearly a matter of right, the litigant must petition the court for a writ of *certiorari* (review), and the application is voted upon by the entire membership of the court. If four or more justices approve the petition, the writ application is granted and the case will be reviewed by the court.

The U.S. Courts of Appeals have only appellate jurisdiction. These courts are assigned a "circuit" covering several states. Each court is assigned from three to nine justices, depending on the work load. Cases are usually heard by three or more judges, with two judges actually present being necessary for a quorum. Senior judges are named as the

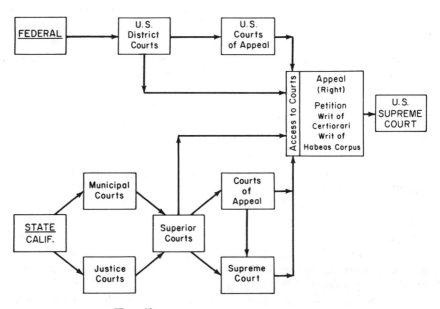

FIG. 5.   APPELLATE JURISDICTION

chief judge of each Court of Appeals. Cases are accepted for review from the lower federal courts, federal regulatory commissions, and several federal agencies.

The U.S. District Courts are the trial courts of the federal court system. Each district covers a geographical area, with the number of judges varying with the case load of the district. It has original jurisdiction of the trial of offenses against the laws of the U.S.; when a "federal question" is involved; in disputes involving a diversity of citizenship among the litigants; cases in which the U.S., its Revenue Department or a national bank is a party; and as noted in federal legislation.

State Court Systems

Each of the 50 states has a system of courts based on the Constitution of the individual state and enforcing the state criminal (penal) code. All states have a bifurcated system of trial courts and courts of appellate review. In the rural states, the lower courts for the trial of petty offenses and the examination of offenders are likely to predominate, while states with a greater number of urban areas are likely to have a court system very similar to the federal court pyramid of lower trial courts, intermediate courts of appeal and a Supreme Court as the highest court in the state.

Basically, the lesser courts in a state system will have jurisdiction in cases up to and including the grade of misdemeanors; the county courts try felony cases and usually have jurisdiction over capital crimes; while the supreme courts and courts of appeals have appellate jurisdiction at the highest levels. However, there is an intermediate staging in the handling of appeals, with appeals from the lower courts moving through the hierarchy of the court system almost as an upward communication in business, with only a small number of cases ending up in the highest state courts.

"Police Court" is a term that sometimes designates the low point in a local court system. For many years the traditional "J.P." of America's system of justice lived up to his title of "Justice of the Peace," and adjudicated many cases of public intoxication and disturbing the peace and quiet of the community. These locally elected or appointed "jurists" usually did not have a legal education or membership in the state bar. In recent years, there has been a trend toward requiring the traditional legal background for the presiding officer of these courts; if this is not possible locally because of politics, then the court is abolished and its workload transferred to the next higher court in the state system. In New York City, the Magistrate's Court is in essence its police court, but the magistrates are all attorneys, and this bench often serves to launch a jurist on a career in the state or federal courts.

California's Court System

California's court complex is a system that is similar to other states; however, no two states have completely parallel court systems. Article VI of California's Constitution, "Judicial Department," assigns the jurisdiction of each court.

The Supreme Court consists of a Chief Justice and six associate justices. This is California's highest court. A justice of this court has power to issue writs of *habeas corpus* (persons in custody in any part of state), *mandamus, prohibition,* and *certiorari;* extensive appellate jurisdiction in civil cases, and in criminal cases involving the death penalty; and constitutional authority to transfer cases to and from the District Courts of Appeals. The Supreme Court also admits applicants to the Bar who have been found qualified by the Committee of Bar Examiners of the State Bar, and passes upon disciplinary recommendations of the Board of Governors of the State Bar. Sessions are held by the Supreme Court at least four times each year in San Francisco, four times in Los Angeles and twice in Sacramento. Regular conferences are held by the Court each week to consider and determine applications for writs, petitions for hearings in cases decided by the District Courts of Appeals, and to pass on other matters pending before the Supreme Court.

California's intermediate appellate court system, the District Courts of Appeals, has five district courts. Justices are assigned to districts and to divisions within districts. In appellate review, three justices staff a district or division court, one presides, and the concurrence of two of them is required for judgments. Justices have the power to issue writs of *habeas corpus* (any person in custody in district), *mandamus, prohibition,* and *certiorari;* and this court has extensive appellate jurisdiction on appeal from the Superior Court and in cases transferred from the Supreme Court.

The Superior Courts of California are the trial courts of general jurisdiction. They have original jurisdiction in all criminal cases amounting to felony, and appellate jurisdiction in cases arising in Municipal and Justice Courts. Judges of this court have power to issue writs of *mandamus, certiorari, prohibition,* and *habeas corpus* (persons imprisoned in county of court). Each county has one Superior Court, and the number of judges is fixed by the legislature, varying from one in rural counties to 120 in Los Angeles County. Superior Court judges are required to be attorneys admitted to the practice of law in California for at least five years immediately preceding election or appointment. The Constitution permits the legislature to establish appellate departments of the Superior Court in counties having Municipal Courts.

The lower courts of California are limited by the Constitution to two types: Municipal and Justice Courts. In each judicial district with a population of more than 40,000, there is a Municipal Court, and a Justice Court in districts with a population of 40,000 or less. Municipal courts have jurisdiction in cases of all misdemeanors with a maximum penalty of one year in jail or a $1,000 fine, and Municipal Court judges sit as magistrates to conduct preliminary hearings in felony cases. Municipal Court judges are required to be attorneys admitted to the practice of law in California for at least five years immediately preceding election or appointment. One judge is provided by law for each Justice Court. These courts have jurisdiction in minor criminal cases in which the maximum penalty is six months in jail or a $1,000 fine, and Justice Court judges sitting as magistrates also conduct preliminary hearings in felony cases.[14]

A Judicial Council was established in California under a 1926 constitutional amendment. It was amended in 1960 to provide additional members. A total of 18 members are now authorized, and service is without compensation. Membership consists of the Chief Justice of the Supreme Court, one associate justice of the Supreme Court, three justices of District Courts of Appeals, four judges of Superior Courts, two judges of Municipal Courts, one judge of a Justice Court, four attorneys, and one member of each House of the legislature. The Chief Justice serves as chairman, and appoints the judicial members for two-year terms. Attorney members are appointed by the Board of Governors of the State Bar, also for a two-year term, and the Assembly and Senate each designate one of their members to serve on the council. The Clerk of the Supreme Court acts as Secretary of the Council. Under authority of a 1960 Constitutional amendment, an administrative director was appointed and directs the Council's newly created Administrative Office of the California Courts. The Administrative Office is a staff agency with legal and statistical personnel for research basic to recommending improved procedural rules and constitutional and statutory amendments, and to collect, analyze and report judicial statistics.[15]

At the request of the legislature, the Council made a study in 1947 of the organization, jurisdiction and practice of the California courts exercising jurisdiction inferior to the Superior Court, and recommended a plan for uniform reorganization. These recommendations resulted in a constitutional amendment (adopted in 1950) which made possible the reduction in the number of courts below the Superior Court from 768 to 400, replacing seven different types of courts by two: Municipal and Justice Courts. There is now only one type of trial court below the Superior Court in each judicial district in California, either a Municipal or Justice Court.

[14]Henry A. Turner and John A. Vieg, *The Government and Politics of California* (2nd ed.) (New York: McGraw-Hill Book Company, 1964), pp. 250–52; California Penal Code, Sections 1425 and 1462.

[15]*Judicial Council of California*, 19th Biennial Report to the Governor and Legislature (San Francisco, Calif.: Judical Council), 1963, pp. 7–8, 115.

Judicial Systems

A judicial system consists of a system of courts and the judicial officials responsible for the legal order embraced therein. While the courts of the United States and the separate states are linked in a chain of appellate review of lower court proceedings, this is a review of the function of the court and the court's end product. It is not the subordination of a judicial official to a higher authority in the normal type of supervision associated with personnel management. In the United States, the judicial systems emphasize the independence of each judge. There is a maximum of judicial autonomy in our criminal justice system, and while it may not contribute to orderly management procedures, it has silhouetted the judges in our court systems as officers of justice and not just officers of government. Within this system of courts and judicial officials, the members of the local legal fraternity—including the prosecutor and public defender—are not independent professional people, but rather officers of the court oriented to this judicial autonomy and functional review.[16]

Each of the court systems in the United States represents a separate but similar judicial system guided by intra-system rules governing practice, procedure and administration; and with varying methods for the selection, tenure, compensation and removal of judges.

Formal judicial status is directly related to the jurisdiction of the court to which the member of the judiciary is appointed, elected or assigned. Generally speaking, appellate and trial judges differ in prestige, with the former being afforded greater deference throughout a court system. Specifically, state statutes will define courts of record, magistrates and members of the judiciary who may issue writs of *habeas corpus,* and all of these provisions of law afford status to the judicial officers concerned.

Independence of the Judiciary

At the time of the Judiciary Act of 1789, no one envisaged the federal judicial power in its present position of strength in both government and public opinion; nor did anyone foresee the social acceptance and recognition accorded to the judiciary of both federal and state court systems. Today's independent judiciary has its roots in the English Act of Settlement and the U.S. Constitution, but its growth is probably due to the high qualifications and the daily influence of the men and women of the judiciary.

[16]Thomas R. Adam, *Elements of Government* (New York: Random House, Inc., 1960), pp. 144–45.

In 1701, an Act of Settlement was enacted by the English Parliament limiting royal powers generally and specifically providing for the independence of the judiciary. This act stated that judges should (1) hold office during good behavior, and (2) only be removable by action of both Houses of Parliament. The U. S. Constitution not only provides for judicial independence in a like manner, but also sustains the judicial morale by providing for a continuing or rising rate of compensation for work performance. Article III (Section 1), as quoted previously, contains a proviso that judges "shall hold their office during good behavior," and shall receive a compensation for their services "which shall not be diminished during their continuance in office." Many federal judges, and some of the justices of the higher state courts, enjoy the morale-boosting effect of a life tenure unless misbehavior is of such a nature as to warrant impeachment or other formal removal action. The social acceptance level of the entire judiciary ensures a rate of compensation which moves upward with the cost of living and comparable salaries in commerce or industry.

The background of the great majority of the judges now holding office in the courts of America is distinguished by some particular eminence while at law school, in the practice of law, or in a social, intellectual or moral environment. The demands of daily decision-making in a judge's adjudicating role in the judicial process is a frightening thing. The late Justice Felix Frankfurter of the U.S. Supreme Court has described this constant demand for appropriate decisions as "the agony" of a judge's duty. All attorneys are aware of this fact, and weigh it carefully when they begin to think of seeking a position on the bench. There's a winnowing aspect in this self-examination: the weak and the incompetent usually rationalize and procrastinate, finding many excellent reasons not to seek judicial office.

Since entrance to the judiciary is either by appointment or election, a further sifting occurs at professional, political and public levels. In most areas of this country, a candidate for judicial office must have a recommendation from his local bar association as the first step in moving toward a judgeship. Oftentimes, a special standing committee exists for processing members' qualifications for judicial office. This is self-policing at its best. Most of the local attorneys with a voice in judicial selection also practice law and will, therefore, submit cases from time to time to courts in which the prospective judge might be presiding. Of course, friendship may help out partially incompetent candidates, but future professional relationships often dictate the rejection of the unqualified candidate and the selection of a person qualified to handle the many problems associated with judicial decision-making.

Secondly, the local press usually initiates comment on the qualifications of proposed candidates or serves as a pipeline to the public for a dissident group in the local bar association. In 1965, a popular eastern Senator was slapped down by the public press when he attempted to place a man without a distinguished background in the federal judiciary. Data on the lack of qualifications of this candidate was supplied to news media by both local and national bar associations, and despite an elaborate campaign of endorsements by persons high in the political life of the nation, the public press prevailed and the candidate's name was withdrawn.

Lastly, politicians prefer candidates who can gain sufficient public support to win at the polls. Unless a substandard judicial candidate is supported by a dominant political "machine," he usually does not gain enough support at the polls. However, even within the area of "machine" politics there is a great deal of sifting and sorting before judicial candidates arrive at the traditional "next in line" step necessary for nomination. Usually, there is enough to distinguish the successful candidate.

The black robes of the judiciary, or the prominent position in the courtroom arena, do not change the character of a new judge. The function of being a judge usually develops judicial character. The need and duty to make a choice between two or more alternatives, to say how far a rule of law or procedure should be extended or restricted, to decide the import of a given set of circumstances and to appraise the value of conflicting arguments of law and reason are important factors in this growth process. This type of decision-making cannot long be based on ties of friendship, party politics or any conflict of interest. Even prejudice and bias, when present in the beginning of a judicial career, will be submerged in the ever present necessity of making public rulings on matters in dispute. Rulings are not only subject to possible appellate review and criticism in news media, but more importantly, subject to review by friends and associates in the legal community. The late James J. Brannigan, leader of New York's National Democratic Club and intimate of several leaders of Tammany Hall—New York's dominant political "machine" through several decades—often commented on this process of personal development. Brannigan complained that no matter how much he or "the party" did for a judicial candidate, it was all forgotten after a few months on the bench.

The present levels of judicial independence do not mean that a community will not find some politics-as-usual in a court system. Judicial patronage is not uncommon, nor is favoritism based on past political debts or "fence-mending" for future consideration for higher judicial positions a thing of the past; but the trend to independence is growing. It is not only socially acceptable, but it is also becoming politically acceptable as more and more of these positions in our court systems are being placed in the nonpartisan classification politically.

Judicial Selection

While appointment and election are the two most common methods of selecting the men and women who are to dispense law and justice in the courts of the United States, there is a middle road in the emerging procedures for bipartisan nomination, for appointment as a prerequisite to nomination, and for election to secure approval of an incumbent judicial officer's continuance in office rather than as a means of securing judicial office by defeating an opponent.

In the federal judicial system, the Constitution grants the President of the United States the appointing power. It is subject to confirmation by a majority of the U.S. Senate. However, if the proposed appointee is "personally obnoxious" to the Senator of his home state, it is unlikely that the appointment will be approved because of a fraternal courtesy common when the Senate considers these judicial appointments.[17] Despite the presence of a means for denying an appointee his right to sit on the federal bench, it is the opinion of many persons interested in good government that the federal judicial system has achieved an intelligent selection of judicial personnel over the years; one which has removed the element of chance common in selection by election, and relieved the candidates for this position of the need for overt political activity.

In order to circumvent the politics associated with political party nomination and gubernatorial appointment, many states sought bipartisan nomination and special bar association advisory committees. The two-party nomination quite frequently degenerated into a parcelling out of judgeships as political awards in agreements between the two dominant political parties. These committees, usually from the local Bar Association, did little more than offer the legal community an opportunity to engage in politics-as-usual. In 1940, a compromise plan between these two alternatives went into effect in the state of Missouri. Termed "the Missouri Plan" by every instructor in public administration and government, this new method of judicial selection pioneered in a field known for its reluctance to change.

The Missouri Plan was conceived as an acceptable substitute for the direct election of judges. Available candidates are screened as to their qualifications by a special commission. The commission for the selection

[17]Henry J. Abraham, *The Judical Process* (New York: Oxford University Press, Inc., 1962), pp. 27–28.

of judges in Missouri's high courts is composed of the Chief Justice of
the Supreme Court as chairman, three attorneys elected by the state Bar
and three citizens appointed by the governor who are not members of
the Bar. The membership is stratified geographically by requiring its
legal and lay members to be appointed from each of the three appellate
districts in the state. The commissioners for the selection of judiciary for
circuit courts in Missouri comprise the presiding justice of the court of
appeals district in which the circuit court is located, two members of
the state Bar who must be residents of the local circuit and who are
elected by similar resident members of the Bar, and two resident public
members appointed by the governor. In an attempt to divorce politics
from this selection process, the terms of commissioners are staggered
over a six-year period (the governor of Missouri has only a four-year
term and cannot succeed himself) to ensure appointment by successive
governors; commissioners are not permitted to hold public office or any
official position in a recognized political party; and no one can be paid a
salary to serve as a commissioner.

The commission makes its decision on the most desirable candidates,
selecting three candidates and proposing them to the governor for every
vacant judgeship within their area of operation. The governor must
choose one of the recommended candidates and appoint him for a one-
year term of office in the vacant judgeship. This one-year period has
been conceived as a probationary period in which the character and
professional competence of the new appointee will become known to the
people of his area. After this probation is concluded, the appointee is
automatically nominated and must have his name placed on the ballot
at the next general election as a candidate for the full term of judicial
office (12 years in appellate courts; six years in circuit courts). The
nominee runs unopposed on a nonpartisan judicial ballot for the decision
of the voters of the area. The Missouri Plan thus combines an intelligent
initial selection method with a final accountability to the electorate of
the area in which the judge will officiate while in office.[18]

In California the present method of selecting justices of the Supreme
and Appeals Courts is similar to the Missouri Plan. The governor selects
a qualified person (membership in the California Bar and having no less
than five years of legal experience) and sends notice of his selection to
the Commission on Qualifications, consisting of the Chief Justice of the
Supreme Court, a presiding justice of an Appeals Court and the Attorney
General. This commission must confirm the appointment before a new
judge can be sworn and seated in either of these two courts. At the next
regular election the appointment is tested at the polls, the new member

18*Ibid.*, pp. 36–37.

of the bench of the Supreme or Appeals Court has his name placed on the ballot for a "YES" or a "NO" vote as to whether he should be continued in office for the term specified. The full term of a Supreme or Appeals Court Justice is twelve years. It is assumed that the voters would have had an opportunity to observe the conduct of the new appointee and an affirmative vote indicates the voters not only approve of the governor's selection, but also approve of the judicial action exhibited between the time of appointment and election day. This methodology does not force the voters to weigh the merits of one judicial candidate as opposed to another one, but rather seeks a review of the gubernatorial action and the probationary period built into California's judicial selection system for its higher courts.[19]

Shortly before the conclusion of the term to which a justice has been elected, he has the opportunity to file a declaration of candidacy to succeed himself, and the voting procedure for continuance in office is repeated. If a justice fails to file such declaration of intent, the governor may nominate a suitable person. However, most justices not seeking reelection will vacate the office in sufficient time to permit the governor to appoint a successor to fill the vacancy and thus qualify the new justice for a place on the ballot as an incumbent.

Judges in California's Superior, Municipal and Justice Courts are elected by the voters of their area on a nonpartisan ballot for a full term of six years. The governor may fill vacancies in both the Superior and the Municipal Courts by appointment, and Justice Court vacancies may be filled by appointment of the County Board of Supervisors. Any county may vote to adopt the California plan—now operating statewide for judicial selection of Supreme and Appeals Court Justices—to the local Superior Court, but local action has been slow in moving away from the nonpartisan ballot. Actually, an incumbent candidate usually wins out in these nonpartisan ballot judicial contests, often despite the fact that the incumbent had only been recently appointed to fill a vacancy.[20]

In fact, recognition of the inherent election-day magic of running as a judicial incumbent is contained in a 1964 Constitutional amendment in California permitting urban counties (over 700,000 population) to omit the incumbent Superior Court judge's name from the ballot when: (1) he has filed nomination papers; (2) no one files in contest for this office; and (3) no one files a petition signed by 100 qualified registered voters indicating a write-in campaign is to be conducted in contest to the incumbent. In such cases, the county clerk declares the incumbent reelected along with his other reports of the voting on election day.

[19]Clyde E. Jacobs and John F. Gallagher, *California Government—One Among Fifty* (New York: The Macmillan Company, 1960), pp. 83–87.
[20]*Ibid.*, pp. 87–89.

Tenure of Judges

The guarantee of tenure assures any employee of a basic security free from concern about termination of employment, and free of pressures to conform to the exigencies of politics, unless misbehavior is of such a nature that any contractural tenure would be jeopardized. In the Constitutional courts of the federal system the justices have a lifetime tenure. Termination is usually through retirement or death. Justices appointed to the special legislative courts in the federal judicial system receive the terms allocated by Congress at the time each of these courts was established. However, several of them also have life tenure for their justices. State court systems offer their judicial personnel a fairly long tenure and most of the states permit a judge to seek reelection without limitation. Therefore, in effect, a judge who performs well in his position at the state level has every reason to expect tenure equal to a federal judge in a Constitutional court. In California, the 12-year terms of justices in the higher courts, and the six-year terms of judges in the lower courts, require only a few elections to equal life tenure when the entrance age for judgeships is normally about 40 years of age, and the desirable retirement age is less than 70.

It is in this lengthy tenure, continued throughout the good behavior of a member of the judiciary, that the community has some assurance of the independent judiciary vital to the basic concepts of law and justice.

Compensation of the Judiciary

The Constitutional proviso that the salary of judges named in its judicial article should not be diminished has originated a salary policy which has spread throughout judicial systems of the United States. Legislative control has not been relinquished in most of the states, but in the history of our court systems legislative approval of salaries of judicial personnel at appropriate levels is quite common. It is quite unusual for a legislative body to lower salaries of their judiciary. It is more common for the same lawmakers to voluntarily increase judicial compensation when the comparable income of attorneys in the community moves upward sharply. However, from the top salary of $35,500 for the Chief Justice of the United States to the average judicial salary of $13,000 for the judiciary of all state court systems, there is little doubt that salaries are no more than adequate.[21]

[21]Abraham, *The Judicial Process*, p. 40.

Removal of Judges

Federal judges are removable for high crimes through impeachment, but this little used and unwieldy method of terminating the employment of a government employee permits notoriously inefficient and unfit federal justices to remain on the bench. The need for a simple majority in the House of Representatives to move the impeachment proceeding, and conviction by a two-thirds vote of a quorum of Senators present and voting, is a definite protection against action by any pressure group in government. Proof is in the history of judicial impeachments: only nine impeachment trials were initiated, and only four resulted in convictions and actual removals. Under such conditions, it is easily understood that only the incompetent and the corrupt judge is threatened with any dismissal from the federal judicial system. However, along with lengthy tenure and adequate compensation, it is likely to be a major factor in protecting the independence of the judiciary from hasty and possibly poorly motivated removal actions.

In 1960 Californians tired of the unworkable procedure of impeachment and censure by a two-thirds vote of both their Senate and Assembly for the removal of judges, and approved a Senate constitutional amendment creating a nine-member Commission on Judicial Qualifications to exercise the necessary administrative discipline when a judge ceases to render good and effective service. This commission consists of five judges appointed by the Supreme Court, two lawyers appointed by the California Bar and two public members appointed by the Governor. An office is maintained for the work of this commission in San Francisco, along with an adequate staff, and consideration is given to complaints and reports on the conduct and capacity of state court judges. The commission investigates, holds hearings and recommends to the Supreme Court, for its final decision, whether a judge should be removed or retired from office. To date, it appears to be an excellent working procedure for investigation and action in the few instances of willful misconduct in office, willful and persistent failure to perform assigned duties, habitual intemperance or other disability of a permanent character seriously interfering with the performance of judicial duties.

California also has an unusual vehicle for removal of any elective public official in its recall, a state Constitutional provision establishing means for the removal of an elective public officer of the state from office at any time by the electors entitled to vote for a successor to such an incumbent; this is accomplished through the filing of a petition having the signatures of a requisite percentage of such electors and a special election. If a majority of the participating voters approve the recall action, they may also vote a successor into office.[22]

Of course, removal follows promptly in every judicial system when a judge is convicted in any court of a crime involving moral turpitude. In California, the Supreme Court will suspend the judge on its own motion, or upon a petition filed by any person, until final judgment of conviction when a permanent order is entered by this court disbarring the judge and removing him from office. In furtherance of prompt action in such instances, the California law[23] provides that when an indictment is returned or an information filed in a superior court against a judge, a certificate of that fact must be transmitted by the clerk to the chairman of the judicial council, who shall designate and assign a judge of the superior court of another county to preside at the trial of such indictment or information.

Juvenile Courts

The modern history of juvenile or children's courts dates back to 1899 and the city of Chicago. The Chicago Juvenile Court was the first attempt by government to handle the problem of youthful participants in criminal activities. A quarter-century later, in 1925, a model Juvenile Court Act was published by the National Probation Association for the guidance of states in establishing statewide juvenile court systems.

The juvenile court, in California,[24] has original jurisdiction in handling children; no other court has jurisdiction to conduct a preliminary examination or trial upon any accusatory pleading charging any crime or other public offense when the accused person is under the age of 18 years at the time of the offense, unless the juvenile court has first reviewed the case and ordered the case removed from the juvenile court for prosecution under the general (adult) law. Also, judges of other courts may certify any case before them to the juvenile court whenever the youngster involved is under the age of 21 years.

Juvenile court judges are usually men and women of legal education selected for their skills in this legal-social area. Some sociological education or experience, or particular interests in the problems of juveniles, have been found in the background of many judges serving on the juvenile court bench. Referees, persons with unusual qualities of interest in youth, specialized education and experience in the social aspects of youth and deviant behavior, may serve in the juvenile courts on a submagistrate

[22]Turner and Vieg, Government and Politics of California, pp. 79–81.
[23]California Penal Code, Section 1029.
[24]Within the Superior Court (Welfare and Institutions Code, Chapter 2, Juvenile Court Law, Sections 550–570).

level and preside at hearings at which juveniles are arraigned, but their decision-making authority is limited.

Management of Court and Judicial Systems

The independence of the judiciary complicates any centralization of the management of a court system. Rising costs of the operation of court systems and the backlog of cases awaiting hearings have led to the initiation of limited management procedures in attempts to ensure effective use of both space and judicial manpower. The present salary levels of court personnel and existing construction costs for necessary facilities have forced every court system to seek means for reducing the basic cost of operation. Better use of the existing staff and facilities of a court system is necessary before attempting any justification for extensive enlargement.

In 1958, Congress authorized the Judicial Conference to seek solutions for the many procedural problems in managing the federal court system. This group is composed of the Chief Justice of the United States, the chief judges of the Courts of Appeals and the several special courts and a district judge from each of the "circuits." The Judicial Conference meets at least once each year and makes recommendations concerning ways and means for improving the operation of the federal court system. There is also a Judicial Council in each of the circuits for the assignment of judges for the efficient disposal of the caseload, and each area also has a Judicial Conference which investigates and makes recommendations for improvement in the circuit's courts.

However, the Administrative Office of the U.S. Courts is the basic management center at the federal level. Its director is appointed by the Supreme Court. It is responsible for budget preparation and disbursement, assists in the supervision of court employees at the subjudicial level, compiles and publishes statistical data regarding court operations, and supplies staff aid to the various committees of the Judicial Conference. While the arrangements for managing the federal courts may appear effective, it is definitely not an authority-centered operation. Its critics describe it as little more than staff assistance to the management of the courts by the judiciary.

This is also true of the many state court systems, with the exception of California. California has not only regrouped its basic courts into a new and streamlined structural unity, but it has also established provisions for authoritative management control in a centralized agency. A Constitutional amendment in 1960 brought the membership of the central Judicial Council to 18 and stratified its composition to ensure representation for each segment of the state court system, the state Bar and the general public. Provision was also made at this time for a full-time and nonjudicial administrative director to serve as executive officer of the new Administrative Office of the Courts.

A review of the responsibilities and functions of the California Judicial Council indicates its potential management role. Its responsibilities and functions are to: (1) survey the condition of business in the courts with a view to simplifying and improving the administration of justice, (2) submit such suggestions as may be in the interest of uniformity and expedition of business to the courts, (3) report to the governor and the legislature at each regular session with such recommendations as it deems proper, (4) adopt rules of practice and procedure for the courts not inconsistent with law, and exercise such other functions as may be provided by law. The Constitution imposes on the Chairman of the Council the following duties: (1) to expedite judicial business and equalize the work of the judges, (2) to provide for the assignment of any judge to another court of like or higher jurisdiction, or to a court of lower jurisdiction with the judge's consent, (3) to submit recommendations concerning consolidation and enlargement of judicial districts with a view toward creating a greater proportion of full-time judicial offices, equalizing the work of the judges, expediting judicial business and improving the administration of justice. The chairman may also assign retired judges (with their consent) to any court. Assignment of judges from courts with light caseloads to those with crowded calendars has helped greatly to reduce congestion and delay in the courts. The Council has adopted rules of procedure for the various courts. From time to time, these rules have been amended to simplify procedure or otherwise improve the administration of justice.

There is little doubt that officials of other court systems are watching the operations of California's centralized group for management improvement and control. To date, reports are very favorable from both the Bar and the bench. It may very well be the breakthrough to improved management of our court systems without sacrificing any of the attributes of the judicial process and power which makes possible fair trials before impartial tribunals.

Selected References

CASES

Barron v. Baltimore, 7 Peters, 243 (1833).
  The leading case, historically, restricting the powers of the federal government regarding acts by state or local government. In 1833, the U.S.

Supreme Court was of the opinion that the first eight amendments to the Constitution of the United States were limitations on the powers of federal government, and not limitations on the powers of state or local governments. The court noted that these constitutional amendments were enacted to guard against the abuse of power by the federal government and contained no expression indicating an intention to apply them to state governments. However, the essence of this decision contributed, in 1868, to the passage of the Fourteenth Amendment with its due process and equal protection clauses.

Douglas v. California, 372 U.S. 353 (1963).

On appeal, a petitioner without funds must be afforded the right to counsel as there can be no "equal protection of the law" if the scope of an appeal and the diligence with which it is prosecuted in appropriate courts have to depend upon the amount of money a petitioner can afford to spend for legal fees.

Gideon v. Wainwright, 372 U.S. 335 (1963).

The appointment of legal counsel established as a fundamental right essential to a fair trial for any person hauled into court, who is too poor to hire a lawyer. At the time of Gideon's trial, the Florida trial court only appointed counsel for indigent defendants in capital crime cases. This landmark decision is an excellent review of a defendant's right under the Sixth Amendment to have the assistance of counsel for his defense because the nature of procedures in modern courts and judicial systems requires legal guidance as a necessity for a fair trial.

Gitlow v. New York, 268 U.S. 652 (1925).

A landmark case regarding the power of the federal court system to recognize certain individual rights as immune from state invasion in any of the courts of a state. In this case, the court explicitly recognized the First Amendment's freedom of speech and of the press as being among the fundamental principles of liberty and justice which lie at the base of all our civil and political institutions and, therefore, protected against state invasion by the due process clause of the Fourteenth Amendment.

Harvey v. Mississippi, 340 2nd 263 (1965).

Right to legal counsel guaranteed to defendants in criminal cases by the Sixth Amendment, and made applicable to the state under the Fourteenth Amendment, extends to and includes legal assistance, retained or assigned, in misdemeanor trials.

Unger v. Sarafite, 376 U.S. 575 (1964).

This court decision held there was no violation of due process where the same judge presided at the trial and the contempt hearing of a witness openly critical of judicial control of the trial, despite the fact that a request for a continuance was refused and the offender only permitted five days to prepare a defense. Excellent reading for a better understanding of the contempt power.

BOOKS

Abraham, Henry J., *The Judicial Process*. New York: Oxford University Press, 1962, 381 pages.

An understanding and penetrating text that probes the significant features of comparative judicial processes. Sections concerned with judicial review offer rewarding reading for police officers and correctional personnel; they concern the processes that have placed the Supreme Court of the United States at the summit of appellate tribunals in this country.

Cardozo, Benjamin N., *The Nature of the Judicial Process*. New Haven, Conn.: Yale University Press, 1921, 180 pages.

These Yale lectures by Justice Cardozo are classics in American jurisprudential thought and have profoundly influenced the techniques of the judicial process. Interestingly, this learned jurist develops as a basic concept the teleological function of judicial decision-making: that the end of the law should determine the direction of its growth and purposiveness and is inherent in the judicial process.

Jacob, Herbert, *Justice in America*. Boston: Little, Brown and Company, 1965, 215 pages.

A study of the U.S. court system. Jacob presents a thorough exposition of court operations, functions and characteristics. This text has a government-in-action view of the courts that develops a delineation of the participants in the judicial process, their basic roles and the regulations for the management of courts and judiciary.

Mayers, Lewis, *The American Legal System*. New York: Harper & Row, Publishers, 1963, 594 pages.

A systematic and comprehensive exposition of the complex legal institutions of the United States. Mayers traces the historical roots of the institutions for criminal justice, describes the total structure and the function of each unit and offers proposals for effective reform.

Murphy, Walter F., *Wiretapping on Trial: A Case Study of the Judicial Process*. New York: Random House, Inc., 1965, 176 pages.

The interaction of both procedure and people is traced in this in-depth study of wiretapping. It is a study of judicial processes, but it does not neglect the public influence as both an action and a reaction, and it really develops the manner in which judges, administrators and legislators often utilize a court proceeding in an appellate tribunal to resolve a pressing problem in the administration of justice.

Pound, Roscoe, *Justice According to Law*. New Haven, Conn.: Yale University Press, 1952, 98 pages.

A basic book in the administration of justice. The author, Dean-Emeritus of Harvard Law School, utilizes his 60 years of practicing and teaching law to develop basic concepts in the administration of justice according to law.

Scigliano, Robert, *The Courts—A Reader in the Judicial Process.* Boston and Toronto: Little, Brown and Company, 1962, 502 pages.

This text deals with judicial policymaking and notes the similarities of the three main branches of American government: the legislative body is concerned with making the laws, or official policy; the executive body with carrying out the policy; and the judicial body with the settlement of disputes arising from this enforcement. From this author's evaluation of the American political system it is apparent that the legislators administer, administrators adjudicate, and judges legislate in a circular pattern of checks and balances.

Turner, Henry A., and John A. Vieg, *The Government and Politics of California.* New York: McGraw-Hill Book Company, 1960, 286 pages.

The primary emphasis of this book is the function of state government in California. The story of one state and its government serves as an excellent text for comparison purposes with other states and their public policy and governmental structures. There is a fine chapter (Law and Justice) detailing the concept and machinery of justice in California.

ARTICLES

Jackson, Robert H., "The Supreme Court as a Political Institution," *The State of the Union,* ed., Robert B. Dishman. New York: Charles Scribner's Sons, 1965, pp. 228–37.

While Justice Jackson's article deals mainly with the U.S. Supreme Court, it is a fine source for basic facts about courts and the judicial process. The book of readings in which it appears has an excellent 56-page section ("Establish Justice") on the administration of justice.

Fischer, Richard S., "The Juvenile Court: New York Returns to the Judicial Fold," *Juvenile Court Judges Journal,* 15, No. 4, (Winter 1964), 32–39.

Fischer writes that the concept on *parens patriae* in juvenile divisions of a court system warped the perspective of the judicial process and projected the courts into a world of shadowy speculation, and praises New York's Family Court Act of 1962 as a bold move in reincorporating the essential ingredients of a fair trial in its judicial proceedings for children, saying: "The court is a court, the judge is a judge, and the child is a full fledged citizen."

Shatten, Michael L., "The Determination of Public Policy," *American Bar Association Journal,* 51 (November 1965), 1048–52.

The relationship of public policy to judicial decision-making. The author writes of public policy as a principle of judicial interpretation founded on the current needs of the community and suggests juristic thought should include social interests (general security, security of social institutions, etc.). The article contains many fine references for further reading in the nature of the judicial process.

8

Writs, Motions
and Appeals

A writ is basically an order of a court. A motion or an appeal is an application to a competent court for an order granting the legal relief specified in the motion or appeal. A motion can be made at any timely place in the criminal action, but appeals are always posttrial procedures because they are timely only when following the verdict and judgment stages of a criminal action.

Writs and court orders in response to motions or appeals are available for the review of any grievance arising from any form of criminal proceeding from arraignment or indictment to final disposition. A motion or appeal is an attack upon the criminal proceeding, and these attacks are divided into two major categories: (1) direct and (2) collateral.

Direct attacks are concerned with the verdict and judgment, and must follow these final stages of a criminal action. These are the motions for a new trial, and appeals from the judgment of a trial court. Collateral attacks may be made at or before any court hearing where evidence is likely to be produced. These are the simple motions made from the time of indictment or preliminary hearing to the court's judgment after trial, and the applications for writs of *mandamus, prohibition, habeas corpus,* and *coram nobis.*

Direct attacks upon a criminal court judgment are dominated by the defendant, and this period between judgment and final disposition in the administration of justice in the United States has been planned mainly to assure the defendant of every opportunity to correct a guilty verdict—if it is a miscarriage of justice. On the other hand, collateral attacks are related to the adversary system; there is the traditional give and take of move and countermove by the opposing attorneys. However, in any of these attacks upon a criminal proceeding, the "side" with an opposing interest has an opportunity to appear and be heard in these actions.

Counsel may seek action in the trial court, in the state appellate courts and in the federal court system. However, most states forbid appeals by the prosecutor. This is also true in federal courts; the government has no right of appeal from an acquittal in a criminal proceeding.[1] However, in a few New England and midwestern states, the prosecutor may appeal if an error of law prejudicial to the "people's" case is claimed. The U.S. Supreme Court upheld such an appeal in Connecticut in the landmark case of *Palko v. Connecticut.*[2]

Depending on the motion pending, the defendant may be held, released on bail until the determination of the action or returned to the county jail from a state prison. The trial court may grant or deny a motion for a new trial, or act for other relief; and appellate courts may affirm, modify or reverse the trial court in their review of the case.

Fortunately, this review of claim, and possibly counterclaim, is by a skilled and legally educated judge. These decision-making officials establish procedures that quickly clear away the unwarranted plea for legal relief. Actually, it is one of the core concepts of the administration of justice in the United States that motions be handled expeditiously and a firm stand be taken on motions that are filed only to achieve delay.

Writs

Writs are formal court orders for securing legal relief in a higher court against the action or inaction of a lower court either through an order directing the offending court or governmental agency to comply

[1]Fifth Amendment, U.S. Constitution, Section 1.
[2]302 U.S. 319 (1937).

with its direction, to forward the lower court's transcript for review or to produce the person alleged to be unjustly imprisoned.

Writs common to American courts are as follows:

WRIT OF MANDAMUS

The writ of mandamus is an order from a higher court[3] to an inferior court or other agency such as the police or prosecutor to compel the performance of an act by that court or agency which the law enjoins as a duty. It is termed "peremptory" when it sets a time for the performance of the act specified, and "alternative" when the lesser court is given the chance to show cause before the higher court as to why the act specified should not be done.

WRIT OF PROHIBITION

The writ of prohibition is also from a higher to a lower court or other governmental agency, but only restrains and prevents the lower court or agency from acting without or in excess of its jurisdiction. It may also be either peremptory or alternative, setting a time for the lower court to cease and desist, or allowing the lower court to show cause why the order should not become permanent.

WRIT OF CERTIORARI

This is a writ of review. It is useful whenever any court has exceeded its jurisdiction and there is no appeal or other plain, speedy and adequate legal remedy. It is frequently used as an alternative procedure for federal review of the state courts and their decisions. The petition for this writ must set forth a "substantial federal question," which was involved in the trial and decided against the defendant, when defense counsel petitions the U.S. Supreme Court to review a case tried in a state court. A vote of four of the nine justices of the U.S. Supreme Court is required to bring the case before this high court. Such action brings the entire record to that court for review.

WRIT OF CORAM NOBIS

This is an extraordinary writ of review that originally had as its principal purpose the enabling of the trial court to review its own judgment so long as the record of the case still remained before the court. The

[3]Superior, Appellate or Supreme Courts.

introduction of adequate and speedy remedies by statute, such as an appeal from the judgment or order of a court or a motion for a new trial has curtailed resort to the writ of *coram nobis*. It is similar to the motion to set aside the judgment of a court. The defendant, through counsel, must show in applying for this writ that some fact existed, and without his fault or negligence it was not presented upon the trial, but that if presented it is quite likely the judgment would have been different. There is also an inherent requirement in this application for *coram nobis* that a normal amount of diligence did not disclose the existence of the fact cited, and that this new evidence is of the nature or quality which would support a motion for a new trial.

WRIT OF HABEAS CORPUS

The writ of *habeas corpus* is the great writ of our American judicial system. It is an order directing the public official detaining a person to produce "the body" in court for a determination of the validity of imprisonment.

Form of Application

An application for a particular legal remedy must be made to a court and must be so worded as to indicate the particular effect desired by the applicant. Usually a motion is made orally, and it has been held that this is required despite a filing of a written application,[4] but this may be no more than an oral declaration that a written application is being made for a specific order from the court and that the papers are then and there being filed with the court clerk. Written applications must be properly supported by affidavits, exhibits, points and authorities if warranted. Grounds for the motion must be stated in whatever detail is required. Usually the "briefs" that accompany the application for a motion will contain the substance of major controlling case law used to bulwark the basic request to the court. In appellate review, court transcripts must also be forwarded. Two 1963 decisions of the U.S. Supreme Court, *Draper v. Washington* and *Douglas v. California*,[5] made it possible for indigent defendants to have equal advantage along the appeal route. *Draper* required a state to furnish necessary reports of criminal trial proceedings to indigents seeking appellate review, and *Douglas* held that an indigent defendant had a right to counsel on appeal.

[4]*People v. Ah Sam*, 41 Cal. 645 (1871).
[5]372 U.S. 487 (1963).
 372 U.S. 355 (1963).

Timeliness

Motions are "seasonal" in that they must be made at certain stages of the criminal proceeding, with the exception of the motion to dismiss in the furtherance of justice. This motion may be made at any time while the trial court can exercise jurisdiction in the case. Other motions are usually timed: (1) at or before the preliminary hearing; (2) prior to trial; (3) during trial; and (4) during the posttrial period. If motions are not timely made, it is presumed to be a waiver in most instances. However, in the move and countermove of motion-making by opposing attorneys, it is possible to "set the clock back" by some motion to get back within the time-machine of the criminal proceedings and offer a "timely" motion. For instance, at the end of a trial or before a retrial, a motion can be made to set aside the plea. If granted, this application will allow motions which should have been made prior to trial.

Motion to Dismiss: Interests of Justice

A motion to dismiss may be granted upon the application of the prosecutor, or the court's own motion, if the grounds are the furtherance of justice. The reasons for the dismissal must be stated for the record and an order to this effect entered upon the minutes of the case. This is not a defense motion, nor is it really a prosecution motion as the prosecutor merely recommends the dismissal. It is a speedy, plain and adequate relief by which the court may dismiss a prosecution in the interests of justice, from the time it acquires jurisdiction until conviction and judgment.

Motion to "Quash" Search Warrant

One of the earliest motions in the "seasonal" sense is the one entitled: "Motion for an Order Quashing Search Warrant and Restoring Property Seized Under a Search Warrant." The defense counsel may attack the validity of the warrant or its processing before the issuing magistrate after the arrest of the defendant. However, failure to act promptly does not act as a barrier to this motion during the preliminary examination or trial of the defendant.[6] While the burden is on the defendant and his

[6]*People v. Butler,* 64 Cal. 2nd 842 (1966).

counsel to provide the court with good and sufficient reasons to "quash," the magistrate's denial of the motion is not final. Defense counsel can secure a review of the denial by petitioning for a writ of *mandamus* to the appellate court, by objections to the evidence directly connected with this search warrant during the trial and by a later direct attack upon the judgment. However, a judgment "quashing" a search warrant, and ordering seized property returned, is likely to be appealed by a diligent prosecutor as a final judgment in a special proceeding.[7]

Pretrial Motion to Exclude Evidence

A motion to exclude confessions or admissions from evidence alleges that such statements were secured against the rights of a defendant. The delineation of the defendant's right not to be a witness against himself places upon police the burden of proof that a defendant knowingly and intelligently waived his privilege against self-incrimination and his right to retained or appointed counsel. However, failure to object to such evidence at the preliminary hearing or to move the confession or admission be stricken from the record at that stage of the proceedings does not preclude the defense counsel from raising the issues at trial.

Motion to Set Aside Information or Indictment

In California the court must set aside the indictment or information when lack of reasonable or probable cause is proven, or the indictment was not procedurally correct (found, indorsed and presented correctly as required by law).[8] The grounds are: (1) erroneous admission of evidence at the preliminary hearing or before the grand jury and a resultant failure of the remaining totality of evidence to show probable cause (if prosecution was by information, there must be evidence of defense counsel's objections and motions to strike[9] which were overruled by the magistrate during the preliminary hearing); or (2) fundamental denial of defendant's Constitutional rights, such as denial of the right of defense counsel to fully cross-examine witnesses at the preliminary hearing, or denial of right to counsel or failure to advise defendant of his rights at that stage of the proceedings. When this "995" motion is denied by the California trial court, defense counsel may seek review of the

[7]*People v. Berger*, 44 Cal. 2nd 459 (1955).
[8]California Penal Code, Section 995.
[9]Remove from the court record.

denial by application for a writ of prohibition to the appropriate appellate court. The "right" to this motion is waived if not made before a plea is entered.

Motion for Severance

Most jurisdictions make some provision for separate trials. In California since 1921, a joint trial is contemplated and a separate trial is a privilege and not a right. The question of whether there shall be a severance and separate trials as to one or more of the defendants is discretionary with the trial judge. For a number of years a basic unfairness has been recognized in trying codefendants in the same trial where one codefendent has made accusatory statements about the other and when such statements are admissible against the declarant. State and federal courts have, in the past, side-stepped the problem by saying that jurors can segment their minds when so instructed and use statements made by the declarant against that declarant and not be influenced by the declarant's statement in deciding the case of the declarant's codefendant.[10] However, in the 1964 United States Supreme Court case of *Jackson v. Denno*,[11] the majority opinion, in quoting Justice Frankfurter's dissent in the Delli Paoli case, stated the problem squarely: "The government should not have the windfall of having the jury be influenced by evidence against a defendant which, as a matter of law, they should not consider but which they cannot put out of their minds."

The most recent state case to establish a specific judicial procedure for this situation is the Califronia decision of *People v. Aranda*,[12] in which the California Supreme Court stated it had "grave constitutional doubts" about the practice of permitting joint trials when the valid confession of one defendant implicates codefendants and declared the practice unfair and prejudicial to the nondeclarant defendant. The court announced the following new rule of practice for these cases:

> The trial court must adopt one of the following procedures:
>
> 1. It can permit a joint trial if all parts of the extrajudicial statements implicating any codefendant can be and are effectively deleted without prejudice to the declarant. By effective deletions, we mean not only direct and indirect identifications of codefendants, but any statements that could be employed against nondeclarant codefendants once their identity is otherwise established;

[10]*Delli Paoli v. United States*, 352 U.S. 232 (1957).
  Federal Rules of Criminal Procedure, Rule 14, 18 U.S.C.
[11]378 U.S. 368 (1964).
[12]63 Cal. 2nd 518 (1965).

2. It can grant severance of trials if the prosecution insists that it must use the extrajudicial statements and it appears that effective deletions cannot be made; or

3. If the prosecution has successfully resisted a motion for severance and thereafter offers an extrajudicial statement implicating a codefendant, the trial court must exclude it if effective deletions are not possible.[13]

Motion for Conditional Examination of Witnesses

This court remedy may be used when witnesses are out of the state or about to leave the state, or are so sick and infirm that there is reasonable apprehension they will be unable to attend the trial. This is a motion that may be made in any case triable in the Superior Court (felony), at any stage of the proceedings from the filing of the complaint or information, the finding of an indictment or the time of trial. Procedurally, when this motion is granted it moves along as follows: (1) witness is brought before a magistrate and examined and cross-examined by the opposing counsel, and (2) testimony is taken and transcribed. This transcript of a witness' testimony is then available in the absence of the witness at the time of trial.

A side-action of this conditional examination of witnesses is the potential of this motion for "discovery" purposes related to out-of-state witnesses. In the Sigal case in California, coauthor Wells was confronted with an out-of-state police officer who had taken polygraph tests of the defendant (Sigal) and refused to disclose the tests when requested. A pretrial discovery motion and court order were useless because the witness was not within the jurisdiction of the California courts and the local prosecutor noted he did not have and would not request the information. A motion for the conditional examination of this witness was granted, and pursuant to that order the witness was subpoenaed in accordance with the Uniform Act for the Attendance of Out-of-State Witnesses and asked to bring the tapes of his polygraph examination. Resultant examination of this witness and his exhibits provided defense counsel with all the information (and more) to which the defendant would have been entitled on pretrial discovery.

Motion to Dismiss: Delay

The court may order the prosecution dismissed, unless good cause is shown to continue with the criminal proceeding, when the information is not filed or the trial not commenced within the required time period.

[13]Similar rules have been adopted in Connecticut, Illinois and Ohio.

In California, the burden of proof is on the prosecutor to show "good cause"—that he has exercised due diligence—but has been unable to prepare the information for filing or get ready for the trial within the allotted time limit.[14] Failure of the prosecutor to prove sufficient grounds for the motion will require the court to grant a defense motion to dismiss. A denial by the court of this motion to dismiss may be reviewed on appeal from the judgment, so long as it is not raised for the first time on appeal. The more approved and popular procedure appears to be application by defense counsel for a writ of mandate or prohibition in the appellate courts before the trial.

Motion to Suppress

A motion to suppress evidence is an application by defense counsel directed to the trial court or the issuing magistrate in cases of search warrants. It is a request for an order to forbid the prosecution to use, during the trial, any evidence obtained through illegal search, or which can be otherwise termed illegal because it was gained by infringing on the defendant's Constitutional rights. Objections can be raised to the admission of such evidence at trial, and in cases where there is some conflict in the evidence of infringement, the courts will not suppress in advance of trial, except under the procedure to quash search warrants or upon the granting of a writ of prohibition by the appellate court. In seeking an order to suppress evidence before trial, the defense counsel is taking advantage of court decisions turning the full force of illegality upon easily delineated practices of the police, and sometimes the staff of the prosecutor's office. The guidelines are now rather clearly drawn and the courts have little difficulty in deciding the issue of admissibility either before trial on a motion under California Penal Code, Section 995, or a petition for a writ of prohibition or mandate, or during trial in a *voir dire*[15] proceeding outside the presence of the jury. If the proffered evidence is found inadmissible, the "fruit of the poisoned tree" doctrine expressed in *Silverthorne Lumber Company v. United States*,[16] could very easily affect other evidence and ruin the entire case for the "people" and result in a dismissal of the accusatory pleading.

Motion for Pretrial Discovery

This motion asks the court to order the prosecutor to turn over to defense counsel specific evidence (statements, reports, photos, etc.) in

[14]California Penal Code, Section 1382.
[15]Questioning under oath to determine competency.
[16]251 U.S. 385 (1920).

the prosecutor's possession or control. Its common use is developing from court decisions recognizing the fact that access to evidence held by the prosecutor is necessary for a fair trial of the accused person.[17]

Motion for Change of Venue

The key question in the motion for change of venue is whether an impartial jury is available to try the defendant. On this issue, evidence of community hostility, prejudicial publicity and the type of crime are all important in determining whether or not the trial should be moved elsewhere.

A change of venue may be granted only on a defendant's motion upon a showing that "a fair and impartial trial cannot be had in the county." Whenever it is "impossible to secure a jury to try the case in the original county," the venue may be changed by motion of any party or on the court's own motion.[18]

In California, change of venue in a lower court (Justice) may be sought in misdemeanor cases. The motion is to be made in writing and must be supported by affidavits setting forth the reasons for the motion. Defense counsel may claim prejudice or bias of the assigned trial judge or the citizens of the judicial district, while the prosecutor may plead the convenience of the "people" if he can secure the written consent of defendant and his attorney, if any.[19] If granted, the case must be removed to another convenient county. If the motion is denied, it is reviewable on an appeal from a judgment of conviction, and may well present a Constitutional issue for the federal courts under the due process clause of the Fourteenth Amendment. Convictions have been reversed because extensive publicity ruined the defendant's opportunity for a fair trial and thus his chance for due process.[20] These recent cases have created new procedures by police and prosecutor which guard against the release of information to personnel of mass media news agencies which may harm a defendant's rights.

Motion to Exclude Evidence

The grounds for such motions during a trial are usually those which have been utilized previously and relate to improper arrest and search and seizure, an improper confession or admission, and, in addition, may

[17]See Chapter 4 for discussion of pretrial discovery.
[18]California Penal Code, Sections 1033 and 1033.5.
[19]*Ibid.*, Section 1431.
[20]*Irvin v. Dowd*, 366 U.S. 717 (1961).
  Rideau v. Louisiana, 373 U.S. 723 (1963).
  Sheppard v. Maxwell, 384 U.S. 333 (1966).

relate to irrelevant or immaterial evidence, hearsay testimony and various types of physical evidence, such as photographs which are prejudicial enough to outweigh their possible materiality.

Motion for a Mistrial

This motion is appropriately based on gross misconduct of someone (usually judge, prosecutor or juror) during the trial, which prejudices the case against the defendant and ruins his opportunity for a fair trial. When the misconduct appears to be deliberately done with the idea of prejudicing the defendant, the courts usually will order a mistrial; but when the conduct relates to the testimony of a witness and a questioner could not have foreseen or avoided an improper unresponsive answer, then the court may deny the motion but agree to strike the answer from the record and order the jury to disregard it.

Motion Requesting Advice to Acquit

A court, on defense motion or its own, may advise the jury to acquit the defendant whenever it deems the evidence submitted, at either the close of the "people's" case or the close of the defense case, to be insufficient as a matter of law to warrant a conviction. A jury does not have to follow this advice. It is not the directed verdict common in some states. Incidentally, opposing counsel may argue the case for this motion before the jury and the court may comment to the jury in connection with the evidence presented during the proceedings related to this motion. If this defense motion is refused, the trial continues as if the motion had not been made.

Motion in Arrest of Judgment

A motion in arrest of judgment is generally limited to an unforeseen lack of jurisdiction by the court, or the same grounds as those upon which a demurrer can be filed at the time of the accusatory pleading before trial, and it appears that a demurrer is a necessary foundation for a later motion in arrest of judgment. California's Penal Code sets forth the grounds in this language:

> A motion in arrest of judgment is an application on the part of the defendant that no judgment be rendered on a plea, finding or verdict of guilty; or a finding or verdict against the defendant, on a plea of a former conviction, former acquittal or once in jeopardy. It may be founded on

any of the defects in the accusatory pleading mentioned in Section 1004 (demurrer), unless the objection has been waived by a failure to demur, and must be made and determined before the judgment is pronounced. When determined, the order must be immediately entered by the clerk in the minutes.[21]

Motion for a New Trial

A motion for a new trial is a request for a reexamination of the issue in the same court, before another jury, after a verdict has been rendered and before judgment. The granting of a new trial places the parties in the same position as if no trial had taken place. At the court's discretion, a defense motion for a new trial may be granted upon the following major grounds: (1) defendant is not present at trial of a felony; (2) jury has received any outside evidence other than a view of the premises concerned in the crime or personal property involved; (3) conduct of the jury after retiring for deliberations has prevented a fair and due consideration of the case; (4) a lottery was contrived for deciding the verdict or any means other than a fair expression of opinion by the jurors was utilized for this decision; (5) court has misdirected the jury or otherwise erred in determining legal questions during the trial, or when either counsel involved is guilty of prejudicial misconduct during the trial and before the jury; (6) verdict is contrary to law or evidence; and (7) new evidence is discovered which is material to the defense case.[22]

Upon the motion for a new trial, a judge may modify the verdict instead of granting a new trial when the motion is based upon (6)— against the weight of evidence. The modification may extend to finding the defendant guilty of a lesser degree of the crime in the verdict. However, the modification of a verdict is appealable by the prosecution.

One of the most dramatic instances associated with the filing of a motion for a new trial occurs when the grounds are the discovery of new evidence. Basically, all jurisdictions require the evidence to be material to the defense case with the strong possibility of a different verdict because of such evidence. There must be a presentation of adequate proof at the time of the hearing upon this motion that the defendant could not have discovered and produced this evidence upon trial with "reasonable diligence." The defendant must also produce at the hearing, in support of this motion, the affidavits of the witnesses by whom such evidence is expected to be given, and if time is required

[21]California Penal Code, Section 1185.
[22]*Ibid.*, Sections 1179–1182.

by the defendant to procure such affidavits, the court may postpone the hearing of the motion for such length of time as, under all the circumstances of the case, may seem reasonable.

Appeals Following Judgment

The basis for an appeal is a question of law, and appeals are limited to those cases provided for by law at either the federal or state level. Basically, an appeal has its foundation in the objections at a trial and the court's sustaining or overruling of these objections, and to a lesser degree to the requests for an "exception"[23] or a motion to "strike" some evidence from the record. When there is a claim that the evidence was insufficient, the appellate review must determine if the evidence as reported to them in the trial record was sufficient as a matter of law for the jurors (or judge) to arrive at their stated conclusions. It is a second-guessing of the "triers of fact." However, the burden of proof is shifted to the defendant to demonstrate that under no analysis of the facts does the evidence show guilt. The appellate court will not substitute its judgment for the judgment of the trier of fact. The appellate court, in reviewing the evidence, will not accord the defendant the presumption of innocence or substitute its concept of reasonable doubt. If there was evidence upon which a jury could base its finding, the court will not reverse on the ground of insufficient evidence. The appellate court must decide if the error led to an erroneous conclusion by the jurors—seeking not so much the legality of the error, but the result of the illegal error in the decision-making process that led to the jury's finding.[24]

An appellate court may reverse, affirm or modify a judgment or order appealed from, or reduce the degree of the offense of the punishment imposed, and may set aside, affirm or modify any or all of the proceedings subsequent to, or dependent upon such judgment or order, and may, if proper, order a new trial.[25]

In California, the defendant appeals from the basic adverse findings; while the prosecutor cannot appeal from the verdict itself, but can seek to block favorable response to a defense appeal by taking an appeal against the court's remedial action. The California Penal Code states: "An appeal may be taken by the defendant: from (1) final judgment of conviction, and an order granting probation shall be deemed to be a final judgment; (2) an order denying a motion for a new trial; or (3) any order made after judgment, affecting the substantial rights of the

[23]Formal objection to a ruling of a court.
[24]California Constitution, Article 6, Section 4½.
[25]California Penal Code, Section 1260.

party."[26] However, the following section only permits appeals by the prosecution as follows:

> An appeal may be taken by the people from: (1) an order setting aside the indictment, information or complaint; (2) a judgment for the defendant on a demurrer to the indictment, accusation or information; (3) an order granting a new trial; (4) an order arresting judgment; (5) an order made after judgment, affecting the substantial rights of the people, and (6) an order modifying the verdict or finding by reducing the degree of the offense or the punishment thereof.[27]

Application for Certificate of Probable Cause

The practice in appeals is for the court to sign a written certificate of probable cause[28] staying the execution of the judgment. This merely certifies that the court recognizes the existence of an honest difference of opinion as to whether or not there may have been prejudicial error in the case. In California during pendency of an appeal, the defendant serves his sentence just as if no appeal were filed. However, bail may be set and accepted, but it is not a matter of right at this stage of the criminal action.

The Great Writ

The writ of *habeas corpus* is a speedy remedy to release a person unlawfully imprisoned or restrained of his liberty; it is issued in order to inquire into the cause of such imprisonment or restraint, or to determine if a person has been denied personal rights and the reason for such denial. It is available to review important questions of law that cannot otherwise be reviewed. It is an order from a court to the person having custody of or restraining the person on whose behalf the application is made, and commands the sheriff or other person having custody of the prisoner to have "the body" of such prisoner before the court issuing the writ at a time and place specified. The person upon whom a writ of *habeas corpus* is served must make a return to the court stating plainly whether or not he has the party for whom the writ was secured in his custody, and the circumstances and authority for such custody.

When the issues have been established by the petition return, a hearing is held in which the return serves as the first pleading or "complaint" and the petitioner files a "traverse" which denies or controverts any

[26]*Ibid.*, Section 1237.
[27]*Ibid.*, Section 1238.
[28]A certificate of reasonable doubt in some states.

matter set forth in the return and sets forth the reasons the applicant is entitled to the relief sought from the court. California law sums up the hearing procedure as follows:

> The court or judge must thereupon proceed in a summary way to hear such proof as may be produced against such imprisonment or detention, or in favor of the same, and to dispose of such party as the justice of the case may require, and has full power and authority to require and compel the attendance of witnesses, by process of subpoena and attachment, and to do and perform all other acts and things necessary to a full and fair hearing and determination of the case.[29]

The writ of *habeas corpus* is in no sense that of review as upon an appeal. Usually, this writ is not appropriate when a conviction can be attacked on appeal. Some jurisdictions will accept a petition for a writ of *habeas corpus* under certain circumstances where the major point raised will dispose of the appeal at the same time. However, in most jurisdictions, the petitioner must show that he has no other speedy or adequate remedy.

Application in a posttrial procedure for a writ to "produce the body" of the defendant can also be presented to a federal court for persons in the custody of the state, and it offends no legitimate state interest in the administration of justice. It is a means for a review of a judgment of a state court by the judge of the federal district court in the area in which the prisoner is confined, and there is also the possibility of review upward throughout the federal court system. Thousands of these applications are being made yearly, and as "novel" cases upholding individual rights are ruled upon in the U.S. Supreme Court, there is every likelihood that this number may increase.

Possibly, the best capsule description of the writ of *habeas corpus* is in the words of one paragraph of the U.S. Supreme Court's decision in the case of *Fay v. Noia*:[30]

> Our decision today swings open no prison gates. . . . Surely no fair-minded person will contend that those who have been deprived of their liberty without due process of law ought nevertheless to languish in prison . . . *habeas corpus* is predestined by its historical role in the struggle for personal liberty to be the ultimate remedy. If the states are without effective remedy, the federal courts have the power and the duty to provide it. *Habeas corpus* is one of the precious heritages of Anglo-American civilization. We do no more today than confirm its continuing efficacy.

The development of this writ into a catch-all device to resolve all wrongs against an accused or convicted defendant may be readily noted

[29]California Penal Code, Section 1484.
[30]372 U.S. 391 (1963).

from the following listing of instances in which it has been used in recent years:

(1) To admit defendant to bail or to set bail at a reasonable amount;

(2) To require defendant to be taken before magistrate or be released;

(3) To test court jurisdiction over subject matter of the offense;

(4) To secure jury trial,

(5) To test sufficiency of accusatory pleading;

(6) To prevent interference with preparation of defense;

(7) To seek discharge from the status of "presently insane" and force trial of pending charge;

(8) To test a conviction when the defendant was not advised of his right to counsel;

(9) To test denial of other Constitutional rights;

(10) To test excess of punishment (habitual criminal status, sex psychopath, etc.); and

(11) To test Constitutionality of a statute or an ordinance.

An appeal following judgment is probably the major guarantee against any injustice during a criminal action, but the great writ, that of *habeas corpus*, is an effective remedy to gain the liberty of a person unjustly imprisoned or to gain relief for an individual whose personal rights have been denied.

Selected References

CASES

Palko v. Connecticut, 302 U.S. 319 (1937).

A decision containing a discussion of appeals and their purpose in the administration of criminal justice.

People v. Ah Sam, 41 Cal. 645 (1871).

A classic California case on the form of motions.

BOOKS

Arnold, Thurman, *Fair Fights and Foul: A Dissenting Lawyer's Life*. New York: Harcourt, Brace & World, Inc., 1965, 285 pages.

The author participated in many famous cases, including *Gideon*, and is an expert in the "battle of writs." An easily read text with a thorough exposition of the diverse means for legal redress.

Lewis, Anthony, *Gideon's Trumpet*. New York: Random House, Inc., 1964, 262 pages.

An in-depth study of a classic case that proves adequate and speedy legal remedies can get results. Gideon, confined in a Florida prison, filed a request for a writ of *habeas corpus* in a Florida court, following his conviction for a burglary. He alleged a denial of "due process' in being tried without counsel because of lack of funds to retain private counsel; upon denial of his application, he submitted a "Petition for a Writ of *Certiorari"* to the U.S. Supreme Court, along with a motion for leave to proceed in *forma pauperis* (without the payment of legal fees in advance). A fine study of one man's use of the great writ.

McCormack, Ken, *Sprung: The Release of Willie Calloway*. New York: St. Martin's Press, 1964, 244 pages.

Is there "adequate and speedy" relief to correct injustice? This is the story of a newspaper reporter's crusade to release Willie Calloway, an illiterate Negro boy, from a life sentence for a murder he did not commit.

Zimmerman, Isidore, with Francis Bond, *Punishment Without Crime*. New York: Clarkson N. Potter, 1964, 304 pages.

The true story of a man who spent 24 years in prison for a crime he did not commit. This is a book that illustrates the hard work associated with seeking relief in court for an alleged injustice. It is also proof that there is no "final disposition" of a convicted and imprisoned defendant, because of the open door to legal relief in the form of applications for writs, motions, and appeals.

ARTICLES

Aaron, Thomas J., "The Dilemma of Judicial Review," *Police* (March-April 1965), 35–36.

A study of the principle of judicial review in America. The author traces the history of this portion of the judicial process from the Judiciary Act of 1789 and the case of *Marbury v. Madison* to the present.

Kronenburg, Jerry, "Right of a State Appeal in Criminal Cases," *Journal of Criminal Law, Criminology, and Police Science*, 49, No. 5 (January-February 1959), 473–82.

This author discusses the basic question of whether the "people" should be allowed to appeal, at the risk of possible harrassment of the accused, or whether the protection of an acquitted person is a more desirable public policy.

McMorris, Samuel Carter, "The Decriminalization of Narcotics Addiction," *American Criminal Law Quarterly* (Winter 1965), pp. 84–88.

This article, while a thorough examination of *Robinson v. California*, 370 U.S. 660 (1962), is also a fine example of legal applications to higher courts to correct any injustice in a criminal action. Robinson was imprisoned in California for being a drug addict; he exhausted state remedies, and appealed to the U.S. Supreme Court.

"Appellate Delay in Criminal Cases: A Report," *American Criminal Law Quarterly* (Summer 1964), pp. 150–58.

An excellent discussion of delay along the appeal route. It suggests uniform rules to reduce the existing time lag.

9

Direct and Cross-Examination

The first questioning of a witness is the direct examination, and it is conducted by a friendly attorney who represents the party who calls the witness. This questioning is followed by the cross-examination, conducted by an unfriendly attorney—the opposing counsel. This is followed by redirect and recross examination, if necessary. Usually, the scope of the preceding questioning limits the area for queries in the following questioning sessions. While cross-examination is restricted to the same matter as covered in the direct examination, it can range to any suppressed or undeveloped facts within the scope of the direct examination; it can range to the remaining and qualifying circumstances of such facts as well as to facts which diminish the apparent trustworthiness of the person being questioned. Generally, attorneys do not relinquish the right to cross-examination. However, ventures by cross-examiners into areas of uncertain responses have often resulted in opposing counsel making an unexpected contribution to his opponent's case.

After the cross-examination, there is an attempt made to "rehabilitate" the witness during redirect examination. When the credibility of the witness appears to be salvaged from the cross-examination destruction, the opposing counsel has one more chance at discrediting the witness in recross examination. Briefly, this alternate mode of questioning has the following order:

1. *Direct* examination of witness (by counsel who issued the subpoena for the appearance of the witness),
2. *Cross-examination* (by opposing counsel),
3. *Redirect* examination (by counsel calling the witness), and
4. *Recross* examination (by opposing counsel).

A witness who has previously testified upon a trial can be recalled for the purpose of testifying about new matter not within the scope of his previous testimony, to correct previous testimony, or to lay the foundation for impeachment; and, at the sound discretion of the trial judge, a witness may be recalled for further examination by either counsel regarding his previous testimony when counsel shows good reason for the recall.

The Privilege of a Witness Against Self-Incrimination

Protection against self-incrimination is a privilege that is based upon Constitutional guarantees and extends to all persons participating in criminal proceedings. The basic guarantee in this respect is contained in the Fifth Amendment: ". . . nor shall any person be compelled in any criminal case to be a witness against himself." The majority opinion of the U.S. Supreme Court in the cases of *Malloy v. Hogan*,[1] and *Murphy v. The Waterfront Commission of New York Harbor*,[2] voiced on June 15, 1964, definitely placed the guarantee against self-incrimination under the protection of the due process clause of the Fourteenth Amendment, and granted a witness complete protection. The court stated in *Malloy v. Hogan*: "It would be incongruous to have different standards determine the validity of a claim of privilege based on the same feared prosecution, depending on whether the claim was asserted in a state or federal court." In *Murphy v. The Waterfront Commission*, the court held that the "correct" construction of the privilege regarding self-incrimination and the immunity of a witness is one that grants complete protection for the witness. This court opinion states that this privilege "protects a witness against incrimination under state as well as federal law," and noted that this meant that the petitioners in this case, as witnesses in

[1]378 U.S. 1 (1964).
[2]378 U.S. 52 (1964).

the state courts, could not be compelled to give testimony which might incriminate them under federal law unless the compelled testimony and its fruits could not be used by federal officials in connection with a federal criminal prosecution against them. Petitioners in that case had refused to answer certain questions about labor trouble at piers in New Jersey during an inquiry made by investigators and officials of the Waterfront Commission of New York and New Jersey. Petitioners pleaded that the questions and their answers might tend to incriminate them, and were granted immunity from prosecution under the laws of both New York and New Jersey; they continued their refusal to respond to questions on the ground that answers might tend to incriminate them under federal law—and the grant of immunity for protection against the laws and authority of two states did not purport to extend to any protection from federal authority. They were held in contempt and the New Jersey Supreme Court affirmed the judgment. In its decision the court overruled three cases:

U.S. v. Murdock:[3] The federal government could compel a witness to give testimony that might incriminate him under state law.

Knapp v. Schweitzer:[4] A state could compel a witness to give testimony that might incriminate him under federal law.

Feldman v. U.S.:[5] Testimony compelled by a state could be introduced into evidence in the federal courts.

The court's opinion in *Murphy* dismisses a 1906 dictum (*Hale v. Henkel*[6]) that the only danger to be considered as prevailing, when a witness invokes this privilege, is one arising within the same jurisdiction and under the same sovereignty. In *Murphy*, the court explained the overruling of *Murdock-Knapp-and-Feldman* by saying that *Murdock* did not adequately consider the relevant authorities, and the legal premises underlying *Knapp* and *Feldman* have since been rejected.

The ordinary witness may be compelled to come forward and give testimony. If he does not wish to testify, he may "take the Fifth," but he must state the grounds upon which he believes he will incriminate himself, and the court will then determine the validity of this claim. The statutes which grant immunity overcome the plea of self-incrimination. A witness may claim that this guarantee of immunity is insufficient to protect him from further prosecution for crime, and again it is the court which must determine the validity of this claim on the individual circumstances. However, in *Ullman v. U.S.,*[7] the majority decision discusses

[3] 284 U.S. 141 (1931).
[4] 357 U.S. 371 (1958).
[5] 322 U.S. 487 (1944).
[6] 201 U.S. 43 (1906).
[7] 350 U.S. 442 (1957).

the privilege against self-incrimination and ends with these words: "Immunity displaces the danger (of self-incrimination). Once the reason for the privilege ceases, the privilege ceases."

An accused person cannot be asked to come forward to be a witness if he does not wish to take the stand or is advised not to do so by defense counsel. A court decision in this area forbids comment by the prosecution on the accused's failure to take the stand in his own defense, and forbids instructions by the court that such silence is evidence of guilt. This was the April 28, 1965 case of *Griffin v. California*,[8] in which the U.S. Supreme Court ruled that California's law permitting such comment was null and void as violating the provisions of the Fifth Amendment which are enforceable on the states by reason of the Fourteenth Amendment.

Witnesses

A court may limit the number of witnesses to a single point or question to save time in court, and may order witnesses other than the witness being examined to be excluded from the courtroom during the examination. Persons who cannot be sworn as witnesses are individuals of unsound mind, children under ten who are apparently incapable of receiving just impressions or relating them truly[9] and those whose communications are privileged because of a confidential relationship: husband and wife, attorney and client, confessor and confessant, public officer and official confidante and a newspaper employee and his source of information.[10] While most of the foregoing individuals may be permitted to testify under certain specified circumstances, their competency depends upon the individual case or the condition of the witness at the time.

Witnesses testify and their words contribute to the evidence which tends to prove or disprove the issue on trial. They testify truthfully and falsely, and with and without bias and interest. Perjury is so common that conflicting testimony is not punished unless it is of such a nature that the court cannot ignore it and its effect upon the case. Often, little more than the ego involvement of being on the witness stand results in slanted testimony.

The witness in a criminal case may be an employee of an administration of justice agency; a member of the community who by chance, friendship or blood relationship became involved in the criminal pro-

[8]380 U.S. 609 (1965).
[9]California Evidence Code, Section 701.
[10]*Ibid.*, Sections 950–1070.

ceedings; or an expert witness in the employ of either the prosecution or the defense. Witnesses may be divided into major groups for a better understanding of their examination by opposing counsel. The six major groups are: (1) police, (2) expert, (3) identification, (4) public-spirited, (5) interested and (6) material witnesses.

POLICE WITNESSES

The police officer often looks forward to his role as a witness, accepting the challenge of cross-examination and the opportunity to engage as an antagonist in a case in which he must have an interest as a result of his own involvement in the process for administering justice. Socrates was tried by his fellow Athenians in 399 B.C. Police had not as yet appeared on the scene, but one of the three prosecutors presenting "evidence" warned the jurors that Socrates would not have been prosecuted in the first place if he were not guilty. That is quite a few years ago, but it is the key to the attitude of many police witnesses. Why has the defendant been arrested by police and successfully arraigned by them? He has been arrested and accused because the police officer concerned believes the defendant is guilty.[11]

EXPERT WITNESSES

The expert witness usually testifies for either the prosecution or the defense with some regularity. The prosecution experts are usually salaried personnel of police units, state investigating bureaus or the Federal Bureau of Investigation. Experts for the defense are usually hired for specific cases and are paid a fee for their work. The distinguishing feature of these witnesses is that their expertise is not only for hire, but such hiring implies pretrial reports and conferences developing the character and nature of their findings and opinions. This does not mean that an expert witness will not be testifying to his honest opinions and findings, but it does mean that the party requesting the appearance of these witnesses expects favorable testimony.[12]

IDENTIFICATION WITNESSES

An identification witness connects the defendant with the crime scene or the victim. Most identification witnesses state a simple and truthful fact when they testify. Others, unfortunately, lie or recollect wrongly.

[11]Henry H. Rothblatt, *Successful Techniques in the Trial of Criminal Cases* (Englewood Cliffs, N. J.: Prentice-Hall, Inc., 1961), pp. 70–71.
[12]*Ibid.*, p. 70.

Probably, ego-involvement is the most meaningful factor in the conduct of the identification witness who testifies falsely. This is the only possible explanation for conduct on the witness stand which has convicted persons who are later cleared of all traces of guilt. Prosecutors do not use identification witnesses who do not identify the defendant.[13]

PUBLIC-SPIRITED WITNESSES

The witness who is asked to appear in court by police or prosecutor is often a reluctant witness. While compulsory court process may be used to ensure the attendance of these witnesses, and their statements may be taken before trial in order to guard against surprise reversals, they usually testify because of some concept of duty regarding the prosecution of the case at trial. In many instances, their testimony may mean the loss of meaningful friendships or business contacts. In cases involving the underworld of organized crime, the lives of these witnesses or the safety of members of their family may be threatened. These individuals are the finest expression of community identification with the problems of administering justice, and their testimony may be the deciding factor in determining innocence or guilt.

INTERESTED WITNESSES

Witnesses with an interest in a case are biased because of their relationship with one or more of the participants in the case. This group of witnesses includes the lying witnesses, the one who recollects wrongly[14] and those who seize every opportunity to help the party aligned with their interest.[15] The role, then, of this witness depends a great deal upon which side served as the agent in bringing him to court. There is no doubt that previous interviews have developed the area of testimony most suited to the particular needs of the side with which the witness is aligned. This person's testimony is oriented to the needs of his "side" and the truth may undergo some slight deviations and change as a result of this loyalty.

The Form of Questions

Specific questions call for a controlled response by a witness. General questions require a narrative type of response and are often termed "open-end" questions. In specific questioning, the witness has responded

13 *Ibid.*, pp. 65–66.
14 *Ibid.*, pp. 73–74.
15 *Ibid.*, pp. 71–72.

when he answers the question. In general questioning, the witness is asked what he observed and often invited to tell the story in his own words and to take his time.

Questions are phrased by the attorneys in a case. Our procedure to determine truth does not invite the trial judge to participate in this questioning—unlike the inquisitorial systems of justice which depend upon judicial questioning. However, and within the judicial limits of implied comment,[16] a judge may question a witness when he believes it necessary to bring out facts which have not been elicited by the parties at trial. A juror may also query a witness, if it is the belief of the trial judge that such action will aid a juror's understanding of a material issue involved.

Leading questions are usually not permitted on direct examination, unless the witness needs help in telling his story because of age, health or other incapacity. These are generally questions calling for a "yes" or "no" answer, but more specifically are questions in which the answer is suggested to the witness by the form of the question. An example of a typical leading question to a witness is:

> Q: Mr. Doe, you saw the defendant pull a switchblade knife and stab the victim four times, correct?

A mere affirmative response includes all the facts suggested in the question. On the other hand, a proper direct examination to elicit the same facts from a witness would be substantially as follows:

> Q: What did you see the defendant do?
> A: He pulled a knife out of his pocket.
> Q: Were you able to determine what type of knife?
> A: A switchblade.
> Q: Did the defendant do anything with the knife?
> A: Yes, he stabbed the victim.
> Q: Did you see how many times he stabbed him?
> A: Yes, four times.

Leading questions are permitted on cross-examination. In this area of questioning, the trial judge has discretion up to the point where his rulings might interfere with the opportunity for a fair trial. This discretionary power is also true of argumentative questions. Many judges will permit extensive cross-examination along such lines; other judges are restrictive. The type of questions most likely to be restricted because of form are misleading questions. These are questions phrased so that the question assumes as true certain facts which are either untrue, in dispute or not related to the direct testimony of the witness being questioned.

[16] *Griffin v. U.S.*, 164 F 2nd 903.

Objections

"I object . . ." is usually a cry heard frequently during the examination of witnesses, with the attorney making the objection rising from his seat in the courtroom to specify the grounds for his objections, and often moving to have the answer stricken from the record and requesting the court to instruct the jury to disregard such evidence.

Unless the possibility of a fair trial is endangered, counsel challenging the legality of the evidence must make timely notice of his objection, and this is usually before the question is answered. However, counsel is entitled to a fair opportunity to object, and when the witness responds very promptly to a question—before the attorney raising the claim can speak out—the court will usually order the response stricken from the record upon motion of the objecting counsel, and will caution the witness to wait before responding to questioning in order to determine whether or not there is a legal question raised in connection with the examination. While the opposing counsel is usually the attorney concerned with objections, the trial judge may also order the witness not to answer a question which he believes to be improper.

The general objection of "incompetent, immaterial and irrelevant" is insufficient unless the testimony would be inadmissible for any purpose, and objecting counsel must specify the grounds upon which he bases his claim for exclusion. When the objection is made, counsel conducting the questioning may make an offer of proof, stating to the court the fact he desires to prove and the manner in which he proposes to prove it. The court may hear the argument from each side, and the arguments and the court's ruling may be made either in the presence of the jury or without the jury being present.

Impeachment

A witness can be discredited on cross-examination by proof that he possesses a bias, motive or interest. However, the formal impeachment of a witness is usually limited to specific instances and formalized procedures. In California, the law states that a witness may be impeached by the party against whom he was called because of contradictory evidence or evidence that the witness had a bad general reputation for truth, honesty or integrity, but not by evidence of particular wrongful acts, except where proof of a felony conviction can be shown—unless the ex-felon has received full and unconditional pardon together with a certificate of rehabilitation. A witness can also be impeached because of previous statements inconsistent with his present testimony; but in these instances, the statements must be related to the witness—along with the circumstances of times, places and persons present—and he must be asked if he made such statements. If he responds in the affirmative, he must be given an opportunity to explain them.[17]

Under cross-examination, a witness may be queried about previous felony convictions. This line of questioning is also permissible even when the witness is the defendant, when a defendant does offer himself as a witness. However, comment of the court of review in *People v. Modesto*[18] indicates this opportunity to impeach a defendant who does take the stand in his own defense because of a past felony conviction may actually be keeping these witnesses from the stand—and possibly affecting the character of justice. The majority opinion in this case notes:

> Defendant contends that the reason a defendant refuses to testify is that his prior convictions will be introduced in evidence to impeach him (C.C.P. 2051) and not that he is unable to deny the accusations. It is true that the defendant might fear that his prior convictions will prejudice the jury, and therefore another possible inference can be drawn from his refusal to take the stand.

In California, a witness can be impeached by either party in a criminal action when the testimony of the witness is adverse. In many jurisdictions the attorney calling the witness is expected to connect the factor of surprise with the showing of adverse evidence in order to impeach a witness.

Direct Examination

The prosecutor and defense counsel do not "coach" their witnesses prior to appearance in court; it is unlikely, however, that a witness will be called to testify without being interviewed on at least one occasion in the course of case preparation. It is usually at this time that the attorney tests the story of the witness and decides just what contribution the witness can make to the attorney's theory of the case.

It is technically necessary in a criminal proceeding for the attorney conducting a direct examination to lay the proper foundation for whatever evidence he hopes to develop through the direct examination of a

[17]California Code of Civil Procedures, Sections 2051–2052.
[18]62 Cal. 2nd 436 (1965).

witness.[19] Not only is it necessary to develop the adequate opportunity of the witness to gain knowledge regarding the facts of his forthcoming testimony, but it is also necessary, in most instances, to demonstrate that his is firsthand knowledge. Evidence handbooks are replete with instances in which hearsay and opinion evidence can be utilized upon a criminal proceeding, but in the reality of a courtroom, the major area of testimony relates to what a witness perceived by his senses; in order to bring the story of a witness out in full detail on direct examination, the groundwork must be laid that the witness had the opportunity to observe (see, hear, smell, touch, taste) the fact. This opportunity must also be related to the date and time of the crime charged, or the date and time of the incident about which the witness is testifying.

It is necessary for the questioner to establish a working relationship between the witness' position at the time of the observation, his physical capabilities for observation, the lack of any obstacles to perception ability and what attracted the attention of the witness initially and what makes it possible for him to relate his observation to a specific time. Then the questioner can develop the testimony of the witness through specific and connected questioning, or by asking a general question. The decision about the form of questioning is an important tactical and strategical aspect of the overall presentation of the case. However, unless the witness has indicated an unusual tendency to digress from an ordinary narrative recital during a pretrial interview, it is the custom to utilize the general questioning technique. The witness is asked to tell what he observed on the occasion and in the place delineated in the preliminary questioning. When the witness has completed his narrative, it is then appropriate for the questioner to ask specific questions about facts omitted from the recital of the witness.

Cross-examination

Cross-examination is the questioning of a witness in a criminal proceeding by opposing counsel, upon his testimony given in response to questioning by the party who produced the witness in court. Cross-examination is a right, not a privilege. The major objective in cross-examination is to weaken the impression made upon the jury (or the judge in nonjury trials) by a witness. The opposing counsel is limited in his cross-examination to the general scope of the direct examination in California and the great majority of other court systems, and attacks upon the testimony itself must be connected in some way with the evi-

19Henry H. Rothblatt, *Successful Techniques in the Trial of Criminal Cases* (Englewood Cliffs, N.J.: Prentice-Hall, Inc., 1961), pp. 84–85.

dence. The attack upon the witness can range over a broad area, and it is the prerogative and duty of the questioner to attempt to elicit answers from the witness which will show his partiality and unwillingness to tell the truth. The destruction of a witness as a person worthy of belief during cross-examination can often be equivalent to the destruction of major portions of the testimony of such witness; a combination of the two achievements can often mean a drastic change in the effect of the witness' direct testimony upon jury or judge, or both.

Cross-examination is at the heart of the adversary system of justice. Most witnesses are able to testify impressively when led through their testimony by a friendly attorney. It is only when their testimony is probed by a hostile attorney that such things as misrecollection,[20] bias or deceit can be discovered and brought to the attention of the jury.

Although the law presumes a witness to speak the truth, every practicing attorney knows that witnesses do lie, even under oath. Even more prevalent is the tendency to exaggerate or misrecollect, or to permit their testimony to be influenced by bias or an interest in the outcome of the proceeding. When a person's life or liberty is at stake, or the protection of the people from hardened or vicious criminals is in the balance, a jury has the right to know—and must know—whether a witness is lying, exaggerating or recollecting wrongly, or whether his testimony is not credible because of bias or some interest in the case.

Thorough investigation and adequate preparation are the best basis for successful cross-examination. The basic facts of the crime originate from the police investigation at the scene and their interviews and interrogations of potential witnesses; data collecting and analysis are the core of effective investigation and must extend beyond the gathering work of the police. Only an attorney who is fully aware of all the circumstances of a crime and their legal significance is prepared to conduct a challenging cross-examination.

A Sacramento County felony case illustrates this point. It involved a killing at Folsom State Prison. Crimes occurring in a prison are ideal for analysis because the witnesses and crime scene compose a closed community. At least in theory, the conditions should be perfect for any investigator. On the day of this homicide, a disturbance brought guards rushing to a hallway just outside of the mess hall of the prison. The first correctional guard to push his way through the seventy or more inmates crowding around the disturbance observed one inmate on top of another inmate lying on his back on the floor. The guard pulled the top man from the prone victim and, as he did so, he saw a sharpened screwdriver drop to the floor. He recovered this lethal instrument as soon as he had control

[20]To recollect wrongly.

of the inmate attacker. The inmate on the floor had several stab wounds and died before he could be taken to the hospital. The attacker was not cut or injured in any way apparent to this correctional officer.

As a result of this killing, the grand jury returned a murder indictment and a trial followed. During the course of this trial, several guards testified to what they had seen of the crime. On cross-examination by the defense counsel, it was developed that the seventy or more inmates who were in the immediate area of the killing had not been searched by any of the guards, nor had the correctional officers made a search of the crime scene, that is, the hallway in which the fatal attack occurred. It was further developed that the hallway had numerous places in which a weapon might be hidden. During the defense case, the defendant testified that he had been attacked by the victim who had a knife, and only then did the defendant pull his screwdriver to defend himself. He further testified the victim threatened physical injury to him on several previous occasions, and these threats caused the defendant to carry the sharpened screwdriver to defend himself. Other inmates testified they had seen the victim attack the defendant, and that the victim had a knife in his hand. They further testified that the victim's knife had been knocked out of his hand early in the fight, and had slid across the floor among the crowd of inmates watching the fight. One witness testified he saw several of the inmates kick the knife further back into the crowd, where he lost sight of it.

Pretrial investigation had indicated that cross-examination of the prosecution's witness would reveal the failure of the prison guards to make a complete investigation at the time of the killing, and the same pretrial fact-gathering suggested that defense witnesses would survive cross-examination. The combination resulted in the jury returning a verdict of not guilty.

Misrecollection

Misrecollection is common and natural with lay witnesses, but should be minimal with police witnesses. Usually the lay witness does not keep notes of what he saw or did at any particular time, and since the trial of a case may be delayed for months, it is not surprising that a lay witness will not recall clearly or accurately the things he heard, saw or did at the time of the crime. In fact, it is rather surprising when a lay witness is positive of events during his testimony several months after the experience, and it certainly raises a suspicion in the mind of the cross-examiner that the witness is filling in blank spots of memory with guesses or fabricated testimony. This is especially true of alibi witnesses who claim to positively recollect a certain date and time many months previously—and for no particular reason. It is strange how many crimes are committed on, or a day before or after, birthdays, anniversaries family reunions and the like. This linking of the day of a crime with a normally recalled day, of course, indelibly imprints the date and time of the defendant's presence in the mind of the alibi witness. The cross-examiner oftentimes finds it useful in cross-examining a lay witness to question him about his recollection of events closely related in time to the witness's main testimony. Thus, in one trial, the defendant had testified on direct examination to being at a certain place at a specific time (the precise time of the crime). After several questions by the prosecutor on cross-examination directed to his memory of other dates and times closely related, but which he could not recall, the defendant finally blurted out "Okay! You've made your point."

The police witness should not have this recollection weakness. His job requires field note-taking and the preparation of reports of his investigation, and he is expected to have reviewed these memoranda before testifying, or he can use them on the witness stand to refresh his recollection. Unfortunately, all investigators do not make complete notes, or do not use their notes to refresh their recollection. This weakness has often been exploited by alert defense attorneys during cross-examination to discredit the police witness.

A case in point resulted from police efforts to curtail the incidence of theft from semiconscious intoxicated persons (drunk-rolling) in an area of a northern California community frequented by transients and ranch workers. The police technique in this campaign was to assign an officer to simulate a drunk lying in the doorway of a building, but in view from the sidewalk, thus enticing persons with a predilection for drunk-rolling to believe a victim was available. These "undercover" techniques usually resulted in the arrest of fifty or sixty drunk-rollers over a period of several weeks. Of course, the details of each of the theft attempts and of the arrests would be essentially similar. To the undercover police officer these arrests became routine, and he neglected the opportunity to refresh his mind on the facts of a specific case. In the course of defending one of these defendants at trial, defense counsel embarked on a line of cross-examination directed at the arresting officer's recollection of this particular offense. During that examination it was discovered the officer had made over fifty arrests in this police campaign against these thefts in a period of just over two weeks, and that he had not made detailed notes of each arrest and its circumstances. A conscientious officer, this witness admitted that it was quite possible that some of his recollections on this case may have been, in fact, recollections of one of the other cases he had during this two-week period.

This cross-examination ruined the state's case, and it was not an attack on the willingness of the officer to testify truthfully, but on the fact his testimony did not truly represent the recall from memory of the facts of the case regarding the accused person on trial.

Another example of the potential of cross-examination in creating reasonable doubt in the minds of jurors occurred during the third trial of Barry Sigal for homicide in Sacramento. Cross-examination of a police officer developed an entirely unexpected misrecollection which was used to cast doubt on the police investigation. Since this was a case in which the prosecution based their case primarily on circumstantial evidence, any attack on the credibility of police witnesses tended to impeach the entire chain of circumstantial evidence. One of a series of incriminating circumstances paraded in court by the prosecution in the Sigal trial was the fact that the keys to the victim's car were missing, although she usually kept them in her purse. Testimony at previous trials, and by the victim's daughter at the trial, established the fact that the purse had been found, but had not been processed ("dusted") for fingerprints or retained as evidence by the police. The police left this purse with the victim's daughter on the night the homicide was discovered and the preliminary investigation conducted.

Aware of these facts and their potential legal significance, defense counsel probed this area during the course of cross-examining the investigating officer. In inquiring about a number of items of physical evidence at the death scene, defense counsel secured several admissions from this witness regarding items of evidence which had not been retained or examined by the investigating team. The line of inquiry and the responses of this police witness, and the resultant damage to the state's case, can be best presented by detailing both questions and answers of this cross-examination:

Q. Glasses. There was a pair of glasses on the floor?
A. Part of a . . . .
Q. Excuse me, sir. Was there a pair of glasses on the floor?
A. Yes, sir.
Q. Eye glasses?
A. Yes, sir.
Q. Did you retain these glasses as evidence?
A. Yes, sir. I think we did.
Q. Do you still have them, sir?
A. No, I don't.
Q. Do you know where they are?
A. No, sir.
Q. Do you know what happened to them?
A. No, sir, I don't.
Q. Are you sure you did retain them?

A. No, sir. At this stage I am not.

Q. You have refreshed your recollection, I assume, before coming to court here, haven't you?

A. Yes, I have.

Q. Now, was there a part of an earring on the floor?

A. Yes, sir.

Q. Did you retain that?

A. I think I did. I think we did.

Q. You're not sure?

A. No, sir.

Q. Do you still have it?

A. I don't know.

Q. Have you ever looked?

A. No, I haven't.

Q. Did you put it on your reports that you had retained that?

A. I can't recall that I read about, that we retained it.

Q. Well, you were doing the investigating, weren't you?

A. A portion of it, yes, sir.

Q. And you were doing the searching?

A. Not within the apartment itself, within the victim's apartment. I was searching elsewhere.

Q. But you did search in the victim's apartment, didn't you? You found the red washcloth?

A. Yes, I did. Within the victim's bedroom specifically, I didn't do, what I meant to say, counsel.

Q. It was what?

A. Within the victim's bedroom I did not do the major part of the searching.

Q. That was Mr. M——?

A. True.

Q. You don't know whether he retained the earring or not, do you?

A. That is true.

Q. You do not?

A. No, sir.

Q. And you did not retain the glasses, did you?

A. I personally did not, no, sir.

Q. And you don't know that Mr. M—— did, do you?

A. No.

Q. And you two were the ones who were doing that sort of thing, weren't you?

A. Yes, sir.

Q. There weren't any other detectives there who were gathering evidence, were there?

A. No.

Q. Was there a towel on the floor?

A. Yes, sir, there was.

Q. Where was the towel?

A. In relation to the body, I don't know.

Q. You don't know?

A. I don't remember.

Q. I assume you did look at things in the bedroom, did you?

A. I looked at them, yes, sir.

Q. And you've refreshed your recollection before coming here?

A. I didn't view any photographs to refresh my recollection.

Q. Was it near the body, the towel?

A. The best that I can recall, yes, it was.

Q. Did you look at the towel at all to see if it had any red substance on it?

A. Yes, sir.

Q. Did it have some red substance on it?

A. Yes, sir.

Q. Did you retain the towel?

A. No, I didn't.

Q. Any particular reason why you did not retain that towel?

A. Yes.

Q. What?

A. I thought the Coroner's office was going to take it.

Q. Didn't the Coroner's office leave before you did?

A. Yes, they did.

Q. Obviously they didn't take it.

A. That's right.

Q. And you decided not to take it?

A. Apparently not, sir.

Q. Even though it had the red substance on it?

A. Right.

Q. Did you find the purse?

A. Yes, there were numerous purses in the closets.

Q. They were on a shelf in the closet?

A. Right.

Q. Did you look through every purse?

A. Yes, sir.

Q. Did you retain any of the purses?

A. Yes.

Q. As evidence?

A. Well, temporarily.

Q. How temporarily, Mr. S———?

A. Until they was dusted for latent prints.

Q. What did you do with—how many purses did you dust? Did you dust them?

A. No, sir, I didn't.

Q. Well, how long did you hold those purses? How long did you retain them as evidence, a day, two days, a week?

A. Long enough to determine whether they were of any evidentiary value.

Q. Well, yes, but how long was it that you retained them, a day, a week, a month?

A. I'll say from a day to a week, until the task was accomplished. We took the purse to the Bureau of Identification.

Q. You took the purse to the Bureau of Identification?

A. Yes.

Q. You did personally?

A. Yes.

Q. What kind of a purse was it?

A. It was a black plastic purse.

Q. And black shiny patent leather?

A. Yes, sir.

Q. Did you take any other purse?

A. No, sir.

Q. When you found this purse it was right up with all the other purses, isn't that right?

A. That is correct, sir.

Q. Did you take it and show it to Mrs. Young?

A. Matter of fact, she was there and she pointed it out.

Q. She pointed the purse out to you?

A. As the one that was being currently used by the victim.

Q. You had left it in the closet and she came to the closet and pointed it out, is that right?

A. Yes.

Q. And then did you take the purse out of the closet?

A. Yes, sir.

Q. What did you do with it then?

A. We took it to the Bureau of Criminal Identification.

Q. Here in the police station?

A. Yes, sir.

Q. Did you give it to Mrs. Young there to look through?

A. Well, I—no, I didn't hand it to her.

Q. Well, what happened?

A. She just opened it by the opening and looked through it.

Q. And you state you kept that purse several days, is that right?

A. No, I didn't keep it.

Q. Who did you turn it over to in the Bureau of Identification?

A. I can't recall.

Q. Who gave—what happened to it after the Bureau of Identification finished with it?

A. I think it was—I—I don't know.

Q. What?

A. I don't know. I don't know whether I took it back, gave it to someone. I just don't recall, counsel.

Q. Isn't it really a fact you didn't take it to the Bureau of Identification at all, that you gave it to Mrs. Young that night, and that you did not retain it at all as evidence? Isn't that really what the fact is, Mr. S———?

A. No, that purse was dusted for latents.[21]

Q. I didn't ask you that, sir. I asked you, isn't it a fact that you did not take that purse to the Bureau of Identification at all, that you gave it to Mrs. Young that night, the night you were investigating on the 12th of January, and you did not bring it into the police station at all? Isn't that really the fact?

A. No, that is not a fact.

Q. That is not a fact?

A. The fact, I did bring it to the Bureau of Identification.

Q. Who did you book it in with?

A. I didn't book it.

Q. Why, isn't that your usual procedure?

A. Well—

Q. Whenever—

A. Not necessarily.

Q. Whenever you have evidence, don't you make out a report on the evidence that you retain and book in or take?

A. If you feel it's really of any value, why, certainly you do.

Q. In other words, there is some evidence or so-called evidence you take into the police station which you do not make out a receipt on?

A. Yes—yes, sir.

Q. And there is some evidence or some articles that you do not indicate in any way that they were ever retained by the police?

A. That is true, sir.

Q. Why?

A. Well—

Q. If they were retained by the police, why?

A. If they are retained—

Q. Yes.

A. Then they are of some value as evidence.

Q. And you made no record of this at all?

A. No, I don't think I did.

Q. You don't know who you gave it to?

A. I'm speaking—I don't know who dusted it and I don't know who I gave it to with respect to dusting it for latent prints.

Q. But you do remember that you are the one that transported that bag to the police department?

A. That is correct.

Q. And you did give it to somebody?

A. Yes, sir.

Q. But you don't know who it was, is that right?

A. That is right, I don't.

Q. No record of that bag being dusted, is there, in your files?

A. No, sir; no, sir.

Q. There's no record of anybody examining it for fingerprints in your files, is there?

A. Maybe there is. I don't know, there may be.

[21]"Latents" are fingerprints not readily visible.

Q. You've never seen one, have you?

A. Well, the report is about 200 pages, and there very well may be a record there.

Q. I asked you, you've never seen one, have you? You are the one that investigated this case, aren't you?

A. Not that I can recall at the present time.

Q. You never made one?

A. I'm not so sure that I didn't. I may have.

Q. Don't you even know the reports that you made, Officer?

A. Yes, I do. I do the majority of them. This is just a questionable one.

Q. Now, sir—

A. I made them four years ago, and I didn't look through all of it. I thought I looked through all of them, but I feel that someone had dusted this purse, that the Sacramento Police Department should have made a report on it.

Q. Should have, it that right?

A. Right.

Q. And if it wasn't—

A. With respect to this person making the report, it could have been an oversight.

Q. You never saw any such report, did you?

A. I haven't recently, no sir.

Q. If I were to tell you, Officer S———, that Mrs. Young just today was on this witness stand and testified that that purse was not taken out of her apartment, would this change your mind at all?

A. Out of Mrs. McAfee's apartment.[22]

Q. Yes.

A. Well, it could, yes.

Q. All right, think back now, Mr. S———. Did you actually personally take that purse to the police station?

A. Yes, I did, but I don't know when. This is my problem.

Q. You don't know when?

A. I think I've said that two or three times. Just as to when I did that task, I don't know.

Q. Let me ask you this. Did you give it to Mrs. Young as she said that night?

A. Possible.

Q. Well then, when did you again recover it from her, a week later, a day later, a month later, two months later, two years later, ten years later, or what?

A. Oh, two weeks later. I'm guessing now.

Q. Are you telling me or are you asking me?

A. Well, you asked me a question. To the best of my knowledge I'm answering it.

Q. Then you got it from her two weeks after this, after the 12th, is that the best recollection?

A. I think I better not—I don't know, is what I'm going to stick to.

[22]Mrs. McAfee was the victim in this case.

Q. Well, are you telling us now you don't know anything about that purse?

A. Yes, I know a few things about it. I won't say anything. That's a broad statement.

Q. But some time after the 12th, maybe a week or two weeks later, you got the purse back again some time afterwards?

A. Yes.

Q. And was it at that time that you took it in to get the fingerprints tested?

A. I don't—I don't remember that.

Q. You just don't remember, Mr. S——, is that right?

A. That's right.

Q. You recall testifying at the last trial in 1964 in April, don't you, sir?

A. Yes, sir, I do.

Q. Let me call your attention to page 344 of the transcript and ask you to read lines 11 through 18.

THE COURT: He's read it, counsel.

MR. WELLS: Thank you, your Honor.

Q. Do you remember these questions being asked and you giving these answers?

A. Yes, sir, I do.

Q. (Reading)   "Q. Did you examine—how many purses did you see?
            A. Several.
            Q. You don't remember how many?
            A. Exact number, no, sir.
            Q. Did you examine each of those purses?
            A. Yes, sir.
            Q. Did you retain any of those purses as evidence?
            A. No, sir, I did not."

Q. Those questions were asked and those answers given?

A. Yes, sir, they were.

These extracts of an investigating officer's testimony under cross-examination should illustrate the fact that the failure of a witness to refresh his recollection can severely injure the prosecution's case, and give a defense counsel (who has not only refreshed his mind by a review of all available data, but who has also researched several areas in which the police failed to follow standard operating procedures) a windfall which could easily affect the final outcome of the case at trial.

Bias and Interest

Bias is often present in lay witnesses' testimony. It may originate in personal experiences of the witness, or reflect his interest in the victim or defendant, or some other person involved in this case. However, a policeman as a witness is not expected to have any bias or interest. The police witness can never let any bias or interest in the case color his testimony. If he does, a skilled cross-examiner will probe it, uncover it in some fashion and use it to discredit the witness. Although the example in the Sigal case of damaging cross-examination has been attributed to misrecollection, there is the possibility that professional pride (which can be a form of bias) played a part in the officer's testimony under cross-examination. Sometimes it's difficult not to relate interest in the outcome of a case to the pride of a police witness in the accuracy of an investigation. This desire not to admit faulty procedures, or failures to perform well, has at times caused an investigating officer to color or exaggerate his testimony. Cross-examination can elicit inconsistencies in the officer's own testimony, or inconsistencies with other testimony or with physical facts. It may even develop inconsistencies with the officer's own reports or field notes, both available to the cross-examiner. Once caught up in such inconsistencies, the same pride that conceived them often bars a ready admission of mistake or error, and an officer ends up confused, angry and discredited—and the prosecutor may be unable to rehabilitate him upon redirect examination.

While a civilian witness may be expected to have some bias or interest, it is not expected to be of such character as to indicate an unusual motivation to testify falsely. Several years ago, in the trial of a prison inmate accused of the brutal and fatal stabbing of his cellmate, the prosecutor produced an inmate witness to testify the defendant threatened the victim only two days before the slaying. The issue in the trial was whether the defendant committed the killing, which he had consistently denied. On cross-examination, it was developed that this inmate witness of the prosecution knew the victim and was, in fact, very friendly with the victim. In a detailed probing of the relationship between the victim and the witness, it was brought out that the relationship was more than friendly and is better described as an intimate relationship. Cross-examination disclosed the witness was an active homosexual and tended to show an unnatural relationship between witness and victim, indicating an interest of the witness in the outcome of the case. This fact was helpful in destroying the effect of his testimony. This cross-examination, together with other evidence, caused a jury to acquit the defendant despite evidence that the victim and the defendant had been locked in their cell for over an hour prior to discovery of the fatal attack!

Deceit

The deliberate lie with intent to deceive is rarely shown during the course of a criminal trial. Usually, the inconsistencies and conflicts of evidence may be reasonably explained by misrecollection or mistake, even though these forays with deception may be explained equally well by terming them wilful misstatements. In the trial noted immediately above, where the bias of the homosexual inmate witness was pointed out on cross-examination, a correctional officer testified (on direct examination by the prosecutor) that he had made a count of inmates after they were locked in their cells and that the procedure for such count required the inmates to be standing at their cell doors with a hand on the cell door bars. If true, this testimony would show that it was impossible for anyone but the defendant to have stabbed the victim, because it showed the victim unhurt at the time of this "standing" count, and the cell doors were continually locked from the time of this count of inmates until the victim was discovered dying of multiple stab wounds. The important portion of the direct examination was as follows:

> A. (Prosecutor) Now, as you made your count on the fifth tier of C section of the number one building last January 28, shortly before five in the afternoon, did you have occasion to go by cell 974?
> A. I did.
> Q. And can you tell us what, if anything, you saw when you went by there?
> A. Well, *the count is a standing count*,[23] and both inmates Miller and Pope were standing up at the bars at the time of the count.

At the conclusion of the direct examination of this witness, defense counsel cross-examined him on all of his testimony except the testimony given on the critical period of the alleged stand-up count. The court allowed defense counsel's request to postpone further cross-examination until later in the prosecutor's case. The next day, the record of prison counts, and prison regulations regarding inmate counts, were subpoenaed by the defense. The prison regulations were found to have no provision for an inmate count at the time period mentioned. The prison record forms for inmate counts had no column for such a count. However, on two of the three days' records of counts returned under the subpoena, numerous figures were penciled in with red pencil and could have been the report of a count, but there were no penciled-in figures on the third day's record. The records of the first two days were unsigned by the officer in charge, the other record was signed. All inmates interviewed from that section of the prison denied any count at that time of day.

The witness was recalled for further cross-examination three days later. After a number of questions designed to test his recollection of what other inmates on that tier were doing or wearing, or if he knew of the actions of the inmates in a particular cell, the following exchange took place:

23Emphasis added.

Q. (Defense Counsel) You are sure inmate Bledson was in cell 1004?

A. Yes.

Q. What was Mr. Bledson wearing at five o'clock on the 28th?

A. I wouldn't venture to say, sir. I don't know.

Q. Who was Mr. Bledson's cell partner, if any?

A. I don't know what his name was. He had a cell partner.

Q. Now, sir, was Mr. Bledson on the right or the left of the door as you faced it at five o'clock?

A. Bledson was on the bunk, sir.

Q. Bledson was on the bunk? How is that?

A. Well, I don't know.

Q. Did you testify that this was a stand-up count?

A. No, I don't believe I did.

Q. Then this was not a stand-up count?

A. No, it was not.

Q. In other words, it is not a requirement that they stand?

A. That's correct.

Further cross-examination brought out that nothing about this count or about the witness seeing the victim and the defendant was placed in any official report. In addition, it was established that this witness had talked to a police captain and the prosecutor before being recalled to testify and was told about the records and regulations having been subpoenaed. The effect of this testimony damaged the state's case far beyond the mere discrediting of one witness.

The "Open Door" of Cross-Examination

The purpose of cross-examination is to discover truth. However, good attorneys will not "open the door," much less "peek," into an area of questioning unless they are fairly certain of the likely answers of the witness. Some years ago, present-Judge Hyman Barshay, a very capable trial lawyer, made this error in questioning coauthor Weston in a Brooklyn, New York, court. The case involved a "common gambler" charge against one of his clients. The prosecutor had fumbled the questioning which normally leads to the qualification of a police witness as an expert on gambling. The state's case alleged the defendant was "banking" a dice game (New York's "permanent, floating crap game") and the prosecutor had qualified Weston on direct examination as an expert on vice and gambling in general, but couldn't seem to phrase the question correctly that would qualify him as an expert on gambling with dice specifically. The judge, exasperated, announced he was only allowing one further question, and the prosecutor phrased a meaningless query. Counselor Barshay could have quit right there, but he wanted to finish the case off without doubt. Assuming that a 20-year police background would pre-clude any admission as to actually playing dice in a game for money, he asked on cross-examination: "Isn't it true, Inspector Weston, that you have never even played dice?" He was shocked and surprised when the answer was, "That isn't true, I have played dice." In response to Barshay's shocked inquiries as to "when," the information was given about playing in World War II dice games halfway across the world over a period of three years. The state now had qualified its expert—with an assist from defense counsel—and the jury voted a guilty verdict at the end of the trial.

Selected References

CASES

Griffin v. California, 380 U.S. 609 (1965).
A case that disallowed court or prosecutor to comment on a defendant's failure to testify at his trial, and which discusses the many implications the jurors may receive from testimony and comment upon it by the presiding judicial official.

Malloy v. Hogan, 378 U.S. 1 (1964).
An excellent discussion of the right of a defendant to refuse to answer questions. The majority opinion notes the American system of justice is accusatorial, not inquisitorial, and recognizes the basic right of an accused person to remain silent unless he chooses to speak and to suffer no penalty for such silence.

Murphy v. Waterfront Commission of New York Harbor, 378 U.S. 52 (1964).
In this case the privilege against self-incrimination was held to protect state witnesses against incrimination under federal law, and the federal government was noted as prohibited from using the testimony of witnesses who gave their testimony under state grants of immunity. The majority opinion contains a thorough review of the concepts of immunity and self-incrimination.

BOOKS

Fenlason, Anne F., *Essentials in Interviewing.* New York: Harper & Row, Publishers, 1962, 372 pages.
A basic book in the social sciences, this text provides an understanding of the interviewing techniques utilized by the skilled social worker and offers insight into the developing of a nondirective type of questioning.

Lake, Lewis W., *How to Cross-examine Witnesses Successfully.* Englewood Cliffs, N.J.: Prentice-Hall, Inc., 1957, 342 pages.

An excellent text for police students. An overview of the entire process of cross-examination.

O'Connor, Richard, *Courtroom Warrior*. Boston: Little, Brown and Company, 1963, 342 pages.

The life story of William Travers Jerome, the first of New York City's "fighting district attorneys," and a devastating cross-examiner. A well-researched exposition of the techniques of destroying defense witnesses in court. The text develops some fine basic principles in cross-examination against the background of one prosecutor's trials—and tribulations.

Rothblatt, Henry B., *Successful Techniques in the Trial of Criminal Cases*. Englewood Cliffs, N.J.: Prentice-Hall, Inc., 1961, 242 pages.

An unusual text about trial strategy and tactics for the successful defense of accused persons in criminal proceedings. A particularly fine section on cross-examination.

Wellman, Francis L., *The Art of Cross-Examination* (4th ed.). New York: Collier Books, 1962, 476 pages.

This book was first published by The Macmillan Company in 1903, and has appeared in four editions and fifty printings since publication. It is an undisputed classic that contains extensive transcripts of actual testimony in which cross-examination proved to be a vital factor in overcoming potentially adverse testimony. Cross-examination is defined as a means of "catching truth," by furnishing an in-court means of destroying false testimony. The "Collier's" edition is in paperback form.

ARTICLES

Appleman, John Alan, "Cross-Examining for the Jury," *The Brief Case*, 24, No. 2 (December 1965), pp. 84–90.

Appleman reviews some general principles of cross-examination and lists as its primary purposes: to destroy or minimize testimony, to destroy the witness as a witness or as a person, to destroy or damage other testimony of the adversary party and to build up a favorable witness. This author also points out that many jurors identify with witnesses and warns of unnecessary cross-examination because of its possible alienation of jurors.

Bellows, Charles A., "Cross-Examination of Prosecution Witnesses in a Circumstantial Evidence Murder Case," *The Trial Lawyer's Guide* (February 1964), pp. 19–41.

A fine resume of successful cross-examination techniques, and profitable reading for a greater understanding of skills used to destroy the credibility of witnesses.

10

The Trial of Offenders

The earliest history of trial by adversary dates back to the neighborhood courts of the early Middle Ages. The two contending parties were neighbors, and court officials served mainly as referees in a complicated medieval religious-legal ritual. Each party had to state his case under oath, and doubts as to the guilt or innocence of the accused person were resolved by either compurgation or ordeal.

Neighbors would be asked to serve as compurgators and swear to the innocence of the accused person. If a sufficient number of neighbors did not come forward, or could not be found, it was concluded that the defendant was guilty. In one type of ordeal, the accused person was forced to carry a red-hot iron a certain distance. If healing was quick, the defendant was innocent. If infection set in, it was assumed the accused was guilty. Justice was swift, and both compurgation and ordeal may have had merit. In the close neighborhood of the Middle Ages, local knowledge of guilt probably worked against a guilty defendant securing enough compurgators to attest his innocence; and the worried mind of the guilty might have had a psychosomatic effect upon infection.

The modern criminal proceeding, termed the trial of an offender, is also a complicated affair which gets under way with the selection of a jury or the decision to waive jury trial, and can conclude anywhere from this point to the time a verdict is reached. Trials may end upon motion of either side, at the court's direction or upon the jury reaching a verdict, or the judge announcing his verdict in trials without a jury.

Trials in the United States adhere to the following outline:

1. Jury selection, empanelling and administration of oath.
2. Opening by both sides (statement, facts only).
3. The state's case.
4. The defense case.
5. Rebuttal (State).
6. Surrebuttal (Defense).
7. Closing by both sides (argument).
8. Charge to the jury (instructions of law).
9. Verdict.
10. Judgment.

There's a partnership in a criminal trial. It is so planned. The assigning of a skilled attorney as a prosecutor to guide the state's case (the "people") is matched by the handling of the defense case by a person of equal attainments. It is a "fight theory"[1] and as long as the adversaries are of equal competency, partisan advocacy develops for each side an effective presentation of their case. The adversary method trusts that in ensuing courtroom scrimmages right will prevail; each side is expected to bolster its own case and demolish its opponent's contentions.[2]

It has been said that a function of prosecutors should be the attempt to save the innocent as well as prosecute the guilty; but when a case gets to the trial stage, the prosecutor has eliminated any potential of innocence and is striving to prove the guilt of the accused person. This is his adversary role in the administration of justice. It has also been said that a defense counsel should never fight to win when he knows a client is guilty, but "guilt" is a jury's or court's determination of the criminal proceeding. Therefore, at any time up to the verdict stage, the defense counsel is fighting to win, as is the prosecutor. And even when there is a "guilty" tag affixed to his client at the end of a trial, a defense counsel may refuse to concede guilt and continue to fight by appropriate motions and appeals.

[1]Jerome Frank, *Courts on Trial* (Princeton, N.J.: Princeton University Press, 1949), p. 80.
[2]Beruard Botein and Murray A. Gordon, *The Trial of the Future* (New York: Simon and Schuster, Inc., 1963), p. 27.

Jurisdictional Territory

Jurisdiction is the power, right or authority of a court to act. Original jurisdiction is held by the court with the power to hear and determine a criminal action in the first instance; concurrent jurisdiction exists when either of two courts may hear and dispose of the proceeding. Trial jurisdiction is the power to try issues of fact; appellate jurisdiction is the power to review cases forwarded from lower courts.

Jurisdiction by subject matter relates to the type of criminal action over which a court has the power, right or authority to act. Some states empower lesser courts to hear, try and determine cases at the misdemeanor level, and reserve felony prosecutions for superior or county courts. The most common division of the work of a court system by subject matter is the assignment of trial jurisdiction to one court, and appellate jurisdiction to another.

A competent court for the trial of a criminal action means any court, the subject matter jurisdiction of which includes the offense charged in the accusatory pleading, and having the territorial jurisdiction required by law. The words "jurisdictional territory," when used in reference to a court, mean the county, city or township; or other limited territory, over which the criminal jurisdiction of such court extends, as provided by law and in case of a superior court mean the county in which such court sits.[3]

Generally, the jurisdiction of every crime and public offense prosecuted under the laws of a state is in any competent court within the jurisdictional territory of which it is committed. The exceptions to this general rule depend upon the nature of certain crimes or their location. In many cases, a "joint" or "concurrent" jurisdiction will exist and the place of trial may be determined by the interests of justice, or the convenience of the counties involved. Jurisdiction is first a matter of law; then it is largely a matter of administration. Budgets are limited in all agencies concerned with law enforcement, and crimes originating in other counties are considered a statistical and moral, and budget, responsibility of the "home" county; this is usually the jurisdiction in which the crime was committed.

All states have complex laws regarding the jurisdiction of numerous crimes. These legislative efforts to bring offenders to account are usually aimed at providing jurisdictional territory in a geographic area in which witnesses and other evidence could be easily assembled, and in which a prosecutor would be willing to prosecute because of the local nature of the crime. This extraterritoriality usually is assigned to areas in which acts are done in furtherance of the crime, a feloniously assaulted person

[3]California Penal Code, Section 691.

dies or such person's body is found, or a crime is committed on a public means of transit. Concurrent jurisdiction is assigned to any of the involved jurisdictional territories when the crime is committed in more than one jurisdictional territory, within 500 yards of the boundary between two such geographic areas or in which any part of a public park or recreation area is located. Jurisdiction in cases such as bigamy, incest, slander and illegal prizefighting, in which it is difficult to isolate the major act of committing a crime or to develop a prosecutor's interest in a case, has even been assigned to the jurisdictional territory in which the victim resides or the perpetrator is apprehended.[4]

Change of Venue

Venue is the territorial jurisdiction in which a case is to be heard. Under normal circumstances, a case is heard by a competent court in the territorial jurisdiction in which the crime occurred or in which specific provisions of law permit it to be tried. However, a criminal action may be removed before trial from the court in which it is pending on the ground that a fair and impartial trial cannot be had in the original territorial jurisdiction.

At all government levels, the basis for concern and action by the courts is the "fair trial" aspects of the due process clause in the Fourteenth Amendment of the U.S. Constitution. The issue is usually raised by a defense motion for a change of venue. It may be based on extensive news coverage in the pretrial period destroying a defendant's opportunity for a fair trial or for some other good and sufficient reason.[5]

In California, a change of venue may be requested by a defendant in any case pending before a superior court on the ground that a fair and impartial trial cannot be had in the county; and the court may, of its own motion or on petition of any of the parties to a criminal proceeding, order a change of venue to an adjoining county whenever it appears as a result of the exhaustion of all the jury panels called that it will be impossible to secure a jury to try the cause in the original county.[6]

The application for the removal of the criminal action before trial must be made in open court, in writing and verified by the affidavit of the defendant. A copy of this application must be served upon the district attorney at least one day prior to the hearing of the application, and this public official may serve and file whatever counter affidavits he

[4]*Ibid.*, Sections 777–795.
[5]*Rideau v. Louisiana*, 373 U.S. 723 (1963).
  Irvin v. Dowd, 366 U.S. 717 (1961).
  Beck v. Washington, 369 U.S. 541 (1962).
  Sheppard v. Maxwell, 384 U.S. 333 (1966).
[6]California Penal Code, Sections 1033 and 1033.5.

deems advisable. The defendant may have an attorney make this application, without appearing personally and notwithstanding the charge pending against him being a felony, if the affidavit of the defendant shows that he can not safely appear in person because popular prejudice might endanger his personal safety.[7]

If the court in which the action was pending is satisfied that the representations of the defendant are true, an order must be made transferring the action to the proper court of a county free from the same objection. An order of removal must be entered upon the minutes of the court, and the clerk must immediately make out and transmit to the court to which the action is removed a certified copy of the order of removal, pleadings, and proceedings in the action, including the undertakings for the defendant's appearance, and of any witnesses. If the defendant is in custody, the order of removal must direct his transfer to the custody of the sheriff of the county in which the action is removed. All costs accruing upon such removal and subsequent trial are charged against the county in which the indictment was found or the information filed.[8]

The court to which a criminal action is removed must proceed to trial and judgment as if the action had been commenced there. If it is necessary to have any of the original pleadings or other papers, the court from which the action is removed must order such papers or pleadings to be transmitted by the clerk, retaining a certified copy of such documents.[9]

Time Factor

Every defendant is entitled to a speedy trial, and it must be commenced before the passage of time outlaws it, without unnecessary delay within the time limits established by law; valid postponements are possible and an insane person can receive a stay of proceedings until declared sane.

STATUTE OF LIMITATIONS

This requirement is concerned with laws prohibiting the prosecution of criminal charges after the expiration of a stated period of time from the completion of a crime, or sometimes its discovery. These laws can be

[7]*Ibid.*, Section 1034.
[8]*Ibid.*, Sections 1035–1037 and 1039–1039.1.
[9]*Ibid.*, Section 1038.

tolled[10] upon the finding of an indictment or proof of absence from the state in which the offense was committed and the prosecution is pending. The time limit in many states for misdemeanors is only one year; felonies may have a span of two or more years; while murder and frauds by public officials or against the government are not included within the statute of limitations. In California, the limit is one year for misdemeanors, and the following limits for felonies: (1) no limit for murder, embezzlement of public moneys or falsification of public records; (2) six years for the acceptance of a bribe by a public official or public employee; and (3) three years for any other felony.[11]

TIME FOR TRIAL

In ordering criminal actions to trial, the first step is a listing in the calendar[12] by the clerk of the court, and the second is an order of procedure. This order usually places felony cases ahead of misdemeanor cases, and actions in which the defendant is still in custody ahead of those in which the accused person has been released on bail. However, many jurisdictions follow California's example of giving top priority to cases in which a minor is the victim of the crime or is detained as a material witness in the case.[13]

After a plea, a defendant in California is entitled to at least five days to prepare for trial, and the trial court will set the date for trial not later than thirty days after the date of the defendant's plea. A defendant is entitled to a dismissal of the pending action, unless good cause to the contrary is shown, when an information is not filed against him within 15 days after being held to answer in a preliminary hearing; he is not brought to trial in a superior court within 60 days after the finding of the indictment or filing of the information, or the granting of a new trial; or he is not brought to trial in an inferior court in a misdemeanor case within 30 days, if in custody, or 45 days if released on a written promise to appear in court. The time for trial may be extended by the consent of the defendant or some mitigating circumstance.[14]

A request for a greater postponement of the criminal action is judged on its merits. The procedure for a continuance, past the statutory limit, begins with a motion and may progress to affirmative proof in open court in the form of an affidavit or the sworn testimony of witnesses. The essen-

---

[10]The time factor halted.
[11]*Ibid.*, Sections 799–803.
[12]A list of pending cases, sometimes termed a "docket."
[13]California Penal Code, Section 1048.
[14]*Ibid.*, Sections 1049–1050 and 1382.

tials of this motion are: (1) the ends of justice require a continuance; (2) the party seeking the continuance has exercised due diligence in trial preparation to locate and obtain the attendance of absent witness or witnesses (specific examples of such diligence are required); (3) that such witness or witnesses are absent, substitutes would not suffice, and the attendance of the absent witness or witnesses can be secured at the trial if a continuance is granted as requested; and (4) a listing of the probable testimony of the absent witness or witnesses, the fact that it is not just cumulative evidence, and that it is necessary, material and competent evidence.

A continuance may also be sought in the absence of counsel for either party to the proceeding. Unforeseen illness, the participation by one of the attorneys involved in another trial or the plea by either attorney that despite due diligence he has been unable to adequately prepare for the trial are all occasions for a motion for a continuance. However, defendants who change their counsel just before trial in a desperate attempt to gain a delay are likely to find a motion for continuance denied, with the court commenting: "Get on with it."

PRESENT STATUS OF INSANITY

If at any time during the pendency of a criminal action, prior to judgment, a doubt arises as to the sanity of the defendant, the court must order the questions as to his sanity to be determined by a trial—without a jury, or with a jury if a trial by jury is demanded. In California, such order acts as a stay of proceedings, suspending the action until the question of the sanity of the defendant has been determined. The trial jury may be discharged or retained, according to the discretion of the court, until the determination of the issue of insanity. If the defendant is found sane, the trial proceeds in its normal order; if the defendant is adjudged to be insane, the trial or judgment must be delayed until he becomes sane, with the court committing the defendant to a state hospital for the care and treatment of the insane, for necessary care and redelivery to the custody of the local sheriff when he becomes sane. If the court dismisses the criminal action prior to the defendant regaining his sanity, the commitment order remains in effect and the defendant is treated as any other mentally ill person.[15]

Counsel for the Defense

The Sixth Amendment to the Constitution assures the assistance of counsel, but it was often denied in past years at the time of trial on the

[15]*Ibid.*, Sections 1367–1375.

grounds that public funds did not permit the assignment of counsel except in very serious felony cases. This is difficult to understand when the very concept of a trial in American courts is based on an adversary proceeding where it is vital to the outcome of the criminal action to have legal assistance of competency equal to the prosecutor.

It is probably for this reason that the U.S. Supreme Court's decision in *Gideon v. Wainwright*[16] received acceptance throughout the United States. In this case, the majority opinion of the court noted the Constitution entitled a defendant to an attorney, and that a defendant who could not afford an attorney had his chances to a fair trial jeopardized. Indigent defendants comprise the great majority of criminal defendants, and this decision orders all courts in this country to provide attorneys for such persons without charge, whether or not they plead guilty or stand trial. Clarence Gideon, when arraigned on a felony breaking-and-entering charge in a Florida state court, stated he was without funds for legal counsel and asked the court to appoint an attorney for him. The court said it regretted that Florida criminal procedure required a denial of his request for counsel as the case was not a capital offense. Under protest, Gideon conducted his own defense, was found guilty and sentenced to five years imprisonment. The U.S. Supreme Court, in its decision in *Gideon*, stated the right to counsel at trial was so fundamental that it was obligatory upon the states by the Fourteenth Amendment of the Constitution to provide counsel when a defendant could not afford to hire an attorney for his defense, saying:

> The right of one charged with crime to counsel may not be deemed fundamental and essential to fair trials in some countries, but it is in ours. From the very beginning, our state and national constitutions and laws have laid great emphasis on procedural and substantive safeguards designed to assure fair trials before impartial tribunals in which every defendant stands equal before the law. This noble ideal cannot be realized if the poor man charged with crime has to face his accusers without a lawyer to assist him.

This doctrine of the *Gideon* case has now been extended to indigent defendants upon the trial of misdemeanors. The Fifth U.S. Court of Appeals ruled in *Harvey v. Mississippi*[17] that defendants charged with this lesser grade of crime were also entitled to legal assistance as noted in the Sixth Amendment to the U.S. Constitution, since the minor nature of the charges of crime did not assure a fair trial before an impartial tribunal unless the defendant had a lawyer to assist him.

[16]372 U.S. 335 (1963).
[17]340 F 2nd 263 (1965).

Mode of Trial

An issue of fact arises upon a plea of not guilty, of a former conviction or acquittal of the same offense, of once in jeopardy or of not guilty by reason of insanity.[18] Issues of fact are tried by jury, but such jury trial may be waived in all criminal cases, by the consent of both parties, expressed in open court by the defendant and his counsel.

Our founding fathers believed in trial by jury as a safeguard against the unjust use of police power. John Dickinson described the jury as "one of the cornerstones of liberty." Alexander Hamilton, in commenting on the Constitutional Convention, remarked that the assembly looked upon trial by jury as a valuable safeguard to liberty and a means to protect free government. There is no such guarantee of trial by jury upon a trial for local laws, for minor offenses such as public intoxication or disorderly conduct. In these "petty offenses" a proceeding in criminal court can be without a jury.

Classically, any less (or more) than 12 persons on the jury while it is deliberating is an error. States can lower this figure, but it is infrequent, and then usually for the trial of lesser crimes. California's basic law requires a jury to consist of 12 persons in felony cases, but in cases of misdemeanor the jury may also consist of 12 persons or of any number less than 12 upon which the parties may agree in open court.[19] To preserve this classic requirement for an even dozen jurors, the "alternate juror" was initiated. Up to four, but usually only two, jurors are picked from the same panel as the regular jurors and examined in the same manner. They sit in the jury box during the trial and have the rights and privileges of other jurors. Their major purpose is to serve as replacements for jurors who are unable to continue because of illness or other disability. Years ago, the jury had to be dismissed and a new trial ordered when a juror became sick or disabled in some manner, and though the trial could continue if the defense waived its right to a 12-man jury verdict, this waiver depended on the approval of the defense counsel. Now, with alternate jurors, the changeover is made smoothly when necessary; and if not necessary, the alternate jurors are dismissed at the time the jury retires to deliberate upon its verdict.

The unanimity requirement is probably one of the dynamics of the jury system. A U.S. District Court case[20] was reversed because a 10-2 verdict was in violation of the constitutional guarantee of due process. However, because of the expense involved when a judge must order a

[18]California Penal Code, Section 1041.
[19]Constitution of the State of California, Article I, Section 7.
[20]*Hibdon v. U.S.*, 204 F 2nd 834 (1953).

mistrial in the case of a hung jury,[21] several states now provide for less than a 12-0 verdict (five-sixths, usually) in certain types of offenses.

A defendant can waive a jury trial. However, a great deal depends upon the specific wording of the state constitutional provision relating to jury trials. Such waiver must be approved by the court, usually requires acquiescence by the prosecutor, and is not a "right." Such waivers are usually made only when the trial is complex or public prejudice is feared (but cannot be proven up to a level commensurate with being awarded a change of venue), or because the effect upon the jury of the details of a revolting crime is feared. It has also been hinted that the behavior of judges is more predictable than juror behavior. Judges, with their technical training and the sedative effect of years of being exposed to the seamy and sordid details of many crimes, are expected to better understand the complexities of a case and have a higher threshold to prejudice and shock than a member of the community called to jury duty.

A jury is a small part of the community transported to the courtroom, and as a pseudo-random selected sample of the universe of the community it should respond to what it sees and hears in the courtroom in the same manner as the community. Its reactions to the evidence in a case should not deviate meaningfully from the reactions of the entire community to similar stimuli. This factor brings to American law enforcement its unusual flexibility. The "heart" of the community is not in the enforcement of some laws, either because of the nature of the crime or some mandatory sentencing provision, and a jury's verdict will often reflect this community dissatisfaction with the law. There is no doubt that legal purists will rebel at the concept of a jury nullifying legislation —but the creed of proof beyond a reasonable doubt leaves a great deal of room for subliminal control of the mind of any juror.

Selecting the Jury

The well-known and highly recommended strategy of getting the "right" people on a jury sometimes threatens the confidence of reasonable people in the entire jury system. It's within the concept of trial by adversary and the constitutional guarantee of a fair trial, however, to seek jurors likely to be favorable to one side or the other in a legal proceeding. Ben W. Palmer, in his book, *Courtroom Strategies*, points out that the real value in an attorney having a hand in the selection of the jury is to keep off the jury persons deemed undesirable and to fill it with those individuals most likely to decide in "your favor and give you the kind of verdict you want."[22]

[21]A jury unable to agree within a reasonable time.
[22]Ben W. Palmer, *Courtroom Strategies* (Englewood Cliffs, N.J.: Prentice-Hall, Inc., 1959), p. 149.

Modern county governments have a "Commissioner of Jurors" who is charged with the responsibility of compiling lists of prospective jurors selected from among the county's citizenry. Certain qualifications are necessary for jury duty, and some occupations are exempt from such duty, though this exemption may be waived. A brief list of qualifications, causes for disqualification and the occupations are as follows:

Qualifications	Disqualified Persons	Exempt Occupations
1. Citizen, 21 and over.	1. Felon	1. Clergy
2. One year as county resident.	2. Convicted malfeasant	2. Attorneys
3. Full possession of all faculties.		3. Teachers
4. Know the English language.		4. Physicians
		5. Dentists
		6. Public officers

Previous jury duty within a year normally disqualifies a prospective juror, or at least puts him in the exempt class. Commissioners of jurors are usually empowered to remove names from lists, excuse exempt persons or postpone jury duty when the prospective juror shows good reasons for such request. However, many jurisdictions hold that the trial judge is the only person who may excuse a juror.

When the commissioner of jurors, or like official, summons a group of citizens to serve as jurors, the group is referred to as the "panel." Jury panels are frequently summoned to serve several "Parts" or "Terms" of the same court. In such instances, the clerk of the court will choose 12 or more of the panel by lot ("jury wheel") to report to a specified courtroom for a specific trial.

In New York City, to secure jurors with above-average intelligence the jury panel is selected from a list of citizens with high-paying occupations or professions. For this reason it has been nicknamed the "blue ribbon" jury and, at times, has earned the sobriquet of a "hanging jury."[23]

If the selection procedure is unfair to the defendant by the exclusion of certain races, religions or occupations from the list of jurors, or the panel itself, then the defense counsel has the right to "challenge the array"—to ask for a new and better panel because of systematic exclusion or other procedure which threatens the possibility of a fair trial for the defendant. This request is usually denied, but the defense attorney frequently reopens the question on appeal after judgment.

Assuming that the panel is acceptable, the trial judge will now group the prospective jurors in and around the jury box, and inform them of

[23]Fay v. New York, 332 U.S. 261 (1947).

the various aspects of jury duty and the procedures which will be followed in selecting a jury. He usually points out that no sense of rejection should be felt by any person if excused by attorneys for either side, as these excusals are part of the jury system which provides *both* sides with jurors as mutually satisfactory as possible.

Many attorneys believe it is desirable to address a few preparatory remarks to the entire panel of jurors. If this is possible, it is a time-saving device for discovering the members of the panel who are in any close relationship with the prosecutor or his staff, the victim or his family or some association with members of the police unit. Usually, it is left to the discretion of the assigned judge to determine whether or not this type of mass *voir-dire* examination is desirable; often, the judge will conduct this screening process. The opposing attorneys may request the excuse of individual jurors by the judge within the limitations of: (1) cause, and (2) the numerical limits of peremptory[24] challenges allowed each "side."

Challenges for cause are without limit, but they must be substantiated by the responses of the prospective juror to questioning by the prosecutor or defense counsel. It may be employment in an occupation in law enforcement, or in the trade or profession of the victim or offender; or a relationship to one of the parties in the case, the witnesses or the attorneys; or when a prospective juror admits to apprehension about his inability (or unwillingness) to join in a verdict based on the law (as it will be explained to him) and the facts of the case as presented during the trial. The judge—who has been presiding over the questioning—bases his decision on the prospective juror's responses, and his own belief as to whether a challenge for cause has been established.

Peremptory challenges are limited. In California, both sides are entitled to ten peremptory challenges in the trial of any offense other than one punishable by death or life imprisonment; and in the latter case, these challenges are doubled for each side. In cases in which two or more defendants are jointly tried for any felony or misdemeanor, California procedure provides for their use jointly of the normal allotment of these challenges and the separate exercise of five additional peremptory challenges for each defendant, and allows the prosecutor whatever additional peremptory challenges as are necessary to equal the number utilized by the group of defendants.

When the selection of the basic 12-member jury is completed, together with as many alternate jurors as permitted and deemed necessary, the judge will order the court clerk to swear in the jury to try the case. Juror's oaths differ from locality to locality, but a common oath reads:

24Dismiss without citing a cause.

You and each of you, do solemnly swear that you will well and truly try the cause now pending before this Court, and a true verdict render therein, according to the evidence and the instructions of the Court, so help you God?

Jury selection is the "Russian roulette" of the administration of justice. The interplay of opposing counsel at *voir-dire* examinations is an attempt to predict human behavior, and it has many of the problems associated with any forecasting. There is little doubt it is the causative factor in many ulcer and coronary cases among members of the legal profession, but no trial attorney would suggest its discontinuance. It is keyed to the adversarial system, and many attorneys develop unusual skill in selecting jurors.

The Voir-Dire Examination

The process of questioning and challenging jurors may not appear to be a part of the trial, and technically the trial does not start until the jury is finally selected and sworn, but it is a formal procedure closely related to the trial. Opposing attorneys indulge in objections and exceptions and the presiding judge works as hard at his decisions at this time as during a trial. Examination is said to be on the prospective juror's "voir-dire"—a legal oath administered to prospective jurors and requiring true answers to questions regarding their qualifications as a juror.

The key to successful *voir-dire* examination is the skill at questioning which will establish the grounds upon which to base a challenge for cause. In this fashion, persons undesirable to one side can be kept from the jury, and the questioner can save his peremptory challenges for jurors he believes to be undesirable, but from whom he cannot fully develop grounds to challenge for cause. Of considerable assistance to defense counsel in this examination is a new type of service which has been initiated in many urban areas. This is the juror information service. It is one of the many legal services available in this country, and it is now allowing the defense attorney as well as the prosecution to know the background of a juror before the *voir-dire* examination is conducted. Previously, the defense counsel did not have the funds to conduct extensive investigation, though the prosecutor has always had ample staff to fully investigate the background of prospective jurors. This background investigation results in a standard report of employment, possible relationships with participants in the trial, previous participation in jury verdicts and other meaningful information.

Voir-dire examination is to discover prejudice and bias, but opposing attorneys make use of it to establish a few preliminary points of advantage. They have found this questioning of prospective jurors an excellent opportunity for: (1) conditioning the prospective juror for an unfavorable aspect of the case; (2) preparing him for the legal terminology and the constant "objecting" common in any trial; and (3) highlighting the elements of the law which are most favorable to his case. Questions along the following lines would develop these points:

> Q. The defendant may not testify. Now, do you promise that if you are selected as a juror you will determine the facts in this case and only the facts, and that you will follow the instructions in the judge's charge to the jury in relation to whether or not the defendant took the stand?
>
> Q. Objecting to a question is part of the rules laid down for the introduction of evidence. I would only object when I think my opponent is attempting something not quite proper; and to protect my client, I will rise and state my objection and its grounds. Do you understand that I do this to ensure a fair trial and not in any way to slow down the trial or harass my opponent?
>
> Q. Do you understand that in a crime of this nature it is necessary for the prosecution to produce evidence that touches upon every essential element of the crime?

Despite the fact that this is an early point in the procedure for trial, many attorneys will have the applicable sections of law listed for the time they will ask the judge to charge the jury relative to the law, and often seize this opportunity to preview the law in the case for the juror. However, it is the judge's discretion to allow *voir-dire* questions pertaining to points of law. Some judges are strict and will not permit this line of questioning; others are liberal in this area.

Diminished Responsibility

Diminished responsibility exists because of a defect in the individual which makes it difficult or impossible for him to form the necessary criminal intent. Any disability that prevents the mind from functioning with normal clarity has always been a defense to charges of crime. The laws of many states, and numerous court decisions, point up the fact that a crime must be the joint operation of mind and body, a criminal intent (*mens rea*) or criminal negligence and an act (*actus reus*). California's Penal Code[25] sums up this relationship in the following words: "In every crime or public offense there must exist a union, or joint operation of act and intent, or criminal negligence."

A person is presumed to intend the natural consequence of his acts.

[25]Section 20.

When defense counsel can offer sufficient evidence of mental incapacity to satisfy a trial court that a defendant is entitled to a finding of diminished responsibility, it is within the concept of justice to avoid "punishing" a sick person. A claim of diminished responsibility may now be based on insanity, the use of drugs with addicting liabilities, and the excessive use of alcohol.

INSANITY

The decision that an accused person or a defendant is not criminally accountable because of insanity is not a simple determination. The *M'Naghten* right-and-wrong rule was handed down in 1843.[26] Daniel M'Naghten was charged with the homicide of an innocent bystander named Edward Drummond during M'Naghten's attempt to kill Sir Robert Peel (founder of the first police force), and upon trial the medical testimony proved M'Naghten's mental disorder to be so great that he was incapable of distinguishing right from wrong. The jury returned a verdict of "not guilty on the grounds of insanity." The key words of this ancient but time-tested rule for testing insanity are:

> The jurors ought to be told in all cases that every man is to be presumed to be sane and to possess a sufficient degree of reason to be responsible for his crimes, until the contrary be proved to their satisfaction; and that to establish a defense on the ground of insanity, it must be clearly proved that, at the time of the commission of the act, the party accused was labouring under such a defect of reason, from a disease of the mind, as not to know the nature and quality of the act he was doing; or if he did know it, that he did not know he was doing what was wrong.[27]

The *Durham* rule is more liberal than *M'Naghten*, and is based on a District of Columbia case reviewed in the U.S. Court of Appeals, *Durham v. U.S.*[28] The petitioner, Monte Durham, was found guilty of burglary despite his defense that he was of unsound mind at the time of the crime. Durham's six-year history, during the period preceding this crime included the following: (1) discharge from the U.S. Navy because of a "personality disorder"; (2) hospitalization for an attempted suicide; (3) commitment to mental institutions by two juries as being of "unsound mind"; and (4) diagnosed psychiatrically as suffering from "psychosis with psychopathic personality." The court, in its decision in Durham's case, rejected the *M'Naghten* "right-wrong" test, saying that a person should not be held answerable for any criminal offense which he may commit if the jury finds beyond a reasonable doubt that he was suffering

[26]*Daniel M'Naghten Case*, 10 C&F 200 (1843).
[27]*Ibid.*
[28]214 F 2nd 862 (1954).

from a "diseased or defective mental condition" at the time of the commission of the criminal act and that this act was the "product" of such mental abnormality.

U.S. v. Currens is a 1961 case in the U.S. Court of Appeals,[29] and it developed what is now termed the "Currens Rule." It is more liberal than any previous doctrine in this area. In this case, the words of the court majority established a rule for extending diminished responsibility: "The jury must be satisfied that at the time of committing the prohibited act, the defendant, as a result of mental disease or defect lacked substantial capacity to conform his conduct to the requirements of the law which he is alleged to have violated." This ruling hews to the line of criminal intent and identifies an insane person as one without the capacity to form the necessary criminal intent.

The various rules regarding criminal responsibility as it may be mitigated by a defense of insanity may be summed up as: (1) the right-and-wrong test (M'Naghten); (2) the determination that the act done was the "product" of a "diseased and defective mental condition" (Durham); and (3) the coupling of substandard mental capacity brought on by mental disease or defect with a lack of the necessary criminal intent (Currens).

DRUG ADDICTION

An emerging question in the administration of justice is whether or not drug addicts, like insane persons, lack criminal responsibility? The crimes of the legally insane cannot be punished. The insane person is sick and not responsible for his or her acts. Since the decision of the U.S. Supreme Court in Robinson v. California,[30] drug addicts are also considered sick people. Drug addiction is an illness (likened to insanity, leprosy, venereal disease and the common cold). Robinson had been found guilty of a California law which rendered drug addiction a crime. It may be that drug addiction, by destroying the power to reason coherently, "pushes" a person into the commission of acts that would never occur if it were not for the illness of drug addiction. It may ruin the capacity of a person to determine right from wrong, or to understand the nature of his act or its consequences.

ALCOHOL USE

Another "status" criminal offense long known to police officers of many localities is "drunkenness" or "public intoxication." At the present time,

[29]290 F 2nd 751 (1961).
[30]370 U.S. 660 (1962).

a jury may take into consideration the fact that the accused was intoxicated at the time of the crime in determining whether or not the defendant's mind was so obscured by the alcohol as to make the accused person incapable of forming the necessary intent.[31] The jury may diminish criminal responsibility by finding the defendant guilty of a lesser degree of the crime or not guilty.

Defendants charged with murder in rage-killings are notorious for utilizing the claim that intoxication was a factor in the crime. Many police officers, first on the scene of one of these fatal assaults, have found the offender asleep. Arraignment of one New York City killer had to be postponed for three days after the crime because of the offender's inability to understand questions. Many of these offenders are "winos" whose mental processes appear to have been impaired by overuse of alcohol for extended time periods.

Some veteran employees in the administration of justice suspect that existing psychiatric examinations do not adequately probe the mind of the confirmed alcoholic. There has been definite evidence that many emotionally bankrupt people use alcohol almost without volition—it is often as involuntary as the taking of drugs by an addict. Therefore, if the U.S. Supreme Court describes the addiction to drugs as an illness and possibly a good and sufficient reason to limit criminal capacity for crime, it is possible that excessive use of alcohol may also be considered such an illness.

Control of the Trial

The judge has the duty to control all proceedings during a trial, and to limit the introduction of evidence and the argument of counsel to relevant and material matters, in order that the proceedings will be an expeditious and effective ascertainment of the truth regarding the matters involved.[32] The court, in its discretion, shall regulate the order of proof, except as otherwise provided by law, and may exclude evidence if its probative value is substantially outweighed by the probability that its admission will: (a) necessitate undue consumption of time, or (b) create substantial danger of undue prejudice, of confusing the issues, or of misleading the jury.[33]

The presumption of innocence is a true presumption, possibly better described as a *prima facie* presumption, or one that can be rebutted by adequate evidence; it is not in existence today because of any honest

[31]*People v. Conley*, 64 Cal. 2nd 321 (1966).
[32]California Penal Code, Section 1044.
[33]California Evidence Code, Chapters 3 and 4.

belief that accused persons who are brought before the bar of justice by sincere members of the police-prosecutor combination are, in fact, innocent. It exists today primarily to establish the formal order of proof.

In general, a party to a criminal action has the burden of proof for each fact whose existence or nonexistence is essential to the claim for relief or defense that he is asserting; the burden of producing evidence about a particular fact is initially on the party with the burden of proof as to that fact. California law specifies the burden of proof on specific issues as follows: (1) The party claiming that a person is guilty of crime or wrongdoing has the burden of proof on that issue; (2) the party claiming that a person did not exercise a requisite degree of care has the burden of proof on that issue; and (3) the party claiming that any person, including himself, is or was insane has the burden of proof on that issue.[34]

Proof is the result or effect of evidence. Evidence is all the means used to prove or disprove a fact in issue. The testimony of witnesses make up the greater part of the evidence presented at most trials. There is a great emphasis on originality in testimony in criminal proceedings in the United States, and although there are numerous exceptions to the "hearsay rule," a trial by adversary sets great value upon firsthand knowledge of the facts.

The credibility of a witness is open to attack or support by any party, including the party calling him. Evidence of character traits other than honesty or veracity, or their opposites, is inadmissible to attack or support the credibility of a witness, as is evidence of specific conduct relevant only as tending to prove a character trait. However, under certain restrictions, for the purpose of attacking the credibility of a witness, it may be shown by examination of the witness or by record that he has been convicted of a felony.

In determining the credibility of a witness courts or juries may consider any matter that has any tendency in reason to prove or disprove the truthfulness of the testimony of such person. It may include, but is not limited to the following itemization in California law:

(a) His demeanor while testifying and the manner in which he testifies.

(b) The character of his testimony.

(c) The extent of his capacity to perceive, to recollect or to communicate any matter about which he testifies.

(d) The extent of his opportunity to perceive any matter about which he testifies.

(e) His character for honesty or veracity or their opposites.

[34]*Ibid.*, Sections 520–522.

(f) The existence or nonexistence of a bias, interest or other motive.

(g) A statement made by him that is consistent with his testimony at the hearing.

(h) A statement made by him that is inconsistent with any part of his testimony at the hearing.

(i) The existence or nonexistence of any fact testified to by him.

(j) His attitude toward the action in which he testifies or toward the giving of testimony.

(k) His admission of untruthfulness.[35]

In addition to in-court evidence, if the presiding trial judge believes it proper that the jury should view the crime scene or any place in which a material incident occurred, or when any personal property which cannot be conveniently carried into court is referred to by other evidence, he may order the jury to be conducted to such place to make necessary observation.[36]

A defendant in a criminal action, because of the presumption of innocence, is entitled to an acquittal unless the contrary be proved beyond a reasonable doubt. In California, reasonable doubt is defined as:

> It is not a mere possible doubt; because everything relating to human affairs, and depending on moral evidence, is open to some possible or imaginary doubt. It is the state of the case, which, after the entire comparison and consideration of all the evidence, leaves the minds of jurors in that condition that they can not say they feel an abiding conviction, to a moral certainty, of the truth of the charge.[37]

In the final control of a trial, the court is to decide questions of law arising during the course of a trial, except that on a trial for libel, the jury has the right to determine the law and fact. In all other cases, the jury will determine only the questions of fact. While a jury has the power to find a general verdict, which includes questions of law as well as of fact, it is bound to receive as law in its deliberations what is laid down to it as applicable law by the court.

Witnesses: Attendance at Trial

The process for compelling the attendance of witnesses is a subpoena.[38] This is a court process signed by a judicial official, the prosecutor, or the clerk of a court in which a criminal action is pending for trial. Such officers of the court must, at any time upon application of the defendant,

[35]*Ibid.*, Chapter 6, Sections 780 and 785.
[36]California Penal Code, Section 1119.
[37]*Ibid.*, Section 1096.
[38]Out-of-state witnesses may be compelled to attend in accordance with the Uniform Act enacted for this purpose. See Chapter 5, Extradition and Rendition.

and without charge, issue as many blank subpoenas for witnesses in the state, as the defendant may require. Disobedience to this court process by failure to appear, or a refusal to be sworn or testify as a witness upon appearance, may be punished by the court as a contempt.[39]

Witnesses whose testimony would be material to the outcome of a criminal proceeding are vital to the administration of justice. In some states, on the application of the prosecutor, a material witness may be held in custody pending testimony upon trial. A claim is made (and supported) to the court in which the trial is pending that the material witness will not be available upon trial because of flight from the jurisdiction, or due to harm at the hands of persons interested in the defense case. In one New York case—the killing of underworld financier Arnold Rothstein—a material witness was confined for over a year pending trial.

California has an enlightened procedure for handling material witnesses when the court in which the action is pending is satisfied by proof on oath that there is reason to believe such witness will not appear and testify. This procedure is as follows: (1) the witness may be required to enter a written undertaking for his appearance and testimony involving a forfeiture of $500.00 or other specified amount; or (2) if unable to procure security or the sureties necessary for the written undertaking, the witness (other than accomplices) may be conditionally examined forthwith on behalf of the people in a question and answer procedure similar to examination at the hearing or upon trial, and this disposition may be used upon the trial of the offender in all cases except the trial of homicides. However, if a witness material to the trial of the offender is capable of providing security or sureties, but refuses to do so, the court must commit such person to prison until he complies or is legally discharged.[40]

Witnesses: Naming Informants

It was recognized over the years that law enforcement agencies were generally privileged to withhold the identity of informers; recently, that privilege has given way if in conflict with the opportunity of an accused person to secure a fair trial. Disclosure is required where the informer participated in the crime with which a defendant is charged, was a witness to a criminal transaction essential to the crime charged or provided information which was the *only* justification for police action. When the informant is clearly a material witness on the issue of guilt or on a necessary showing of reasonable cause for the police search and seizure, dis-

[39]*Ibid.*, Sections 1326 and 1331.
[40]*Ibid.*, Sections 878–883.

closure of the identity of the informer by the police or prosecutor is necessary for the accused to fully and fairly prepare his defense.

When the informer is a material witness to facts relating directly to the question of guilt, the policy conflict involved is best described as: (1) the encouragement of the free flow of information to law enforcement officials, as opposed to (2) the right of the defendant to prepare and present a full and fair defense on the issue of his guilt or innocence. When the communications between police and informant are necessary to the issue of reasonable cause to make the arrest and search, the policy conflict may be defined as : (1) the encouragement of the free flow of information to law enforcement officers, as opposed to (2) the policy to discourage lawless enforcement of the law.

When it appears from the evidence that the informer is a material witness on the issue of guilt, because of participating in or witnessing the crime, and the defense attorney seeks his identity on cross-examination, the people must either disclose his identity or incur a dismissal.[41]

If information from a confidential informant established the legality of a search, the defendant must be given a fair opportunity to test police reliance on such information. He must, therefore, be permitted to ascertain the identity of the informer, since the legality of the officer's action depends upon the credibility of the information, not upon facts that the officer directly witnessed and upon which he could be cross-examined. If an officer were allowed to establish the lawfulness of a search through a simple statement under oath that this action was justified on the basis of information received from an informant whose identity would not be revealed, this would make the officer the sole judge of what is probable cause to make the search. It would prevent any defense probing into the credibility of the officer or the information. Only by requiring disclosure and giving the defense counsel an opportunity to present contrary or impeaching evidence about the officer's testimony, and the reasonableness of his reliance on the informer, can the court make fair determination of the issue.[42]

Mr. Justice Douglas summed up the case for naming informants in *U.S. v. Nugent*[43] in the following extract from the minority opinion:

> The use of statements by informers who need not confront the person under investigation or accusation has such an infamous history that it should be rooted out from our procedure. A hearing at which these faceless people are allowed to present their whispered rumors and yet escape the test and torture of cross-examination is not a hearing in the Anglo-American sense.

[41]*People v. McShann,* 50 Cal. 2nd 802 (1958).
[42]*Priestly v. Superior Court,* 50 Cal. 2nd 812 (1958).
[43]346 U.S. 1 (1953).

This fairly recent shift in the balance of public policy from nondisclosure and the free flow of information from informants, to disclosure and fair opportunity to prepare a defense, casts many hardships on law enforcement. The policy of disclosure certainly tends to destroy the future usefulness of an informant and, in some instances, the underworld even follows up a disclosure by murdering or maiming the informant.

There are, however, ways in which the police may have the benefit of informants without the detriment of disclosure. Where the informant's information indicates a search or arrest, the officer has the choice to search and arrest based solely on the information given and then disclose the source; or he may use the information as the beginning of his investigation and gather other facts, within his own knowledge, which would give reasonable cause for search or arrest or both. In this latter situation, the officer need not disclose his informant because there are sufficient facts within his own knowledge to show probable cause to search or arrest.

In the *McShann* situation, the law enforcement agencies may certainly use their own paid officers in undercover work, and when the undercover assignment is completed the agency can place the officer on regular police duty or perhaps use him in another area where he is not known. A derivative advantage of this system over the system of an informant working with the police is that the credibility of the informant is very low with the lay citizen who will hear the case as a juror; while the policeman, working undercover, will not only be more credible to the juror but will also have the juror's admiration for the dangerous job he performs.

Transfer Evidence

As far as protection against giving incriminating evidence against himself, the accused person upon trial is afforded the maximum protection. The Fifth Amendment's words are clear and unambiguous: "... nor shall (any individual) be compelled in any criminal case to be a witness against himself." However, accused persons have been fingerprinted, their body fluid analyzed, their blood typed, their hair examined, their clothes "vacuumed" for lab examination of dust and debris and they have been directed to speak for voice identification and to give handwriting samples. Shoes of an accused person have been removed and fitted to impressions at crime scenes; dirt and mud from an accused person have been examined. In fact, any item of physical evidence which might tend to connect the accused with the crime has been subjected to physical, optical, chemical, microchemical and spectrographic analysis.

This kind of evidence has been acceptable to public and courts in most instances. It has only been when such inspections or comparisons have invaded some basic concepts of fairness that any of these examinations have been rejected. For instance, a stomach pump was rejected by a review court, as a means to secure evidence from a subject which would serve to incriminate him in a narcotic drug-selling case.[44]

The near future may see a growing use of such examinations by police, as a substitute technique to make up for the loss of the police interrogation process. An indication of the extensive use of such examinations may be found in the fact that police have developed a title for physical evidence amenable to an objective analytical examination and some correlation with a suspect. This is "transfer evidence," or "TE." TE occurs when some clue or trace will link up the accused person with the crime scene or the victim, or vice versa. It is a case of the clues or traces being transferred from the crime scene or the victim to the criminal, or from the criminal to the crime scene or the victim.

Closing Argument

The purpose of the summation or closing argument is to provide each of the adversaries in a criminal trial with an opportunity to persuade the jurors to adopt the prosecution or the defense view of the trial. The order of presentation is slightly different than the opening statement, in that the prosecutor has the first closing argument, and is then followed by the defense attorney; the prosecutor has a right of rebuttal, or a "last chance," after the defense attorney has completed his summation of the case.

The entire prosecution summation is usually based on the facts which establish the *corpus delicti* of the crime and identify the defendant as being connected with it. Each major point of evidence is "taken apart" to show how it applies to important facets of the case against the defendant. Lastly, the prosecutor attacks the defense case generally and attempts to stress the fact that the defendant is guilty as charged.

The defense attorney usually bases his closing argument upon the failure of the prosecutor to establish guilt beyond a reasonable doubt. He casts doubt upon the veracity of the prosecution's witnesses, pointing out that it is the business of police to testify in support of their arrests and of police "experts" to support their brethren. He notes some of the backgrounds of the witnesses, and when they are of doubtful character glibly expounds upon the basic unreliability of such people—particularly accomplices or informers. He attacks weak or absent facts to prove ele-

[44]*Rochin v. California*, 342 U.S. 165 (1952).

ments which are necessary to conviction, and may attack only a part of the prosecution case and tacitly admit the remainder. He repeats the important points of his case and the law involved, and ends on the theme that the law forbids a juror to find against a defendant unless convinced beyond a reasonable doubt that the prosecution has proved their case.

After the closing arguments, the judge instructs the jury, and the jury retires for its deliberations prior to rendering its verdict.

Juvenile Court Proceedings

Juvenile court proceedings under the concept of *parens patriae*[45] are inquisitorial to a greater degree than they are accusatory. The accusatory pleading is a petition, rather than a complaint, information or indictment. There is no adversarial relationship. There is no prosecutor, no jury and usually no defense counsel. These proceedings are in a class by themselves (*sui generis*). California is one of the states that permits or assigns a defense counsel to be present at these hearings, either at the request of the juvenile or at the discretion of the court—and an indigent youth can secure the services of the public defender.

The judge or referee presiding at a juvenile court hearing must first determine if the acts or condition alleged in the petition bring the juvenile within the jurisdiction of his court; and secondly, whether the facts as stated will support an adjudication of the child as dependent (neglected), wayward (verging on delinquency) or delinquent (criminal, if adult). When the juvenile and his parents (if present) deny the allegation set forth in the petition, the juvenile court judge will adjourn the hearing in order to permit the policeman or probation officer to bring in witnesses who will support the allegations in the petition and the probation report.[46]

In California, the procedure in juvenile court for hearing these cases is as follows: At the beginning of the hearing on a petition, the judge or clerk reads the petition to those present and upon the request of the minor, or of any parent, relative or guardian, the judge explains any term or allegation contained therein and the nature of the hearing, its procedures and possible consequences. The judge ascertains whether the minor and his parent or guardian or adult relative have been informed of the right of the minor to be represented by counsel; if not, the judge advises the minor and such person, if present, of the right to have counsel present. If such person is indigent and desires to have the minor repre-

---

[45]Parental.

[46]Martin H. Neumeyer, *Juvenile Delinquency in Modern Society* (New York: D. Van Nostrand Co., Inc., 1961), pp. 332–34.

sented by counsel, the court may appoint counsel to represent the minor;
in such cases the court must appoint counsel if the minor is charged with
misconduct constituting a felony if committed by an adult. The court
may continue the hearing for not more than seven days, as necessary to
make an appointment of counsel, or to determine whether the parent or
guardian or adult relative is indigent and unable to afford counsel at his
own expense.[47]

The Juvenile Court Law of California also outlines the informal at-
mosphere and procedure for these hearings. This law reads as follows:

> The judge of the juvenile court shall control all proceedings during the
> hearings with a view to the expeditious and effective ascertainment of
> the jurisdictional facts and the ascertainment of all information relative to
> the present condition and future welfare of the person upon whose behalf
> the petition is brought. Except where there is a contested issue of fact
> or law, the proceedings shall be conducted in an informal nonadversary
> atmosphere with a view to obtaining the maximum cooperation of the
> minor upon whose behalf the petition is brought and all persons interested
> in his welfare with such provisions as the court may make for the dis-
> position and care of such minor.[48]

All the elements of a criminal action are present at a hearing in
juvenile court, but despite the assistance of legal counsel, it is apparent
that the paternalism of this tribunal emphasizes cooperation rather than
controversy. The juvenile is not on trial. These judicial proceedings are
to determine truth and the most likely corrective program for the juvenile
when it appears such action is warranted.

Selected References

CASES

Douglas v. California, 372 U.S. 355 (1963).
> This decision relates to the extension of the *Gideon* doctrine (the right
> to legal counsel assigned by the court to indigent defendants) to indigent
> defendants seeking legal relief on appeal.

Fay v. New York, 332 U.S. 261 (1947).
> This decision details New York's law for empaneling a "blue ribbon"
> trial jury in complex and important criminal actions. It is also a fine
> discussion of "impartial" means for selecting a trial jury.

Gideon v. Wainwright, 372 U.S. 335 (1963).
> The landmark case in support of the Sixth Amendment's guarantee of

[47]California Welfare and Institutions Code, Chapter 2, Juvenile Court Law, Section 700.
[48]*Ibid.*, Section 680.

the right to counsel. It extends this right to every "one charged with crime," and if a defendant is without legal counsel because of lack of funds, legal assistance must be assigned by the court without cost to the indigent defendant.

Harvey v. Mississippi, 340 F 2nd 263 (1965).

This is the 1965 decision of the U.S. Court of Appeals holding that an indigent defendant charged with a minor offense, the maximum punishment for which was a fine ($500.00) and a short jail term (90 days), was entitled to assigned counsel.

In re Johnson, 398 P 2nd 420 (1965).

A California decision extending the right to counsel to a defendant charged with a traffic offense, and citing numerous precedents for considering the right of a defendant to counsel as fundamental in every criminal case, large or small.

People v. Conley, 64 Cal. 2nd 321 (1966).

A decision in the California courts indicating a diminished responsibility because of intoxication in certain crimes requiring specific intent. A great deal of the discussion is in support of the "condition" precept of *Robinson v. California,* 370 U.S. 663 (1962), in which the U.S. Supreme Court establishes new concepts of drug addicts as sick persons.

People v. Lawrence, 149 Cal. App. 2nd 435 (1957).

Case law on disclosure of the identity of informant—participant to an offense to the defendant, upon demand and showing the testimony of informant-participant is material to the facts at trial.

Priestly v. Superior Court, 50 Cal. 2nd 802 (1958).

A leading case regarding the disclosure of the identity of informants. The decision upholds the right of a defendant to the identity of an informant when the lawfulness of the arrest, search and seizure depends upon information supplied by informant. The court notes the purpose of disclosure is to permit testing the truth of the testimony of police witnesses and the reasonableness of police reliance upon such information.

Robinson v. California, 370 U.S. 663 (1962).

The landmark case in narcotic drug law and control of illegal drug use. It declares a state law establishing drug addiction as a crime to be unconstitutional. A fine decision for examining the nature of acts rather than "conditions" as subject for sanction law, and an equally fine delineation of an emerging doctrine of diminished responsibility for drug addicts charged with the commission of crime while addicted to habit-forming drugs.

Sheppard v. Maxwell, 384 U.S. 333 (1966).

An extensive discussion of the effect of unfair, distorted publicity upon the jurors at the time of trial, and this decision notes that neither prosecutors, counsel for defense, the accused, witnesses, court staff nor enforcement officers coming under the jurisdiction of the trial court should be permitted to frustrate its function by actions or statements threatening the fair trial of the defendant.

U.S. v. Currens, 290 F 2nd 751 (1961).

A decision establishing new standards of legal insanity, and new horizons for diminishing criminal responsibility because of insanity at the time of the commission of a crime.

BOOKS

Cohen, Louis, *Murder, Madness, and the Law*. Cleveland and New York: World Publishing Co., 1952, 173 pages.

An excellent evaluation of the various aspects of legal psychiatry. Cohen discusses the role of the psychiatrist when called upon to help determine legal responsibility; the extent of "expertness" in this field; and the techniques of psychiatric evaluation and examination.

Frank, Jerome, *Courts on Trial*. Princeton, N.J.: Princeton University Press, 1949, 429 pages.

The entire process of trial by adversary is critically examined for faults and errors as well as for meritorious features. The make-up of the court and the jury, the legal process, the theory of trial law are all examined. Of major interest is this author's views on the "fight theory" of trial by adversary.

McCart, Samuel W., *Trial by Jury*. Philadelphia: Chilton Books, 1964, 204 pages.

A complete guide to the jury system. McCart details the jury system from its primitive beginnings to its evolution into the fine and independent institution it is today. This text covers developmental history, jury selection, powers and duties, the verdict and notations on constitutional provision for jury trials in each state.

Palmer, Ben W., *Courtroom Strategies*. Englewood Cliffs, N.J.: Prentice-Hall, Inc., 1959, 392 pages.

A text for young attorneys primarily, but a fine delineation of effective procedures for trial attorneys. Palmer covers the trial from jury selection to appeals, writing: "It has been my intention to provide a practical guide to the effective use of those strategies that have proved their worth to me in my many years in the trial of lawsuits." Recommended to police readers for its potential insight into the conduct of opposing counsel.

Silverstein, Lee, *Defense of the Poor in Criminal Cases in American State Courts, A Field Study and Report*. Chicago: American Bar Foundation, Vol. I, 1965, 280 pages.

An examination of the present methods for providing counsel to defendants unable to hire lawyers of their own choosing. There is a comparison of the "assigned counsel" system and the emerging "Public Defender"; a discussion of the problems of attorneys for indigent defendants; and a strong plea for creative research which will lead to improved techniques of legal defense for the poor—so the indigent defendant will have more than a "splendid poor man's chance" when accused of crime—an equal chance with everybody else.

Soderman, Harry, and John J. O'Connell, *Modern Criminal Investigation*, (4th ed.). New York: Funk & Wagnalls Co., Inc., 1952, 557 pages.

A classic text in criminal investigation since its first publication in 1935. Soderman and O'Connell were the first authors to recognize the importance of "transfer evidence," or the emerging role of the police laboratory in criminal investigation, and of the unassailability of the scientific analysis of otherwise-mute physical evidence.

Inbau, Fred E., ed., *Free Press—Fair Trial*. Evanston, Ill.: Northwestern University School of Law, 1964, 202 pages.

The papers and proceedings of a conference on prejudicial news reporting participated in by representatives of the police, prosecutor, defense counsel, courts and the press. A well-edited mass of resource material regarding the administration of justice in America and the challenge to a formidable opponent: the press, traditionally, an adversary who always has the "last word." There is excellent coverage of the conflict between the two cherished rights in America: the right of a free press to access to information of public concern, and the right of a defendant in a criminal case to a fair trial by an impartial jury.

ARTICLES

Arnold, Thurman, "The Criminal Trial as a Symbol of Morality," in *Criminal Justice in Our Time*, ed. A. E. Dick Howard. Charlottesville, Va.: The University Press of Virginia, 1965, pp. 139–61.

Arnold writes of the significance of trial by adversary, of the notion that every man, however unsavory and however guilty he may be, is entitled to a fair and impartial trial in which he must be presumed to be innocent and in which he has the right to counsel.

Davis, Bruce E., and Richard E. Wiley, "Thoughts on Jury Selection," *The Trial Lawyer's Guide* (May 1965), pp. 110–15.

Davis and Wiley offer 49 suggestions for effective "jury-calling," and note that while the *voir-dire* examination is designed to ensure an intelligent, alert, and impartial jury willing and capable of performing assigned duties, it is also an opportunity for an attorney to: (1) introduce himself and his case; (2) engender feelings of friendship, respect and understanding among the selected jurors; and (3) create a foundation for the development of trial strategy and tactics.

Hollopeter Charles, "The Trial of a Drunk-Driving Case," *The Trial Lawyer's Guide* (November 1964), pp. 118–29.

An outline for the defense in a specific criminal proceeding, but the techniques cited may be employed in trials for murder, burglary, and other crimes. Hollopeter covers jury selection, police witnesses, and scientific tests; and concludes with notes of "preparation for trial," and the classic need for establishing guilt beyond a reasonable doubt.

Kuh, Richard H., "A Prosecutor's Thoughts Concerning Addiction," *Journal of Criminal Law, Criminology and Police Science* (September-October 1961), pp. 321–27.

A study of the role our existing laws assign to prosecutors and to the criminal courts in dealing with drug addicts. Kuh writes that in viewing drug use as an illness—rather than as a penal matter—it must be recognized as the equivalent of a highly contagious disease within particular segments of our community.

LeWine, Jerome Martin, "What Constitutes Prejudicial Publicity in Pending Cases," *American Bar Association Journal* (October 1965), pp. 942–48.

A very fine examination on publicity likely to be prejudicial and which should be forbidden under the "clear and present danger" test. LeWine notes the greatest danger of prejudicial publicity extends to the time the jury is selected and lists areas of hazard as: (1) confessions; (2) prior convictions; (3) evidentiary facts generally; (4) out-of-court statements of witnesses; (5) personal opinions as to guilt; and (6) comments on evidence or proceedings.

Platt, Anthony M., "The Origins and Development of the 'Wild Beast' Concept of Mental Illness and Its Relation to Theories of Criminal Responsibility," *Issues in Criminology*, 1, No. 1 (Fall 1965), 1–18.

A tracing of the "wild beast" test of criminal responsibility in a legal context and in the treatment of insane offenders.

Powell, Lewis F., "The Right to a Fair Trial," *American Bar Association Journal* (June 1965), pp. 534–38.

Reconciliation of the conflict between the rights of a free press and a defendant should be focused on the pretrial period, this author writes, and must be mindful of the fact that the essence of the guarantee of a free press is to allow unlimited discussion about public and political matters.

Riave, Lionel, "Fair and Impartial Trial by Jury in the United States and in England," *American Bar Association Journal* (March 1964), pp. 232–34.

The author compares the trial systems for criminal proceedings as they exist in the United States and in England. Riave works with the NATO Status of Forces Agreement and the requirement that commanding officers of American troops stationed abroad must examine the safeguards provided by local law when an American serviceman stationed overseas is charged with a crime.

11

Judge's Charge to the Jury, Verdict and Judgment

After the closing statements in a criminal action have been completed, the judge must charge the jury with instructions as to applicable matters of law and its responsibilities as trier of fact, arrange a safe place for its deliberations upon the issues at trial, accept its verdict when it is rendered in court and pronounce judgment and a sentence best planned to serve both the offender and the community.

The mutual obligation of the trial judge to instruct the jury, and of the jury to follow such instructions, is a joint enterprise that ensures an accused person against arbitrary or capricious acts of the jury. This joint action and the many safeguards established for the manner in which a jury, or a judge in trials without a jury, will return a verdict and the many forms of possible verdicts are all procedures for securing fair trials for all accused persons.

The trial of the offender concludes with the judgment and sentence.

The sentencing function of a trial judge is a lonely function heavy with the requirement of predicting future behavior and responses to the correctional process. It is a little less lonely, however, because of modern presentence investigations and reports, new arrangements for committing convicted offenders before sentencing to diagnostic and treatment facilities and the emerging concept of indeterminate sentences. Offenders convicted of less serious crime and without extensive prior arrests and convictions may be placed on probation or sentenced to a short term in a county jail often with a work-furlough arrangement of daytime release. More hardened convicted offenders are sentenced to state prison for an indeterminate sentence, with modern state-wide parole boards determining the exact sentence length (within legal limits) and the time period of parole supervision required.

Charging the Jury

While a trial judge may admonish and otherwise instruct jurors during a trial, his formal instructions after opposing counsel has completed his closing statements relate primarily to the law in the case. This final segment of a criminal action is known as "charging the jury."

By 1700, Anglo-English law had formalized the summing up of a presiding judge in a criminal action tried by jury as an essential feature distinguished by the fact that it is the sole means by which a trial jury could gain legal assistance. The function of instructions to juries by trial judges is to enlighten the jury on the law. This requires the trial judge to phrase his instructions simply and concisely in order that every juror may comprehend the statement of law being made, and such delineation of the law should be sufficiently inclusive to cover any relationship in which the jury may place evidence in the case.[1]

Additionally, instructions to juries are a legal methodology by which appellate courts control juries and trial courts, trial courts maintain their integrity, and defense counsel often traps a trial judge into action which will serve not only as grounds for an appeal, but also action likely to incur a reversal upon appeal. Appellate courts do not reverse cases on findings of fact, but if they find the judicial instructions were in error as given, or in error when not given as requested, and such judicial action or inaction wrongfully influenced the jurors, they can reverse the case on the law. Cautionary instructions guard against sympathy and prejudice on the part of the jurors and serve to warn the jury of questionable aspects of specific items of evidence. And every defense counsel has a

[1]Charles W. Fricke, ed., *California Jury Instruction—Criminal* (St. Paul, Minn.: West Publishing Co., 1958), p. 1.

wee hope, when he believes a case is going poorly, that something in the judge's instructions to the jury will serve him if he appeals the case and will offer an opportunity for reversal and a new trial.[2]

The judge's instructions serve as legal advice to the jurors to assist them in properly considering the evidence in their deliberations and decision. These words are the totality of the legal principles which should be applied by the jury to the facts of the case. Trial judges will, whether or not counsel on either side so requests, instruct the jury on all necessary and pertinent general principles of law; the law of the offense charged, and of lesser variations of such offense, if warranted; the doctrine of reasonable doubt; on the nature of circumstantial evidence, if such evidence may be substantially relied upon by the jury in its deliberations; and the understanding that the jurors are the exclusive judges of all questions of fact submitted to them and of the credibility of the witnesses.

The adversarial system still prevails at this stage of a trial, as each attorney may request the court to instruct the jury on certain aspects of the law favorable to their case. In full pursuance of the fight theory, even at this late stage of the trial, these requests usually counter each other.

A "request to charge" asks the court to instruct the jury on the law as set forth in the request. These requests must be in writing, and should be submitted before the commencement of the closing arguments, although there is a potential for amending a request if issues are raised during the argument phase of the trial which have not been covered in the request. The request should state the law accurately and concisely and appellate authority should be paraphrased equally simply. These requests relate to the nature of the charges within the scope of the trial, the elements of such charges which must be proven, the principles of the burden of proof and the concept of reasonable doubt; and extend to the credibility of witnesses, physical evidence, and cautions that the jury restrict its deliberations to the evidence "at trial," and exclude any bias or prejudice from its deliberations.

Either of the opposing attorneys may also take exception to the judge's charging of the jury, giving such common grounds as bias, errors in citing law and refusal to charge in accordance with a written request. However, the determination as to the correctness of a judge's instructions to a jury depends upon the entire charge of the court, and not an isolated phrase, sentence or paragraph.

Once charged, it is the jury's final decision whether or not to convict and the manner in which its verdict will be returned to the court.

[2]Lester Bernhardt Orfield, *Criminal Procedure From Arrest to Appeal* (New York and London: Oxford University Press, 1947), pp. 449–51.

In California, the duty of a trial judge in charging a jury includes placing all instructions in writing, either in advance or by means of stenographic note-taking, except in misdemeanor cases when opposing counsel stipulate the instructions may be given orally. Also, trial judges should accept from either party to the action any written requests to charge on the law, but not with respect to matters of fact; the court must endorse his decision to give the charge or part or to refuse it or any part, sign this endorsement and a statement showing the party making the request and place it in the court record.[3]

California also has a section of its penal code which was enacted for the purpose of establishing one standard for every jury in regard to the conflict between the presumption of innocence and the doctrine of reasonable doubt, and the same law provides that no further instruction on the subject of the presumption of innocence or defining reasonable doubt need be given if, in charging the jury, the court reads this section of law to them:

> A defendant in a criminal action is presumed to be innocent until the contrary is proved, and in the case of a reasonable doubt whether his guilt is satisfactorily shown, he is entitled to an acquittal, but the effect of this presumption is only to place upon the state the burden of proving him guilty beyond a reasonable doubt. Reasonable doubt is defined as follows: "It is not a mere possible doubt; because everything relating to human affairs, and depending on moral evidence, is open to some possible or imaginary doubt. It is that state of the case, which, after the entire comparison and consideration of all the evidence, leaves the mind of jurors in that condition that they can not say they feel an abiding conviction, to a moral certainty, of the truth of the charge.[4]

In most jurisdictions, judges will also charge the jury regarding expert testimony and the import of evidence of flight by the defendant, if these factors have entered into the case. California also provides standard instructions in these two fields in order that a trial judge will uniformly discharge his responsibilities in these important areas. No further instruction on the subject of expert testimony or evidence of flight need be given if the court instructs the jury substantially as follows:

> Duly qualified experts may give their opinions on questions in controversy at a trial. To assist the jury in deciding such questions, the jury may consider the opinion with the reasons stated therefor, if any, by the expert who gives the opinion. The jury is not bound to accept the opinion of any expert as conclusive, but should give to it the weight to which they shall find it entitled. The jury may, however, disregard any such opinion, if it shall be found by them to be unreasonable. The flight

[3]California Penal Code, Section 1127.
[4]*Ibid.*, Section 1096.

of a person immediately after the commission of a crime, or after he is accused of a crime that has been committed, is not sufficient in itself to establish his guilt, but is a fact which, if proved, the jury may consider in deciding his guilt or innocence. The weight to which such circumstance is entitled is a matter for the jury to determine.[5]

The case of *Griffin v. California*[6] curtailed the freedom of judges to comment on the failure of the defendant to take the stand and testify in his own behalf, in the few states permitting it. The decision in *Griffin* reasoned that to permit such conduct seriously threatened Constitutional safeguards against forcing a defendant to incriminate himself, despite the fact that California's Constitution and Penal Code permit such comment by a trial judge in charging a jury.[7] Eddie Dean Griffin was convicted of murder in the first degree after a jury trial in California. He did not testify at the trial of the killing. The trial court instructed the jury, saying that a defendant has a constitutional right not to testify, but adding:

> . . . As to any evidence or facts against him which the defendant can reasonably be expected to deny or explain because of facts within his knowledge, if he does not testify or if, though he does testify, he fails to deny or explain such evidence, the jury may take that failure into consideration as tending to indicate the truth of such evidence and as indicating that among the inferences that may be reasonably drawn therefrom those unfavorable to the defendant are the more probable.

Since the court had held in a decision[8] prior to *Griffin* that the self-incrimination clause of the Fifth Amendment was applicable to the states by the Fourteenth Amendment, it now held that neither comment by the prosecutor on the accused's silence, nor instructions by a trial court to a jury that such silence is evidence of guilt were permissible.

Judicial instructions in charging a jury must not invade the juror's role of determining questions of fact, nor is it proper for the court to submit to the jury for decision any matter within the duty of the court to decide, but since it is the duty of the court to charge the jury appropriately in each individual case, it is also the duty of the jury to act on the law as received by it from the court. Of course, opposing attorneys in a criminal action seek to influence the jury as to the law in the case in their closing arguments, but this segment of the trial occurs before the judge charges the jury. Therefore, at this conclusion of a trial, each juror should be aware that the final summing up was the law to be applied in

---

[5]*Ibid.*, Section 1127b-c.
[6]*Griffin v. California*, 380 U.S. 609, 614 (1965).
[7]California Constitution, Article VI, Sec. 19; California Penal Code, Section 1127.
[8]*Malloy v. Hogan*, 378 U.S. 1 (1964).

the case, as the judge "charged" them, and not as they might remember it expounded by one of the opposing counsel.

The great import of these instructions to a jury are difficult to imagine correctly. All through the trial, the presiding judge or justice has held the position of authority in the court, and this has been supplemented by his sombre robes of office and the courtroom courtesy required of spectators and participants in the trial toward this authority figure on the court's raised "bench." The learned judges of the U.S. Supreme Court indicated the tremendous potential weight of judicial comment in this charging of a jury when they noted in the *Griffin* decision: "What the jury may infer given no help from the court is one thing. What they may infer when the court solemnizes the silence of the accused into evidence against him is quite another."[9]

The Verdict

A verdict is the decision of a jury, or of a judge in criminal actions prosecuted without a jury, on the matter submitted in a trial. It is a formal statement by the "trier of facts."

Jury trials may be terminated by a directed verdict of acquittal. This is possible at any time after the evidence on either side is closed, and the court deems it insufficient to warrant a conviction. The court "advises" the jury to acquit the defendant. However, each of the states has overriding provisions of law which modify the force of the court's "advice" in so directing a jury. For instance, New York provides full force and effect to this advice, making it mandatory upon the jury to accept it, while California jurors are informed they are not bound by such advice. The New York law concludes: ". . . may advise the jury to acquit the defendant thereof and they must follow the advice."[10] The California law concludes with this sentence: ". . . But the jury are not bound by the advice."[11]

A jury is provided with a place to conduct its deliberations without molestation and one which guards against communication with everyone except other members of the jury, the court bailiff or the trial judge. The jurors are escorted to meals, and are frequently locked up for the night. They may, during this period of deliberation, seek assistance of the court for the examination of physical exhibits or the court record, or further instructions. Exhibits are usually sent into the jury room, but most jurisdictions require the trial judge to recall the jury to the trial room to have

[9]*Griffin v. California*, 380 U.S. 609, 614 (1965).
[10]New York Code of Criminal Procedure, Section 410.
[11]California Penal Code, Section 1118.

the transcript of the record read to it or to enlarge upon his charge to the jury, and it must be in the presence of opposing counsel and the defendant.

A jury is given a reasonable time to deliberate, and except as provided by law in the various states, it will not be discharged unless there is no reasonable probability that it can agree on a verdict. This is a matter for the court's determination.[12] Many juries have returned to open court and reported they were unable to agree upon a verdict, but did reach a verdict when the court directed they return and make another attempt at their deliberations.

When the jury informs the member of the court's staff having them in charge that they have arrived at a verdict, he will conduct them into court and the name of each juror will be called. In California, if all jurors do not appear, the rest of the jury must be discharged without giving a verdict.[13]

The verdict must have the necessary unanimity, agreement in the verdict by all 12 jurors, and the jury is polled to so determine—with the trial judge or court clerk querying each juror in turn. Any doubt, as to the juror's vote during this questioning[14] must be resolved before the trial judge can accept the verdict. A negative vote by any juror requires the court to send the jury out for further deliberation.[15] When the verdict given is such as a court may receive, it must be recorded in full upon the minutes and the court must act upon the verdict.

In most jurisdictions, juries may also find the defendant guilty of a lesser offense committed in the course of the crime charged; an attempt to commit the offense charged; the degree of the crime of which the defendant is guilty; the existence of a previous conviction, if it is not admitted by the defendant; and whether a weapon was involved in the crime. When the verdict is for acquittal, the court must accept it. Only when there is a verdict of conviction can the trial judge direct a reconsideration of the verdict, and the circumstances of the jury's action should indicate to the court the jury has mistaken the law in the case. In such instances, the trial judge explains to the jury his reasons for this opinion, and directs it to reconsider its verdict. When the jury returns after its reconsideration of the case, as directed, the court must accept its verdict, even if it returns the same verdict.[16]

In California, a jury must return a general verdict, except when it is in doubt as to the legal effect of the facts proved in an action

[12]*Ibid.*, Section 1140.
[13]*Ibid.*, Section 1147 (action may be tried again).
[14]Polling the jury.
[15]California Penal Code, Section 1164.
[16]*Ibid.*, Section 1161.

prosecuted in the Superior Court (other than a trial for libel) it may
render a special verdict. When a jury trial is waived, the judge or justice
before whom the trial is had shall, at its conclusion, announce his findings upon the issues of fact and they shall be in substantially the same
form as the general verdict of a jury.[17]

A general verdict upon a plea of not guilty must be either "guilty" or
"not guilty" (which means either conviction or acquittal—respectively—
of the offense charged in the accusatory pleading); upon a plea of former
conviction or acquittal of the offense charged, or of being once in jeopardy, it must be either "for the people" or "for the defendant"; and
when the defendant is acquitted on the ground of a variance between
the accusatory pleading and the proof, the general verdict should be
worded: "not guilty by reason of variance between charge and proof."

A special verdict must be reduced to writing. It is a finding by the
jury of conclusions of fact. It is insufficient if it only details the evidence
which will prove the conclusions of fact without specifically presenting
the jury's conclusions of fact as established by the evidence; or if it does
not intelligibly present the facts found by the jury. A special verdict, to
be received by a court, need not be in any particular form, but it must
be carefully worded as to its conclusions of facts, and thus put the court
in a position to do nothing more than draw conclusions of law upon them.

In California, except on a plea of not guilty by reason of insanity, a
general verdict or judicial finding—in trials without a jury—in favor of a
defendant who had pleaded not guilty must be followed by a judgment
of acquittal and the discharge of the defendant; and upon a special
verdict, if the court finds the facts as found by the jury do not prove
the defendant guilty of the offense charged in the indictment or information, or of any other offense of which he could be convicted under that
indictment or information, judgment must also be of acquittal and the
defendant is also to be discharged.

If the plea of the defendant is of former conviction or acquittal or
once in jeopardy of the same offense, the court must order a judgment
of acquittal and discharge the defendant if a general verdict is "for the
defendant" or the facts presented in a special verdict prove the former
judgment or acquittal, or jeopardy. When the acquittal is because of a
variance between the accusatory pleading and the proof, and a new
accusatory pleading may correct this variance, the court need not discharge the defendant and may continue his detention for a reasonable
time to permit the preparation of a new accusatory pleading. When the
general verdict or judicial finding is "guilty" or "for the people," or the
facts presented in a special verdict cause the court to adjudge the de-

[17]*Ibid.*, Sections 1150 and 1167.

fendant as "guilty" or as failing to prove the plea of former conviction or acquittal or once in jeopardy, the defendant is remanded if in custody, or he may be committed by the court if free on bail.[18]

In California, when the verdict is conviction in capital cases in which the penalty is the alternative of death or life imprisonment there is a penalty trial which follows this verdict. In fact, when the judge is charging the jury, in these cases, his instructions will be that the jurors should not discuss or consider the question of penalty when weighing the guilt or innocence of the defendant. Evidence at the secondary proceeding[19] is presented on the issue of penalty, the circumstances of the crime, the defendant and his criminal history and background, and any facts in aggravation or mitigation of the crime or penalty.[20]

There is a similar provision in cases involving a pleading of not guilty by reason of insanity, when the verdict in the primary criminal action on the offense charged is adverse to the defendant. This permits the trial of the offense to move smoothly and not be confused with the issue of the insanity defense. The secondary trial on the issue of insanity may hear evidence restricted to the determination of the mental condition of the convicted defendant, and shall be concluded with a verdict either that the defendant was sane at the time the offense was committed, or that he was insane at the time the offense was committed.[21]

If the verdict is that the defendant was sane at the time the offense was committed, the court shall proceed as with other convicted defendants, but if the verdict is that the defendant was insane at the time of the crime charged, the court should order the defendant confined to a state hospital for the criminal insane until such time as his sanity is restored. At that time, or if it appears at the time of the jury's verdict that the defendant had fully recovered his sanity, the defendant will be held in custody until his present mental status is determined in accordance with law.

Judgment

Judgment is the official pronouncement of a sentence at the conclusion of a criminal proceeding. It follows the verdict and may be postponed beyond the statutory time limit,[22] until the completion of a reasonable

[18]*Ibid.*, Sections 1155, 1165–1167.
[19]The trier of fact in these secondary proceedings depends upon the circumstances of the original trial of the offense. It may be the presiding judge, when no jury was involved; the same jury; or a new jury—when good cause is shown for drawing a new jury.
[20]California Penal Code, Section 190.1.
[21]*Ibid.*, Section 1026.
[22]California's base period is 21 days.

period, for presentence investigation and report by the probation agency, defense applications for writs and motions, diagnostic examination as to defendant's mental illness, and the possibility the defendant may be adjudged a sex psycho.[23] The normal limit in most states is a 20 to 30 day period from verdict to judgment, but a 90-day period is not unreasonable if a defendant is sent away for observation and examination.

For judgment, the defendant is brought before the court if in custody, and voluntarily appears or is placed under arrest on a bench warrant if out on bail. He must have his counsel present unless he knowingly waives an attorney at this stage, and he is queried by the court as to whether there is any legal cause why sentence should not be pronounced. In California, the defendant must be informed by the court or its clerk at this appearance for judgment of: (1) the charge against him; (2) his plea, and (3) the verdict, if any; and must be questioned whether he has any legal cause to show why judgment should not be pronounced against him.[24]

In California, if the judgment is for a fine alone, the execution is similar to a judgment in a civil action; but if the judgment is for a fine and imprisonment until it is paid, the defendant is committed to custody until the judgment is complied with. If the judgment is for imprisonment, and is not a judgment of death, a certified abstract of the judgment should be forwarded by the court to the officer whose duty it is to execute the order of judgment. An abstract of judgment requires: (1) designation of crime or crimes (and degrees, if any) of which defendant has been convicted; (2) a statement (a) of prior convictions which affect the sentence of defendant, (b) as to whether or not the defendant was armed with a deadly weapon or a concealed deadly weapon when that fact will affect his sentence, (c) as to whether or not the defendant has been adjudged a habitual criminal, (d) of how the sentence imposed on each count of which defendant was convicted shall be served; and (3) a copy of the remand order to the sheriff for the defendant's custody or delivery to a state prison. Judgments of death require a more formal abstract, a commitment signed by the judge and attested by the clerk of the court under the seal of the court, and a notation in the remand order that the defendant is to be held pending the decision upon his appeal (automatic in death judgments).[25]

The judgment is the final determination and decision of the court in a criminal proceeding; the sentence is that portion of a court's judgment establishing the penalty pronounced upon the person convicted. Modern

[23]This is an involved procedure that varies from state to state, but usually requiring expert testimony from qualified psychiatrists to guide the presiding jurist.
[24]California Penal Code, Section 1200.
[25]Ibid., Sections 1213–1227.

sentencing procedures are based on the assumption that the correctional process of probation, institutional treatment, and parole will result in less recidivism or any kind of reinvolvement in criminal behavior.

Selected References

CASES

Griffin v. California, 380 U.S. 609 (1965).
   While basically a decision regarding self-incrimination, there is considerable discussion of the weight of the judge's instructions to the jury in the final outcome of a trial.
People v. Alotis, 60 Cal. 2nd (1964).
   The leading case on the discretionary power of a sentencing judge in granting probation, despite the fact a deadly weapon was involved in the commission of the crime.

BOOKS

Fricke, Charles, *et al.*, *California Jury Instructions—Criminal* (rev. ed.). St. Paul, Minn.: West Publishing Co., 1958, 742 pages.
   The definitive text in California for the guidance of the judiciary when instructing a jury. Comprehensive yet concise, this is the book which guards trial judges from action or inaction likely to lead to reversal upon appeal, and assists in developing a set of instructions to the jury in each trial which is well within the intent and meaning of a fair trial before an impartial tribunal. (Similar texts are available for each state.)
Mathes, William C., and Edward J. Devitt, *Federal Jury Practice and Instruction*. St. Paul, Minn.: West Publishing Co., 1965, 724 pages.
   A legal text establishing guidelines for the federal judiciary in instructing jurors.
Murphy, Walter F., and C. Herman Pritchett, *Courts, Judges, and Politics*. New York: Random House, Inc., 1961, 701 pages.
   An account of the way the American judicial system actually operates. Necessary reading for an improved understanding of the impact upon jurors of a judge's instructions and his rulings as to what evidence they may or may not consider in their deliberations.

ARTICLES

Alexander, Myre E., "A Hopeful View of the Sentencing Process," *American Law Quarterly* (Summer 1965), pp. 189–97.
   A critical analysis of the concept of mandatory sentences and a strong plea for the repeal of mandatory penalty and habitual offender's laws.

Alexander calls for sentencing procedures aligned with the belief that criminal offenders have varying personalities, problems, and criminal patterns.

Jackson, Bruce, "Who Goes to Prison," *The Atlantic Monthly*, Vol. 217 (January 7, 1966) pp. 52–57.

A discussion of who goes to prison; the author believes imprisonment after judgment has definite social implications: the poor and the stupid are sent to institutions.

Schmideberg, Melitta, "The Offender's Attitude Toward Punishment," *Journal of Criminal Law, Criminology and Police Science*, Vol. 51, No. 3 (September-October 1960) pp. 328–34.

The effectiveness and desirability of various forms of punishment are the subject of this article. The author writes that the penalty provisions of court judgments require an adequate appraisal of the offender's attitude toward punishment.

V

PROBATION, INSTITUTIONS, PAROLE

The correctional process describes all the means contributing to the reform and rehabilitation of convicted offenders. It is the terminal aspect of the administration of criminal justice in the United States in the prosecution of offenders. Unfortunately, it is not the endpoint of many criminal careers. It includes conditional release after sentence on probation; custody, discipline, treatment and medical care in correctional institutions, schools and other facilities for juveniles and youths, and medical facilities

for the criminally insane or inmates requiring
psychiatric care; and conditional release
on parole after institutional confinement. Its
major objective is not "punishment," but
the reform and rehabilitation of offenders.
Clemency, historically, is an executive function
for righting injustices to accused persons
wrongfully convicted of crime. In modern
techniques for administering justice to the
convicted offender in the United States,
clemency is emerging as a postrehabilitation
supplement to the correctional process.
The final disposition, legally, implies the
exhaustion of legal remedies and court
access, but it has developed as the term best
describing the objective of the entire
sequential process of criminal justice: to end
a criminal career.

12

The Correctional Process
and Final Disposition

The correctional process ranges from the sentencing function to probation, imprisonment care and treatment in a correctional institution, and
later release under parole supervision.

The final disposition of a criminal action against a convicted person
follows the correctional process and coincides with the exhaustion of all
legal remedies to effect a change in the court's judgment. As Clarence
Gideon proved in his famous fight from a Florida prison cell, a convicted
criminal can secure adequate and speedy legal relief despite the "final
disposition" status of his case legally.[1]

More importantly, from a socio-judicial viewpoint, the correctional
process and final disposition of a case coincide with the complete
rehabilitation of the convicted criminal offender. The only final disposition really acceptable in the administration of justice is when the "output"

[1]*Gideon v. Wainwright*, 372 U.S. 335 (1963).

of the process does not produce individuals who become "input" statistics again and again.

Clemency is now being used to further reform and rehabilitation. It supports probation and parole, and offers new goal incentives to convicted offenders. Prison life and criminal attitudes learned while in prison often ruin reform and rehabilitation, despite every attempt to help the offender. Today and the distant past are now joined in the administration of justice. In the distant past, the only act of mercy was executive clemency; today, there is no "punishment," all of the postsentence period is devoted to helping the offender.

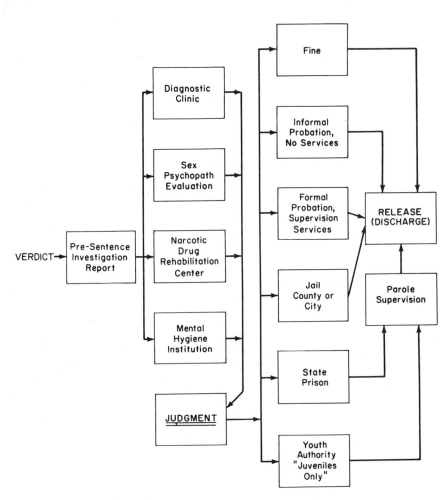

FIG. 6.   THE SENTENCING FUNCTION

The Sentencing Function

In California, as in many of the states, the determination of the length of the sentence in felony cases has been taken away from the trial judge and is now fixed by the Adult Authority.[2] In effect, the trial judge sentences for the maximum term allowed by law and the Adult Authority determines the sentence so that the actual time served is less than the allowable maximum.

Many states also have laws such as New York's "Baumes Law",[3] or California's "Habitual Criminal Act",[4] which punish continual felony commitments with lengthy mandatory sentences. Other states have provisions in their laws requiring either a mandatory sentence, or a mandatory extension of the basic sentence, when the crime involves narcotic drugs, guns or other deadly weapons, violence or sexual misbehavior. In these instances, not only must the trial judge state in his sentence that the defendant is a first or second offender (or third or fourth), but he must also follow the statutory sentencing provisions.

These laws requiring mandatory sentencing interfere in the exercise of the sentencing function by the sentencing judge and prevent him from fully utilizing every aspect of the correctional process from probation to state prison when sentencing an offender, and from adapting the sentence to the profile of the offender as it develops from data in the presentence investigation report and new diagnostic aids available to guide the sentencing judge.

Presentence Investigation and Report

More and more states are enacting laws requiring a presentence investigation and report in all cases in which the offender has been convicted of a felony. In California,[5] such investigation and report must be ordered by the court in all felony cases in which the defendant is eligible for probation, but its use is discretionary in misdemeanor cases. The presentence investigation and report is a splendid opportunity to review the history of the offender as a person as well as his criminal history. It not only provides information regarding the many things that a judge must learn about an offender before the day for sentencing arrives, but it also provides data for the use of parole personnel and others within

[2]*Ibid.*, Sections 1168, 3000–3025.
[3]New York Code of Criminal Procedure, Section 510.
[4]California Penal Code, Section 644.
[5]*Ibid.*, Section 1203.

the correctional process. The extensive coverage of a probation investigation may be gleaned from the following resume of a presentence investigation:

1. *Legal History of the Offender*
   a. Court and institutional record;
   b. Statement describing present offense;
   c. Complainant's statement;
   d. Offender's statement describing offense;
   e. Mitigating (or aggravating) circumstances:
      (1) *Offender*
      (2) *Crime*
      (3) *Codefendants*
2. *Social History of Offender*
   a. Early life and education;
   b. Employment and socio-economic condition;
   c. Character, habits, associates, leisure-time activities;
   d. Social condition and history;
   e. Religious training and observance; and
   f. Mental and physical condition.
3. *Family History of Offender*
   a. Wife and children;
   b. Parents; and
   c. Previous marriages.
4. *Home and Neighborhood Background*
5. *Community Attitudes*
6. *Other Information*
7. *Disposition Recommended*
8. *Summary*

A copy of this report is delivered to the court, the prosecutor and the counsel for the defense. After sentence, it becomes part of the record of the case, and if probation is denied, a copy of the report is forwarded to the officer in charge of the place of imprisonment to which the defendant is committed.

If the probation officer recommends probation as the best remedy for the offender, most judges will so sentence an offender. Of course, there's some reality testing in these reports and their recommendations. Probation officers usually learn what circumstances are most likely to be relied upon as justification for recommendations for probation by each trial judge, and make recommendations as a result of this conditioning process. Possibly because of this attitude, a very high percentage of the offenders who were recommended for probation in the presentence report were subsequently granted probation by the court.

Presentence Commitments

TO DIAGNOSTIC FACILITY

This new procedure in sentencing is a service to the judiciary by state correctional or mental health facilities. Their studies and reports provide specific knowledge as to the emotional and personality adjustment of the offender. This practice is being used by more and more judges as part of the presentence procedure. It is a step forward in finding out more about an offender, and brings to the judge the type of knowledge normally available only to corrections personnel after commitment. The medical officer of the diagnostic facility usually has 90 days to report to the court as to his findings and his recommendations for treatment. New York City and California pioneered extensive use of presentence diagnosis. New York City works at the court level; California provides this service to the courts by specialists of the state-wide Department of Corrections. Reports are available only to the court, the prosecutor, defendant and his counsel, and the county probation department. After disposition of the case, all copies of this report are sealed and are available only to the Department of Corrections, the court, the prosecutor and the defendant or his counsel.

OF SEX "PSYCHOS"

Many states now have "sexual psychopath," "defective delinquent," or "mentally disordered sex offender" laws. The Welfare and Institution Code of California[6] defines its "mentally disordered sex offender" as "any person who by reason of mental defect, disease or disorder is predisposed to the commission of sexual offenses to such a degree that he is dangerous to the health and safety of others"; and its "mentally abnormal sex offender" as "any person who is not mentally ill or mentally defective, and who by an habitual course of misconduct in sexual matters has evidenced an utter lack of power to control his sexual impulses and who, as a result, is likely to attack or otherwise inflict injury, loss, pain or other evil upon the objects of his uncontrolled and uncontrollable desires."

Laws of this type are a device to remove such offenders from society until cured, or no longer a menace to the safety of others. Once reported as "safe," the court may reschedule the sentencing and impose whatever

[6]Sections 5500 and 5700.

sentence is warranted. This is a procedure that offers the offender a real chance for help with his problems, and encourages cooperation while under care and treatment. Judges are in a much better position to reward any cooperative offender at the time of sentencing, and at the same time serve the community by utilizing a new area in medico-legal cooperation.

FOR DRUG ADDICTION

Since California's law for incarcerating drug addicts as criminals was declared unconstitutional by the U.S. Supreme Court,[7] new laws provide for the civil commitment of such addicts following a conviction for crime and before final judgment and sentence. The procedure is similar to the "sex psycho" determination. There is a court hearing as to whether or not the defendant is addicted to drugs with habit-forming liabilities, and if an affirmative finding is made by the court, the offender is committed to a "rehabilitation center" for care and treatment. When the offender's drug habit is arrested and it appears to the rehabilitation center official that the offender can live in a community without drug use, he is returned to the court's jurisdiction and considered for sentencing as a convicted offender without a drug habit. Again, judges are in a position to reward self-help, and utilize a new aid to effective sentencing.

Probation

Trial judges know that probation is a basic tool of rehabilitation with first offenders, but even these beginners-in-crime often have hidden propensities which erupt into a crime of violence while on probation—and seriously embarrass the court that made the decision for probation in lieu of a jail or prison sentence. Trial judges also know that recidivists are not good prospects for probation, but suspecting the prison community capacity as a "crime school," a trial judge may risk a probation order to change an emerging pattern of criminal behavior in a young defendant.

The suspension of any possible imprisonment while the offender is conditionally released after conviction not only involves total mitigation of sentence during good behavior, but also involves some help to the offender by the probation agency. The first helpful aspect of probation is the indication of a certain trust and confidence placed in the offender by the judicial order of probation. Secondly, there is the actual supervision and guidance by a probation officer. Most probation agencies stratify the case loads of their agents so that individuals who require

[7] *Robinson v. California,* 370 U.S. 663 (1962).

more active supervision will get it, and persons who require little or no supervision to succeed on probation will be let alone. The self-policing inherent in the "trust and confidence" factor of a probation order is more than enough with many offenders, and this fact permits more active help to offenders who need it. Many judges use "summary" probation, which begins and ends with the order of probation, when they believe the offender can be rehabilitated without supervision.

Rules establishing eligibility for release after conviction provide sentencing judges with a listing of types of convicted persons who may be admitted to probation, or who must be denied probation. In most states, the major limitations on eligibility for probation concern the nature of the crime, its seriousness; whether drugs, minors or a dangerous weapon were involved; the infliction of great bodily injury or torture to the victim in the commission of the crime; if a public official is accused of bribery, extortion, or embezzlement; and the criminal history of the convicted defendant. If never previously convicted of a felony in California, a defendant can usually be admitted to probation, unless the sum total of factors such as listed above indicates such release would be unwise. A previous felony conviction makes probation unlikely, and two or more prior felony convictions will indicate to most judges the need for a sentence in prison as most likely to benefit the defendant and certainly likely to protect the community while the defendant is in prison.

In misdemeanor cases, most states allow a sentencing judge the right to grant summary probation unless the offender has an extensive criminal history. However, a nationwide lessening of the restrictions on probation in misdemeanor cases may occur in the near future because of the 1964 California court decision in *People v. Alotis*,[8] in which the doctrine that any convicted misdemeanant is eligible for probation was established.

County Jail

Sentences to this type of institution are for less than one year and are limited to misdemeanants and lesser offenders. The local jail may have several security levels of custody, including an "honor" camp or farm. There is little or no treatment of offenders at this county level, except that good behavior or assignment to a work detail will secure "good" time reduction of the sentence (five to ten days a month). In county jails, drunks and "winos" dry out; "hypes" lose their addiction to drugs "cold turkey;"[9] and criminals have time to leisurely plan their next criminal foray, or attempt rehabilitation on a do-it-yourself basis.

[8]60 Cal. 2nd 698 (1964).
[9]Without medical care.

A sentence to a county jail can now be integrated with a work furlough plan in several areas of the country. It is useful for persons who would not be granted the full freedom of probation, but who profit from an opportunity to work outside of the jail in the day time. The idea was first tried in 1913 in Wisconsin, and is now in use in over 75 percent of the counties in Wisconsin, and about a dozen counties in California. The California Penal Code[10] permits judges to endorse upon a county jail commitment order a direction that the inmate be permitted to continue his regular employment or to secure employment in the county, and only be imprisoned during non-working hours, nights and weekends. The working inmate pays from $3.00 to $6.00 a day for his board and room, and can support his family during the period of the sentence. This often saves the county some of the cost of supporting a prisoner's family by welfare payments. Many insightful judges utilize this new plan when sentencing habitual minor offenders.

Indeterminate Sentence

When a defendant is not eligible for or is denied probation, and is not sentenced to the county jail, the trial judge will sentence him to a term in the state prison. Regardless of the length of the sentence, or its future adjustment by conditional release on parole, the individual is subject to both custody and treatment. Treatment is defined as explicit procedures deliberately undertaken to change conditions or attitudes believed to be responsible for a violator's misbehavior.

In California, every prisoner committed to the Department of Corrections by the courts is first sent to a special diagnostic facility for the purpose of discovering the causes of the inmate's criminality and suggesting a program of proper clinical measures for eliminating those causes. The staff of a diagnostic facility includes persons skilled in medicine, psychiatry, psychology and sociology. Staff recommendations are integrated with the report of a person with extensive administrative experience in a correctional institution, and the new or returning inmate is sent to a specific institution for his treatment program. It is a great step forward in support of the sentencing function.

The indeterminate sentence is basic to a correctional process keyed to a state-wide parole board[11] with sentencing functions of establishing the minimum limit of the indeterminate sentence. The state-wide parole board sets a prison release date somewhere between the required mini-

[10]Section 1208.
[11]The Adult Authority in California.

mum of the sentence and its lawful maximum time. Unlike the sentencing judge, these boards can examine the offender and review the reports of his prison behavior and attitudes six months to a year after he has been in prison, and more intelligently determine the most advantageous length of sentence to be served in prison and the most useful period to be served on parole in the community.

A study of various factors upon which the California Adult Authority bases its decisions indicates actions very similar to the sentencing function. The major factors used in decision-making regarding parole eligibility are: (1) *the nature of the crime*, primarily social damage and offense to the community; (2) *the crime itself*, all the planning, aggressiveness and criminal techniques involved; (3) *previous criminal history*, both arrests and convictions; (4) *prison behavior and attitude*, attitudes exhibited and conduct while in prison; (5) *evaluation of progress*, any clues of sincerity of purpose, or motivation for improvement, or understanding of emotional difficulties and drives and of a willingness and an ability to solve present and future problems, and (6) *the protection of society*, all factors indicating sufficient self-control for management of behavior upon release on parole.

Parole

Indeterminate sentences for serious felony offenders allow the flexibility vital to the successful rehabilitation of such individuals: release on parole or continued custody until such time as the felon is no longer a threat to the peace and order of the community and can live among free people without committing crime against them, their property, or their government.

The effective management of parole lessens the loss of liberty and provides inmates with an opportunity to live in the community, and is far less expensive than the custody and treatment of an inmate in a state prison. New concepts of classifying parolees in a "point system" of need for supervision may also lessen costs while contributing to effective management. A total number of points, rather than parolees, will be used to determine an appropriate case load for each parole officer, with the closest supervision of three hours each month going to parolees with a background of instability and violence.

Release on parole should have maximum flexibility, and not be hamstrung by restriction as to either the time or length of parole before discharge. In this way, an inmate can be rewarded for adjusting to a nondeviant and law-abiding life while on parole by action suspending his parole or discharging him from its obligations.

Parole is an extension of the correctional treatment program in that the parolee must live in accordance with an established set of regulations and the laws of the community. Parole agents help the parolee in finding employment and adjusting to life on the "outside" under parole regulations; and they must take action when a parolee violates a condition of parole or is arrested for a crime. Appropriate action varies from a verbal admonishment and warning through counseling to a recommendation the parolee be returned to prison for further treatment.

Success on parole can lead to restoration of civil rights under executive clemency, and a real final disposition of a criminal action in the administration of criminal justice.

Juveniles

Juvenile courts have been established with their own processes for correction of young violators. These range from intake sections at spacious Juvenile Halls to psychiatric clinics, extensive probation supervision and boys' "ranches." The child may be assigned to a program involving some degree of custody, very similar to a commitment and prison sentence, instead of probation. State youth agencies offer custody and treatment similar to adult programs. At the end of a juvenile offender's treatment in a custodial institution, the youth will be released on parole —the same as his adult counterpart—and supervision will be provided until discharge from this conditional release when the juvenile attains maturity or concludes the term of parole without difficulty.

Juvenile court judges are fully aware of their responsibility for the general security of the community and also fully aware of the harm a dangerous child can do when allowed at large. However, it is notably difficult to gauge a delinquent's capacity for rehabilitation by the enormity of his offense, and "sentencing" judges in these courts believe the potential for the rehabilitation of these offenders to be very high because of their ages.

Clemency

The discretionary power of a sentencing judge is paralleled by the power of the executive branch of government to commute[12] a sentence or to grant a full pardon. Executive clemency is closely related to the power of king or crown in any historical review of the Anglo-American legal system. In transport to the American colonies, this power passed to the Colonial governors who served as "heads of state" to some extent and

[12]A reduction in the sentence, often to the time served.

exercised a delegated royal prerogative. The new federal government vested the clemency power in the executive role of the president. The Constitution gives the president unlimited areas for clemency, except in cases of impeachment, when the offense committed is against the laws of the United States. This section of the Constitution, conferring this power upon the executive branch of the government, reads as follows: ". . . and he shall have power to grant reprieves and pardons for offenses against the United States, except in cases of impeachment."[13]

The various states also placed this power within the executive department, either vesting it in the governor or in a "Board of Pardons" or like commission of state officials, usually with the governor serving as an ex-officio member of such group. In some states, the governor delegates the investigation of applications for clemency to a similar commission charged with advisory responsibilities.[14]

The major use of the power of clemency today is not to interfere with the sentencing power of the courts, but rather to correct errors in justice which cannot be adjusted by any legal remedy in the courts, to support a rehabilitated offender by "removing guilt" and restoring the civil rights of the offender, and to serve as a reward for some meritorious act on the part of a prisoner.

Executive clemency is a check and a balance within the concept of the separation of powers. Any grossly excessive action by the judicial branch of government can be corrected by executive reprieve or pardon. However, this power can be misused for political and other ulterior purposes, and the fine work of the judicial branch of government set aside by executive action. Fortunately, there has been little misuse of this power. In fact, the power is not used to any great extent in the United States, and its disuse indicates the esteem in which the acts of the judiciary are viewed by most of the top executives in government in the United States.

At the federal level, the president seeks the advice of the attorney general, and makes little use of the full pardoning power. Unbelievably, only about one convicted person a year has been pardoned at the federal level in the past twenty years.[15] Use of the power to reprieve[16] became more extensive during the incumbency of recent attorney generals, as a device by which various inequities in sentence length could be adjusted by executive commutation of sentences of convicted offenders. Since

[13]United States Constitution, Article II, Section 2, Clause 1.
[14]Lewis Mayers, *The American Legal System* (New York: Harper & Row, Publishers, 1963), p. 138.
[15]Walter A. Lunden, *Facts on Crimes and Criminals* (Ames, Iowa: The Art Press 1961), pp. 286–87.
[16]Withdrawal of a sentence.

persons imprisoned in federal correctional institutions originate from a vast nation-wide complex of courts, it is not unexpected that there is some gross disparity in the sentences of offenders with similar criminal histories for like crimes. Executive clemency is now moving into this area to right this wrong, particularly in reprieving prisoners serving consecutive sentences.

At the state level, an average of one hundred persons a year have received full pardons in the United States in the past 20 years.[17] However, the use of executive clemency to restore the civil rights of offenders is now used as one of the means by which a better "final disposition" can be secured in a criminal action, by helping a convicted offender back to full status as a citizen of the community.

In California, clemency may be judicial as well as executive, with many provisions of law established to aid the offender in making a better final disposition of his problem with the law. Probationeers and misdemeanants can be rehabilitated and criminal records of minors sealed by judicial action; parolees pardoned for service with the armed forces by the Adult Authority or a local parole board; and felons receive clemency through executive and judicial action.

REHABILITATION OF PROBATIONEERS AND MISDEMEANANTS

At the time of sentence, a misdemeanant is informed of the process for his rehabilitation by law. Every defendant who fulfills the conditions of his probation[18] for the required time period, and every imprisoned misdemeanant who has served his sentence and is not under charge of the commission of any crime after the lapse of one year from the date of sentence, may utilize this procedure. This type of clemency is based on the fact that the offender has lived an honest and upright life and has conformed to and obeyed the laws of the land for a necessary period, and such removal of the stigma of criminal conviction is helpful to the rehabilitation of the offender. The convicted defendant seeking rehabilitation must apply to the sentencing court for permission to withdraw his plea of guilty and enter a plea of not guilty, or if he has been convicted after a plea of not guilty, for the court to set aside the verdict of guilty. In either case, the court shall thereupon dismiss the accusatory pleading against such a defendant, who shall thereafter be released from all penalties and disabilities resulting from the offense of which he has been convicted. However, in any subsequent prosecution of such rehabilitated defendant for any other criminal offense, the prior conviction

[17]Luden, *Facts on Crimes and Criminals*, pp. 286–87.
[18]May be a person classed legally as a felon.

may be pleaded and proved and shall have the same effect as if probation had not been granted or the accusation or information dismissed.[19]

SEALING CRIMINAL RECORDS OF MINORS

In any case in which a person under the age of 21 years at the time
of committing a misdemeanor (except a traffic violation) was arrested
but not convicted of any crime, or if arrested and convicted, availed
himself of the legal procedure for rehabilitation of misdemeanants,
it is possible to apply to the sentencing court for an order sealing the
record of arrest, or arrest and conviction. Only sex perverts and persons
who violate the laws against drug use are excluded. The court may
issue an order granting the relief prayed for in the youth's petition, and
thereafter such arrest, or arrest and conviction, shall be deemed *not to
have occurred,* and the youthful offender is authorized to answer any
question relating to the occurrence of arrest, or arrest and conviction,
accordingly.[20]

SPECIAL ARMED SERVICES PARDON

Men in state prisons or county jails, who are qualified for service in
the armed forces may be granted special service paroles by the Adult
Authority or a county board of parole commissioners. Under this special
parole, persons favored by it will be sent directly from custody into the
hands of military authorities and shall in no case be paroled to civilian
life. When such persons complete their service in some branch of the
armed forces and receive an honorable discharge, they may be eligible
for a full pardon from the governor, even though they have not served
their full period of parole by the end of their period of military service;
such persons may petition the paroling authority for a full discharge
from parole, and such authority may consider the honorable discharge
of such person from the military service as grounds for granting such
discharge from parole.[21]

REPRIEVES, PARDONS AND COMMUTATIONS

In California, clemency bridges the three branches of government in
a fine example of checks and balances for the control of a power that
might be misused. The general authority to grant clemency is conferred
upon the governor by the Constitution of the State of California. This
section reads as follows:

[19]California Penal Code, Section 1203.4–4a.
[20]*Ibid.*, Section 1203.45.
[21]*Ibid.*, Sections 3100–3116.

> The governer shall have the power to grant reprieves, pardons, and commutations of sentence, after conviction, for all offenses except treason and cases of impeachment, upon such conditions and with such restrictions and limitations, as he may think proper, subject to such regulations as may be provided by law relative to the manner of applying for pardons. Upon conviction for treason, the governor shall have power to suspend the execution of the sentence until the case shall be reported to the legislature at its next meeting, when the legislature shall either pardon, direct the execution of the sentence, or grant a further reprieve. . . . Neither the governor nor the legislature shall have power to grant pardons, or commutations of sentence, in any case where the convict has been twice convicted of a felony, unless upon the written recommendation of a majority of the judges of the Supreme Court.[22]

The Adult Authority may report to the governor, from time to time, the names of any and all persons imprisoned in any state prison who, in its judgment, ought to have a commutation of sentence or be pardoned and set at liberty on account of good conduct, or unusual term of sentence, or any other cause which, in its opinion, should entitle the inmate to a pardon or commutation of sentence. Either the Adult Authority or the governor may request the sentencing court, or the district attorney who prosecuted the offender for the crime for which he is imprisoned, to furnish a summarized statement of the facts proved on the trial, and of any other facts having reference to the propriety of granting or refusing clemency, together with his recommendation for or against clemency and his reasons for such recommendation. Prior to any executive action, the district attorney of the county in which the conviction was had must be served with written notice of the application for clemency, and proof of such notice, by affidavit, shall be made part of the executive record of the case.[23]

Applications of twice-convicted felons, however, are made directly to the governor, but assigned to the Adult Authority for investigation. The governor may refer any application for clemency to the Supreme Court, but usually only refers applications which have received a favorable recommendation from the Adult Authority. If a majority of the justices recommend that clemency be granted, the clerk of the Supreme Court shall transmit the application, together with all papers and documents filed in the case to the governor; otherwise the documents shall remain in the files of the court.[24]

At the beginning of each legislative session, the governor must send to the California legislature a complete listing of each reprieve, pardon,

[22]Article VII, Section 1.
[23]California Penal Code, Section 4800–4807.3.
[24]*Ibid.*, Sections 4850–4852.

or commutation of sentence, stating the name of the person convicted, the crime concerned, the sentence and its date, and the date of executive clemency and the reasons for granting it.[25]

RESTORATION OF RIGHTS

Almost any person convicted of a felony in California may apply for restoration of rights and a pardon, with the exception of persons under a mandatory life parole, who were committed originally under death sentences, or to persons in the military service. Briefly, the procedure starts with a "notice of intention," filed by the felon with the county clerk of the county of residence, and a service upon the chief of police of the city of residence, or the sheriff of the county of residence if living in an unincorporated area, of a certified copy of such notice. The applicant must also provide the police official with his photograph, fingerprints and a personal history; and agree to supervision by such official and to conform to any reasonable requirements by him during this period of rehabilitation. Basically, the applicant is required to live an honest and upright life, conducting himself with sobriety and industry, exhibiting a good moral character, and conforming to and obeying the laws of the land during this period. At the end of the three-year period, the applicant may file in the superior court of the county in which he then resides a petition for a certificate of rehabilitation. The court must notify local law enforcement agencies, permit the applicant to have counsel, and may require such testimony and the production of documents as it deems necessary for adequate review of the case. If, after the hearing, the court finds the applicant has demonstrated by his course of conduct his rehabilitation and his fitness to exercise all of the civil and political rights of citizenship, the court shall make an order declaring that the petitioner has been rehabilitated, and recommending that the Governor grant a full pardon to the applicant and transmit certified copies of its order to the governor, the Adult Authority and the Bureau of Criminal Identification and Investigation, and in the case of persons twice convicted of a felony, to the Supreme Court.[26] The certified copy of a certificate of rehabilitation transmitted to the governor shall constitute an application for a full pardon upon receipt of which the governor may, without any further investigation, issue a pardon to the person named therein, except that the Governor must secure the recommendation of a majority of the judges of the Supreme Court prior to granting a pardon to any person twice convicted of felony.

[25]*Ibid.*, Section 4807.
[26]*Ibid.*, Sections 4852.01–4852.2.

EFFECT OF FULL PARDON

A full pardon acts to restore to a convicted person all of the rights, privileges and franchises of which he has been deprived in consequence of said conviction or by reason of any matter involved therein.

Final Disposition

The final disposition in relation to individual convicted criminal offenders should be viewed as the rehabilitation of the offender. A continuing career of crime, resulting in a chronological array of arrests, prosecutions, court determinations and sentences, does not indicate agents of law enforcement have successfully disposed of such offender with any finality.

Two basic roadblocks to successful final disposition of criminal actions may be summed up as the element of chance inherent in an offender's view of law enforcement, court action, and the correctional process; and the influence of the prison community on offenders.

ATTITUDES OF OFFENDERS: CHANGE IN LAW ENFORCEMENT

Efforts to create in the mind of the offender a desire for rehabilitation are difficult because of the element of chance that is connected with the detection, apprehension, prosecution, trial, and commitment of offenders. People in crime know the percentages of risk involved in violating laws. Young hoodlums toll off the "odds" in the manner of a bookmaker accepting bets on horses at a race track. Crime does "pay" to some extent. There is a diminishing order in the number of persons who are apprehended, prosecuted, and convicted of crime, and sent to prison after sentence.

The setting of a release date by a parole board or the decision of a parole officer to "violate" a parolee and return the erring offender to prison involves executive decision-making based on known facts, and modern techniques achieve remarkable objectivity in the vital area of corrections. Members of a parole board work to release deserving prisoners and only reject those inmates not deemed worthy of this opportunity to return to the community. The "violation" of a parolee by his parole officer is also generally within the scope of effective direct supervision. Inmates, however, rationalize that a major element of chance also exists in this procedure.

While the adventitious nature of the process of the administration of justice does not appear to be resented by prison inmates, it does condition their minds, and permits rationalizing their presence in prison without any loss of self-image, or experiencing any feelings of doubt or even guilt. This mental meandering usually leads toward the rejection of rehabilitation efforts by department of corrections treatment personnel. While true repentance may not be necessary for rehabilitation, it is certain that some insight is necessary that will at least rationalize future conforming behavior with past nonconforming actions which violated laws and resulted in the prisoner's processing in the administration of justice. However, can insight be gained into criminal behavior and the need for correction, when there is also a cynical and smug appraisal that detection, arrest, prosecution, conviction, imprisonment, and release on parole resulted only from the offender's failure to "luck out"?

ATTITUDES OF OFFENDERS: ORIENTATION TO CRIME AND CRIMINALS

The prison community is predominantly antitreatment and handicaps the best programs for rehabilitation. This community within the institutional setting is dedicated to the criminal code that an inmate who cooperates with the administrative staff is a "rat" or a "fink"—and this cohesive cultural nucleus defies most prison authorities with day-after-day regularity. The prison community accepts and rewards the same skills and attitudes that make a life of crime possible and profitable and interesting. There is a cynical acceptance of every kind of immorality in the prison's lingo's term of jocker.[27] There is rejection of authority in the words "right guy," the inmate who does not "rat" or "squeal" on his friends, even if a witness to murder. And the inmate-criminal's attitude toward lawbreaking is inherent in the term "route," for systematic stealing in prison. The fact that these terms do exist in the lingo of a prison is indicative of the fact that the attitudes and prevailing practices they represent exist in the culture of the prison community, and reflect the moral and ethical standards of the community of prisoners.

Inmates exposed to this subculture of crime learn that conniving and scheming and deception can go on despite prison authorities or with their cooperation, just as it did in the crime-and-politics jungle of the underworld life. Their frame of reference is still the criminal's outlook that authority can be hoodwinked, bought off, or manipulated.

RECIDIVISTS

A recidivist is a person that resorts to crime again and again. This is the prison inmate who ignores the correctional process or rejects it.

[27]The male prisoner who persuades, buys or forces himself into a homosexual relationship with other male inmates.

Investigation of the impact of correctional treatment upon specific offenders is a problem in research. However, to effectively appraise the impact of any portion of the correctional process, there is a need to know the facts of failure—or even the facts of limited success. Again, California has pioneered in this area. Within the structure of the youth and adult system of corrections in California, there are many ongoing studies. Research has ranged from community treatment projects to intensive correctional experiments, with the major objective of gathering evidence that a certain specific program of correctional treatment has accomplished an alteration of the behavior of offenders in the group under study. Improved treatment programs can be developed when research reports indicate a high success with one form of treatment and a much lower success rate with "competing" treatment programs.

California's corrections unit has accomplished a fine job because of facts secured through extensive research, and the many rehabilitated offenders now contributing to the support of the government in California as working and conforming community members are the result of such work, but California's jails are still full, and parolees still commit crimes while on parole.

Again, it is a simplification of a problem to say that the correctional process is to blame for recidivists. Police, prosecutor and court personnel must accept major responsibility for the chance factor in today's criminal justice operations. The differential association of convicted criminals in the prison community is beyond the control of the personnel of any department of correction, so long as the individual criminals were not of the type who could be trusted to succeed in the community on probation. Even release under strict parole supervision cannot completely prevent a parolee from seeking associates in the underworld with a like criminal background.

Billions of words have been written about the defects of practice theory in corrections, and there is mounting evidence that neither psychogenic nor sociogenic images of crime causation are sufficient by themselves to explain the variety of deviant forms of behavior common to the universe of criminal offenders. The people who are the subjects of the correctional process may be abnormal, normal, or subnormal. And while the sociological and criminological literature is replete with encouragement, it is still a fact that diagnostic models upon which most of the treatment in corrections is based do not match the scope and diversity of the problems of inmates. The colloquialism, "people are funny," is a capsule explanation.

Donald R. Cressey, a top sociologist and one of the finest writers in this field of correctional practice and theory, has developed one of the best descriptive titles for an occupation in the administration of justice.[28] Cressey writes of the great need for a new group of correctional technicians, whose occupation titles he believes could properly be "people changers." According to Cressey, there are not now and never will be enough professionally trained (postgraduate university level) persons to man our rehabilitative agencies.

"People changers" may be a dynamic breakthrough in correctional treatment. Failure of other methods of treatment with antitreatment and antistaff prisoners certainly warrants further working models to prove or disprove the emerging belief that criminals can be changed to noncriminal status by using criminals and delinquents to introduce guilt and shame into the psychological makeup of problem prisoners: the recidivists of today's correctional process.

There is an existing lack of success in rehabilitating criminals, but there are significant indications that radically new concepts are likely to have unusual success. It may be "people changers," or it may be some other helping process. There has to be some innovation, because each and every community in the nation should face the issue squarely: do something effective to achieve greater success with the last-ditch correctional process of treatment or face a permanent, predatory, hostile group of repeating criminals battling the forces of law enforcement.

Measuring Success

No data are available as to how many persons are convicted wrongly in the courts of the United States. However, the history of persons being convicted though innocent of the crime charged is almost totally absent of accusations against the police and prosecutor for unjust arrests, accusations or prosecutions. The majority of the relatively small percentage of known injustice in the administration of criminal justice in this country results from the unintended-but-false identification of the accused person by an eye-witness. This is certainly continuing support for the concept that the administration of justice should not be entrusted to a single functionary, and that the participants in this complicated process have accepted both their responsibility and accountability for working together to achieve justice, despite the fact that "the awful instruments of the criminal law" could send innocent men and women to prison.[29]

Data are available as to the manner in which each agent and agency of

[28]Donald R. Cressey, "Social Psychological Foundations for Using Criminals in the Rehabilitation of Criminals," *Journal of Research in Crime and Delinquency* (July 1965), pp. 49–59.

[29]*McNabb v. U.S.*, 318 U.S. 332 (1943).

law enforcement and criminal justice operates, and the cost of such operation can also be ascertained, but data as to the cost of achieving results by function have never been compiled or computed. Management in criminal justice agencies has been guided mainly by the executive assumption that the best results were being obtained for the budget monies allocated to each agency! Subliminally, there is a nebulous hypothesis that better results could be achieved if greater sums of money were to be made available.

Measuring success in the management and operation of criminal justice agencies must be upgraded to full acceptance of modern cost accounting, an auditing procedure which will not only establish dollar values for each percentage point of improvement in measurable areas, but which will also establish penalties for wasting money on useless procedures or gaining success by any diminishing of the rights of the individual accused of crime.

However, basic to cost accounting as a measure of management efficiency is the development of modern electronic data processing centers at no less than state-wide levels to serve as central information pools for the storage of accurate and inclusive and relevant data which would provide the required system capability for both day-to-day information service and evaluation procedures.[30]

This collected data on the administration of criminal justice are likely to permit a definition of the extent of both overall and specific problems, and thus make them amenable to scientific analysis.

California awarded a contract in this field of cost accounting and management evaluation to a leading aerospace firm whose engineers and consultants have worked on scientific problems of space travel. One of the new findings to emerge from this comprehensive study was "career costs"—the total costs of the entire system of criminal justice to process an average offender over his entire lifetime.[31]

Justice in America is a costly enterprise. California alone spends $600 million a year for the control of crime and delinquency.[32] Research will cost additional money, but its promise is that future expenditures can be reduced because research will provide meaningful information on how to allocate resources to most effectively reduce crime and reduce the damages resulting from crime. This is the prime objective, unless today's crime rate is considered a ghastly coefficient of modern living!

[30]*Feasibility Report and Recommendations for a New York State Identification and Intelligence System* (Santa Monica, Calif.: System Development Corporation, 1963), pp. 1–2.
[31]*Prevention and Control of Crime and Delinquency* (El Monte, Calif.: Space-General Corp., 1965), pp. 14–23.
[32]*Ibid.*, p. 3.

No matter the cost of today's system of criminal justice, the return to the "input" stage of the administration of justice by an offender previously processed after a police arrest is a total loss. Actually, a saving could be computed if twice as much money was expended in per capita cost per offender to attain an "output" result for the control of crime that dissuaded the offender from again violating the laws. A greater saving could be computed if cost accounting and management evaluation indicated methods for expending reasonable funds to prevent susceptible persons, particularly juveniles, from entering the criminal justice system at all. In the future, an extensive "case management" program may replace today's techniques of arrest and prosecution, with the accent on early identification of susceptible crime groups, and such modernization of operational procedures will not only reduce the public cost of crime, but also mitigate its tremendous social cost.

Our existing system for administering criminal justice in the United States is not a formal management system. The agencies of justice have unusual administrative independence and often conflicting objectives. It is a system, however, in which procedural and substantive safeguards ensure fair trials before impartial tribunals in which every defendant is equal before the law; in which the social responsibility of police in suppressing crimes has been reconciled with the right of the criminal defendant to be tried according to constitutional requirements; and it can be a system in which the measurement of success in agency operations will be based on a scientific comparison of results and costs.

Selected References

BOOKS

Arens, Richard, and Harold D. Lasswell, *In Defense of Public Order: The Emerging Field of Sanction Law.* New York: Columbia University Press, 1961, 314 pages.

A system of law must be viewed as a whole, and sanction law in the American legal system is wider in scope than the mere "punishment" of offenders for criminal behavior. Arens and Lasswell cite as the major objectives of their text: (1) establish the conception of sanction law in social control; (2) delineate the American sanctioning system (to justify the claim that the field is sufficiently important for further development); and (3) briefly outline how the field of sanction law can be useful in the administration of justice.

Clemmer, Donald, *The Prison Community.* New York: Holt, Rinehart & Winston, Inc., 1958, 341 pages.

An authoritative text on the people who make up the population of a prison—both inmates and staff personnel—and their groupings and relationships. This book is a sociological study of a social unit: a prison. Clemmer delineates the prison community as supportive to criminalistic attitudes and behavior, but believes the impact of the existing prison culture can be decreased by: (1) increasing humanitarianism toward offenders; (2) good men entering prison work; (3) smaller prisons; (4) improved scientific treatment techniques.

Gibbons, Don C., *Changing the Lawbreaker*. Englewood Cliffs, N.J.: Prentice-Hall, Inc., 1965, 306 pages.

Gibbons groups offenders into typologies, suggests specific treatment practice, and recognizes and identifies obstacles to treatment. A very fine text that hews to the theme that changing criminals to the status of noncriminals requires: (1) identification of the causal factors in the development of specific types of criminality; (2) understanding of the nature of the deviant behavior to be corrected; and (3) contriving methodologies which will (a) "unlearn" criminal behavior, and (b) reinforce new noncriminal behavior and fresh attitudes favoring conformity.

Glasser, Daniel, *The Effectiveness of a Prison and Parole System*. New York: The Bobbs-Merrill Co., Inc., 1964, 596 pages.

This book is a major resource for planning research activities into the merits and deficiencies of specific methodologies for changing the lawbreaker. It is a report of a massive study of the institutions under the supervision of the U.S. Bureau of Prisons, and is concerned with: (1) ascertaining offender failure rates; (2) determining factors related to reversion or nonreversion to crime; and (3) discovering practical measures and programs likely to be successful in reducing recidivism.

Schur, Edwin M., *Crimes Without Victims*. Englewood Cliffs, N.J.: Prentice-Hall, Inc., 1965, 180 pages.

A study of abortion, homosexuality, and drug addiction, in paperback form. Schur raises the question between "deviance" and "crime," as each of these crimes involves the willing exchange between consenting individuals of a desired product or service forbidden by law.

Spergel, Irving, *Racketville, Slumtown, Haulberg*. Chicago, Ill.: University of Chicago Press, 1964, 211 pages.

Spergel explores three subcultures: (1) young delinquents living in areas where an organized crime syndicate offers the top means for reaching success-goals (Racketville); (2) the "conflict" environment of sub-standard slum areas with its short-circuiting of access to conventional success-goals and the substitution of "rep" as a gang-fighter as a desirable success-goal (Slumtown); and (3) the social setting offering limited legitimate and illegitimate opportunities to achieve success-goals through some form of stealing (Haulberg). A well-organized report of extensive field studies, and a book that offers new and inviting guidelines for dynamic research projects which will delineate possible community action in dealing with delinquent subcultures—rather than relying upon police action and current arrest-to-release procedures of the administration of justice.

Tyler, Gus, *Organized Crime in America*. Ann Arbor, Mich.: The University of Michigan Press, 1962, 421 pages.

A selection of writings, joined by interpretive essays of the author. The concept of organized crime as both a product and reflection of today's national culture is studied and discussed. This is a comprehensive text about a phenomenon that intrudes upon the successful rehabilitation of many offenders, and which permeates the prison community.

ARTICLES

Braithwaite, Lloyd, "Executive Clemency in California: A Case-Study Interpretation of Criminal Responsibility," *Issues in Criminology*, 1, No. 1 (Fall 1965), 77–107.

Philosophic and ethical motivations underlying acts of executive clemency in commuting sentences in a selected sample of death penalty cases. A fine exposition of the methodology and soul-searching involved in the use of clemency to make an improved final disposition of serious offenders.

Brancale, Ralph, "Diagnostic Techniques in Sentencing," *Law and Contemporary Problems* (Summer 1958), pp. 442–60.

A thorough discussion of the differences between people who engage in antisocial behavior, and the wide range of personalities and motivations likely to be present in any group of offenders. Brancale points out the same punishment cannot be applied to all offenders, and holds that each offender must receive an individual psychonanalysis and diagnosis, with "work up" clinicians providing the court with data to guide sentencing. The following information is suggested for effective sentencing: (1) a clinical evaluation of the seriousness of the offense, and the underlying psychological significance of the act; (2) the psychological and environmental aspects of the offense; (3) the offender's diagnostic category; (4) the chronological sequence of offender's deviant behavior and any evidence of compulsive, repetitive factors; (5) offender's insight into the nature of his crime (guilt, remorse, etc.); (6) motivations and responsiveness to rehabilitation; (7) hazard to the community in the probation or parole of offender; and (8) overview and professional recommendation of diagnostic "team."

Cressey, Donald R., "Social Psychological Foundations for Using Criminals in the Rehabilitation of Criminals," *Journal of Research in Crime and Delinquency* (July 1965), pp. 49–59.

Differential association and symbolic interactionist theory provide foundations for developing a theory and techniques for utilizing criminals and delinquents as "people changers" in the rehabilitation of offenders. Cressey notes that words reflect attitudes and social conduct can be changed to noncriminal status by introducing substitute verbalizations which develop feelings of guilt and shame about criminal conduct.

Fox, Vernon, "Analysis of Prison Disciplinary Problems," *Journal of Criminal Law, Criminology, and Police Science* (November-December 1958), pp. 321–26.

A very fine exposition of disciplinary problems as a threat to the orderly administration of a custodial institution. Fox writes that treatment ceases in most prisons when rules are violated, though "problem" inmates causing discipline problems demonstrate a need for treatment. This author states the three most common major disciplinary problems in any prison are the control of gambling, sex and fighting; believes repeated misconduct is related to emotional immaturity, psychopathy and chronic neurosis; and suggests a moratorium on punishments to permit incorrigible offenders to develop emotional maturity.

Green, Paul S., "A National Approach to Rehabilitation," *The Police Chief*, 33, No. 6 (June 1966), 16–18.

An article detailing the planned operations of the Joint Commission on Correctional Manpower and Training. Against a backdrop of hope for the future, Green notes that the correctional process has been neglected, poorly supported financially and lacking in the necessary percentage of professionally trained personnel. He writes: "Man's relations to his criminal fellows have been a succession of three 'R's'—revenge, restraint and reformation."

Irwin, John, and Donald R. Cressey, "Thieves, Convicts, and the Inmate Culture," *Social Problems* (Fall 1962), pp. 142–55.

A stimulating article about the prison community and the resistance of inmates to rehabilitation. The authors note that fine distinctions between "prison culture" and "criminal subculture" make understandable the behavior patterns of various categories of inmates, and conclude that recidivism rates are not affected significantly by incarceration in the traditional prisons studied.

McGee, Richard A., "The Administration of Justice: The Correctional Process," *Crime and Delinquency* (July 1959), pp. 225–39.

An article on the enormous problem facing America today: what to do with the offender after he has been convicted? McGee writes that punishment may be meted out, or an attempt made to bring about psychological and social changes in the offender. The first, he notes, has failed dismally for centuries, and the second has never been accomplished fully or fairly for several reasons: (1) expense; (2) lack of skilled personnel; (3) poor leadership; (4) misunderstanding of rehabilitation as a concept; (5) absence of statistics and records; and (6) lack of research.

Index

DATE DUE

DEMCO 38-297